Moral Behavior in Chinese Society

Moral Behavior in Chinese Society

Edited by:

Richard W. Wilson
Sidney L. Greenblatt
Amy Auerbacher Wilson

Foreword by:

Thomas A. Metzger

PRAEGER SPECIAL STUDIES • PRAEGER SCIENTIFIC

Library of Congress Cataloging in Publication Data
Main entry under title:

Moral behavior in Chinese society.

Includes index.
1. China--Moral conditions--Congresses.
I. Wilson, Richard W., 1933-   . II. Greenblatt,
Sidney L. III. Wilson, Amy Auerbacher, 1934-
HN740.Z9M65   951   81-4581
ISBN 0-03-056922-2   AACR2

Published in 1981 by Praeger Publishers
CBS Educational and Professional Publishing
A Division of CBS, Inc.
521 Fifth Avenue, New York, New York 10175 U.S.A.

© 1981 by Praeger Publishers

123456789   145   987654321

Printed in the United States of America

PREFACE

The papers collected in this volume on moral behavior in Chinese society were presented by a group of scholars at conferences at East Asian Legal Studies of Harvard Law School, Harvard University on October 13 and 14, 1979 and at the Center for Chinese Studies of the University of California, Berkeley, on November 10, 1979. These conferences addressed the fourth topic in a series, which has had, as an overall objective, the application of selected social science paradigms to Chinese data.

Our goal in this volume is to present a set of studies related to a common theme that can reveal the value of a focus on moral behavior as an aid to understanding Chinese society. Moral behavior as a framework of analysis has been of interest to students of social and political life for centuries. In contemporary social science literature, however, this topic has fallen into disuse. Only recently has moral behavior again become of major interest following extensive theoretical and empirical work in psychology on the bases of moral judgment and behavior. Increasingly, this work has come to the attention of scholars in a broad variety of fields and has stimulated a reexamination of the usefulness of moral behavior as an intellectual focus. As a consequence, both the conferences and a subsequent volume devoted to an examination of moral behavior in Chinese society seemed appropriate and timely.

The scholars who contributed to this volume represent a variety of disciplines, and each addressed the question of moral behavior in Chinese society from a unique perspective. Prior to the conferences the editors set forth for those who were invited definitions of moral behavior derived from contemporary literature. The authors were asked to explore the problem of moral behavior in terms of work that they knew best, and the conferences themselves were then organized in such a way as to maximize discussion concerning the utility of a concentration on moral behavior for the study of Chinese society. As a consequence, the papers reflect, in their discussion of Chinese materials, problems and issues drawn from the general field.

As editors, our tasks have been of several kinds. Initially we formulated the general parameters for an intellectual focus on moral behavior in Chinese society. We then wrote to a number of scholars who we felt might have an interest in pursuing this topic from the vantage point of their own scholarly perspectives. During the conference organization phase we maintained close liaison with the authors informing them about progress toward our goals. All three of us as editors helped in the general selection of conference topics, the preparation of guidelines, the selection of participants, the organization of the conferences, and the subsequent editing of the proceedings.

Several participants at the conferences did not present papers, but their participation was invaluable. We would especially like to thank Thomas A. Metzger and William Shaw. Special appreciation is also owed to East Asian Legal Studies of Harvard University and the Center for Chinese Studies of the University of California, Berkeley for hosting the conferences. For help in organizing the conferences and for their invaluable assistance in the preparation of the manuscript, we extend our gratitude to Catherine Tranfo, Grace Kurkowski, and Phyllis Telleri of the Rutgers University International Center. Our thanks also go to Betsy Brown of Praeger Publishers for her many valuable suggestions and her help in the preparation of this volume.

CONTENTS

LIST OF FIGURES

FOREWORD

Thomas A. Metzger

THE QUESTION OF MORAL DEVELOPMENT
AND THE CONCEPT OF CULTURE

Exemplifying the secularization of Western thought, the anthropological theory of culture has yielded many insights. Indeed much more will be learned when this concept of culture is applied as vigorously to Western, urbanized, and educated people as it has been to the rural, uneducated folk of exotic lands. To be sure, as pointed out by Edward Said and others, this idea has often been ideologically misused to put "natives" into a moral/intellectual position inferior to that of the Western area specialist and so to suggest their political inferiority as well. The remedy for this abuse, however, is not to stop dissecting foreign cultures but to start dissecting our own. The idea of shared culture orientations has also been criticized as a reification contradicted by the nature of human reality, which, we are told, actually consists only of discontinuous events. This thesis, however, leads to the *reductio ad absurdum* that shared languages do not exist. Indeed, as Clifford Geertz suggests in *The Interpretation of Cultures,* the idea of a culturally shared, structured pattern of meaning can be fruitfully used without raising unanswerable questions about the ultimate physiological or ontological status of its referent.[1] If cultures, especially the cultures of urbanized elites, have often been described simplistically, we should now try to do justice to their complexity, not hastily throw out the idea of culture.

Another criticism, however, has to be taken more seriously. The theory of culture to a large extent disentangles the description of human life from moral

ix

judgments. Yet, since moral judgment is integral to human experience, an amoral approach cannot do full justice to this experience and indeed disrupts its phenomenological integrity. Anthropologists themselves worry about how to integrate the "emic" approach, based on an empathetic understanding of indigenous ideals, with the "etic," which bypasses such an understanding. Moreover, outside scholars describing an indigenous moral perspective cannot really avoid morally evaluating it. Max Weber claimed they should, but he himself repeatedly inserted value judgments into his empirical studies, as Leo Strauss pointed out in *Natural Right and History*.[2] Marxist scholars openly make value judgments, and although we may not agree with their judgments, their decision to make them has its appeal.

In the case of China, moreover, the moral evaluation of culture is particularly inescapable, not only because the Chinese frequently compare themselves morally to other peoples but also because Westerners observing the Chinese have, since the days of Marco Polo, inevitably oscillated between admiration and contempt. Thus, today three major critiques of Chinese culture are prominent.

First, there is a powerful negative critique based on the idea that the full development of freedom and morality is impossible without "individualism," a complex Western cultural pattern that has not taken root in China. This vague term is admirably defined by Steven Lukes. He sees "individualism" as a normative pattern of thought emphasizing that individual autonomy cannot be realized unless the individual is free to be skeptical about all moral pronouncements, free imaginatively to redefine himself in relation to his social context, and free to hold back the power of authority figures over him by using the vocabulary and the institutions of a legal system, that is, by asserting "rights."[3] From this individualistic standpoint, Chinese culture is criticized as leaving the individual too dependent on authority figures.

Second, some Chinese scholars such as the late Tang Junyi have developed a powerful negative critique of this Western individualism, defending the Confucian ethos as a more effective way of "completing the realization of the self and of others" *(chengji chengwu).*[4] According to Tang, self-realization can come about only through a "merging" *(herong)* of ego's and alter's natural feelings of empathy, which are distorted by any "individualistic" struggle to establish ego's idiosyncratic identity. From a partly different standpoint, one might argue that the pathologies of the Confucian ethos are less serious than those of individualism. Is a relative shortage of individual autonomy worse than an uninhibited, morally relativistic individualism rejecting the traditional constraints of bourgeois civilization? Third and finally, many admire the Chinese Communists' revolution, believing it promoted that spirit of self-sacrifice that is the highest form of morality.

The prevalence of these three ways of morally evaluating Chinese behavior suggests the futility of trying to divorce study of this behavior from moral evaluation. Yet, if moral evaluation is inescapable, this does not mean we should discard the findings of the social sciences. What behavioral scientists like Richard

W. Wilson have discovered, therefore, is a two fold challenge: defining the criteria of moral development in a maximally explicit, reflective, and systematic way; and applying them to a particular social structure, knowledge of which has been provided by the behavioral sciences. At least in the case of Chinese studies, this is a very new approach indeed.

To be sure, this approach is not a way of measuring the amount of nasty behavior in a particular society. There is always plenty of that everywhere. The issue, as I see it, is rather the extent to which cultural and social patterns facilitate the moral development of the individual. Nor can we be sure that this approach can yield any final evaluation of such patterns. It can, however, lead to a more balanced understanding of them than can less systematic approaches like the three critiques above, clearing away misunderstandings and pinpointing the remaining areas of uncertainty.

Collected in the light of such considerations, the articles in this volume are provocative and based on a sensitive understanding of the Chinese scene. Although not all angles can be covered, the authors use a wide variety of data ranging from theatre pieces to information from field surveys, ideological statements, and linguistic data. Their complex discussion can perhaps be broken down in terms of the following issues:

1. What were some of the main visions of moral action that existed in modern and premodern China?
2. To what extent were these various visions legitimated or viewed indigenously with reservations?
3. What was the genesis of the modern visions of morality, and how was this genesis related to the tradition?
4. What were some of the relations of these visions to the concrete behavior characteristic of different social strata or personality types?
5. What should be the main criteria of moral development, and to what alternative evaluations of the Chinese scene do they lead?
6. How do these evaluations differ from the three critiques above?

THE MAOIST VISION OF MORALITY
AND THE QUESTION OF ITS ORIGINS

There is not much controversy about the content of the Maoist vision of heroic moral action. As discussed in this book, this vision emphasized a cult of "sincerity" stressing uninterrupted self-abnegation for the sake of the total moral community ("the people"); the realization of this self-abnegation through disciplined work and what Pusey calls the "gladiatorial virtues"; the simultaneously egalitarian and elitist, collectivistic and individuating aspects of this cult, which aimed for equality while identifying a moral vanguard as well as an absolute moral leader, and which aimed for collective action while emphasizing the moral autonomy needed to oppose immoral authority; a special emphasis on youth as a likely attribute of the morally responsive person, though not of the absolute moral leader; the definition of the moral community in terms of both this universalistic cult of sincerity and Chinese nationalism; the voluntaristic belief, contradicting Marx, that economic backwardness cannot prevent this community from realizing the highest moral ideals and even serves as the best medium for the moral struggle; and a Manichaean definition of this struggle.

There is, however, considerable controversy regarding the origin of this Maoist vision. Pusey argues, convincingly I think, that even though Mao was more egalitarian, more iconoclastic, and more enchanted with young people, his vision has much in common with that of Liang Qichao, a famous modernizer at the turn of the century, on whom the Marxist influence was minimal. At the same time, the extent to which Liang broke with Confucian values is a controversial question on which scholars like Zhang Hao, Zhang Pengyuan, and Wang Ermin do not agree. Comparing these traditional values with Liang's and Mao's visions, many have been struck by seeming continuities such as the nonindividualistic emphasis on the individual's moral autonomy, the cult of sincerity and self-abnegation for the sake of the moral community, and the Manichaean approach to struggle and conflict.

Thus, readers of this volume may well be struck by the resemblance between the Manichaenism in the traditional dramas analyzed by Peter Li and that in the communist propanganda dramas analyzed by Lowell Dittmer. A Manichaean perception of society and history was as basic to the Neo-Confucianism of late imperial times as it was to all the main ideologies of modern China, right, left, and liberal. Except for differently identifying heroes and villains, the Maoist vision of heroic, Manichaean moral action differs little from the official Guomindang vision in Taiwan today. In both cases, the hero, filled with a spirit of pride and sincerity while supported by both "the people" and the force of history, seeks to translate his "spirit" into an externally effective "struggle," which invariably consists of responding in an angry, Manichaean way to the *cuozhe* (humiliating setbacks) inflicted on him by evil people with power.

The centrality of this image of *cuozhe* is illustrated not only by the Communists' perception of the hardships thrust on them by domestic and imperialistic enemies but also by the Guomindang's perception of the loss of the Mainland. In both cases, these "humiliating setbacks" were defined as a challenge revitalizing the heroic spirit. Precisely because it saw the loss of the Mainland as that kind of "setback" integral to heroic struggle, the Guomindang on Taiwan, no matter what the practical considerations, could not agree that this loss was irreversible without discarding its own sense of heroic identity, without which it would have dissolved into a faction-ridden collection of ineffective politicians united by no common purpose. Similarly, no matter what the practical considerations or the theoretical dictates of Marxism, Mao could define economic backwardness not as an obstacle to rapid change but as the field of an heroic struggle effecting an unlimited transformation of society. In both cases, that of military defeat and that of economic backwardness, it was precisely an agonizing situation almost empty of hope by any practical standard that was seized upon as the most suitable occasion for realizing the highest moral ideals, which in turn were perceived as inherently and inevitably leading to practical success. One can, moreover, see a connection between the Manichaeanism of this widespread image of "struggle" and the tradition-rooted psychology of "shame" as analyzed by Wilson. Thus, his Figures 1.3 and 1.4 describe how common reactions to shameful behavior could escalate into that mood of moral condemnation integral to this Manichaeanism.

If, then, the Maoist vision of heroic action seems to be part of a broader, tradition-rooted pattern, continuities with the past are suggested also by the epistemological, cosmological, and historical framework with which this normative vision has been habitually intertwined. For instance, while Mao's cosmological and historical theory of "materialism" is often viewed as a Western import, it depended on the following assumptions, all of which were often made in modern China by non-Marxists as well as Marxists, and all of which had traditional roots: the assumption that cosmic and historical processes are linked; that they follow fixed principles; that the units of historical development, such as dynasties or evolutionary stages, can be characterized in simple, monistic terms as shaped by a single, dominant quality; that this cosmic/historical process is filled with a "power" that is inherently moral; that this flow of power is inherently susceptible to control through heroic action, which is carried out at the center of the polity and/or initiated in ego's mind, and which is based on a correct, architectonic doctrine about the nature of the cosmic/historical process *(xitong);* that evil, wrong ideas about this process can also have a powerful influence on people; that the right ideas were discovered in the past and are available today, though in an insufficiently clear form, while the wrong ideas have often determined the course of history; that, as a result, history is a dualistic, Manichaean process constantly generating "humiliating setbacks" but currently moving upward with more hope of progress than in previous centuries; and, finally, that the main physical locus of this historical process is a territory so abundantly stocked with resources that there can be no imbalance between resources and population. Admittedly, in this set of perceptions, the vision of current progress arose only with the Western impact.

While some scholars thus discuss the relation to tradition of Mao's normative vision and its conceptual framework, Alfred H. Bloom touches on this question of continuity by studying linguistic patterns. He argues vividly that the Chinese language leans more to "rather direct categorizations of perceptual reality" than to "rather complex, abstracted perspectives on reality." This suggestion perhaps helps us understand why Chinese thought, modern and premodern, has been so free of skepticism about the validity of universal categories and the possibility of deducing "ought" from "is." To be sure, one factor is the above-noted belief, so contrary to the Greek tradition, that universally right ideas about both "ought" and "is" were discovered in the past, whether in western Europe or north China, and are available today in published form. Thus, exegesis largely replaced epistemology. Moreover, any growth of philosophical skepticism would have clashed with the prevalent, traditional Chinese pessimism about the free play of ideas. Lacking John Stuart Mill's optimistic view that good doctrines would emerge victorious out of a free marketplace of ideas, Chinese since Mencius and Xun Zi have instead emphasized the human tendency to become deluded through the interplay of "false" and "correct" doctrines. Given this fear of delusion, uninhibited skepticism could not easily appear as a valuable heuristic tool. At the same time, if modern and premodern Chinese, as Bloom holds, have to a large extent phrased statements about universals in terms referring to concrete particulars, then it is easy to see why the ontological status of universals did not appear to them as a salient problem, and so why skepticism about the existence of moral universals never really arose.

Moreover, while Chinese thinkers, traditionally and in modern times, have thus usually been free of skepticism about the possibility of universal, absolute moral knowledge, they have also to a large extent agreed specifically about the content of morality. In modern times virtually all ideologies, right, left, and liberal, have stressed not only self-abnegation but also a tradition-rooted bundle of norms that can be termed Apollonian, bourgeois, and civilizational, and that called for hard work, love of learning, manners, reverence for nature and art, and, in a peculiarly Chinese way, a certain "oneness" of all human and material things.

While a variety of arguments thus can be made about the traditional roots of the Maoist vision, however, a prominent school of thought holds that the most important aspects of this vision contradicted traditional values. In accord with Max Weber's view of Chinese culture, this school today is represented by scholars such as Benjamin I. Schwartz, Zhang Hao, Richard H. Solomon, and, in this volume, Richard P. Madsen. Madsen contrasts the Maoist "inner-worldly asceticism" with the Confucian "ethic of adaptation to the world." This asceticism, he holds, was similar to that of the Puritan, who lived "*in* but not *of* the world," and who emphasized "an individual's personal integrity." By contrast, according to Madsen, the "traditional Chinese [person] ... lived in and very much of the world." His Confucian ethos put the "social obligations" of a "narrow, local world" above any emphasis on personal integrity and so resulted in a pattern of individual life "determined from without."

This thesis seems impressively supported by the contrast between the mass ascetic activism of Maoist China and premodern conditions. Yet, nothing was more basic to the Neo-Confucian vision than determination from within, the total integrity of the individual according to a transcendent, cosmic principle of morality, and the moral transformation of the whole world, not just "adaptation" to the "narrow, local" status quo. Moreover, there was a definite ascetic streak in Confucianism going back to Confucius' repeated injunction to put moral obligations above material desires.

True, a prevalent thesis holds that the Confucian emphasis was on fitting into a "social hierarchy," not preserving one's moral autonomy. In fact, though, our word "hierarchy" fails to encompass the variety of social relations Confucians valued. Moreover, discussing the "serving" of "superiors," Confucians had in mind an ideal relation partly distinct from the status quo. At the same time, in defining superiority, the traditions of both Mencius and Xun Zi explicitly used three partly conflicting criteria of hierarchy, that is, age, position in society, and virtue. Thus, their consequently ambiguous concept of hierarchy was compatible with their emphasis on moral autonomy.

Again, some might argue that the Neo-Confucian emphasis on autonomy and the moral transformation of society was an ideal less connected to overt social behavior than Mao's "asceticism" and mostly reserved for an elite minority. This point is plausible. In that case, however, the Maoist ethos could have arisen more as an effort to implement, externalize, and popularize rather than to reject this Neo-Confucian ideal. Indeed, as is especially clear from the studies of Wang Ermin, the modernizers of the Liang Qichao generation to a large extent saw modernization precisely as a project realizing in the "outer" world and popularizing the ancient ideals celebrated in Neo-Confucianism.[5]

To be sure, there were cultural discontinuities with the tradition, such as those marked by the rise of nationalism and iconoclasm, factors emphasized particularly by the Levensonian school. Such discontinuities, however, were not necessarily more important than the continuities. Moreover, the rise of iconoclasm, thanks to Lin Yu-sheng, has now been identified as a major historical puzzle, while nationalism is too ubiquitous a modern phenomenon to explain the cultural development of any modern society in particular.

Moreover, if Mao's vision of heroic action did not have traditional roots, where did it come from? Aware today that this vision filtered out key Western values and appealed often to millions of Chinese too uneducated to understand exotic values, many scholars today hesitate to view it simply as a Western import. Another possibility often favored today is that it was largely created in the historical present, arising possibly out of a quest for integration in a time of chaos, or out of a revolutionary response to economic backwardness and to the perceived victimization of the Chinese people by domestic and foreign exploiters.

It seems to me, however, that this thesis contradicts anthropology's impressive testimony about the persistence of cultural patterns and dubiously endows human beings with an enormous capacity to transcend these inherited patterns, to confront experience as raw fact rather than a situation partly defined in terms of native cultural forms, and to act creatively in the present. As Wang Ermin has argued, the new intellectual developments of modern China can be best seen as arising out of a combination of creative contemporaneous efforts with traditional as well as Western influences.

ACCOMMODATIVE VISIONS OF MORALITY AND THE QUESTION OF THEIR LEGITIMATION

Yet, however the transformative Maoist vision originated, we have to keep in mind that competitive though sometimes overlapping visions of morality also have existed in modern China. One of the most important is best contrasted with Maoism in terms of the dichotomy between transformative thinking and accommodative thinking. Does morality require the total transformation and moral purification of society, or can suffering be alleviated more effectively by accepting the persistence of some evil and aiming for slow, gradual progress? In other words, should one wholly dissolve or partly yield to the given hard edge of an unsatisfactory world? This dichotomy refers to the basic moral problem of negotiating the tension between utopia and practicality. It goes back especially to Ernst Troeltsch's distinction between "sect" and "church" and also is close to Max Weber's distinction between the Sermon on the Mount's "ethic of ultimate ends" and a more realistic "ethic of responsibility." It also roughly corresponds to a dichotomy between an ethics of defiance, putting truth above the dictates of authority figures by *gan* (daring) to challenge them, and an ethics of compliance, stressing the need to *shi* (serve) authority figures and so to repress egotistic impulses. To be sure, defiance is one thing, defiance in the name of a utopian ethic of ultimate ends is another, and a utopian act of defiance aiming at a transformation of the actual structure of society is still another. For the purposes of our discussion here, however, we can use these categories a bit loosely, sometimes regarding them as overlapping.

Certainly it is clear that in contrast to Mao's utopian, "sect"-like "ethic of ultimate ends," there has also been prevalent in modern China an accommodative vision of morality evading Mao's Manichaean emphasis on heroic action, emphasizing the objective problems that limit the pace of progress, respecting those particularistic "natural human feelings" *(renqing)* condemned as "selfish" by Maoism, and encouraging compliance with the wishes of authority figures.

This accommodative vision is often expressed in the views of those Chinese individuals described by some behavioral scientists as "dependent" and "authoritarian." It is rooted in the traditional familism, which emphasized filial piety while leaving to others the Confucian dream of combining filial piety with that broader mission of world transformation epitomized by the "eight steps" of the *Great Learning.* It was expressed in late imperial collections of popular proverbs, and it continued to be important in republican times. Eclipsed by Maoism after 1949, it now reappears in Deng Xiaoping's pragmatism. An excellent example of its role in contemporary Mainland villages is provided by Madsen's portrait of Old Pepperpot in this volume. In Taiwan, it has been central during the last

decades. There it complements but does not coincide with the official philosophy, the Three Principles of the People. A fascinating version of it can be found
in a popular book published under Guomindang auspices in 1972, Gu Ying's
Yige xiao shimin di xinsheng (An Ordinary Citizen Speaks Out).[6]

Curiously enough, however, despite its prevalence, its legitimation in the
minds of many influential Chinese has traditionally been a major problem.
This is a most important fact, since the reservations and ambivalences attached
to a moral vision are more than a cultural penumbra; they can facilitate the
abandonment of this vision in favor of another.

True, the accommodative viewpoint was legitimated in China. Indeed, it is
the viewpoint we usually associate with "traditional China," and which Max
Weber identified as the Confucian ethos. Yet, it was never legitimated in the way
that the Aristotelian and Burkean philosophies arose in the West, intellectually
recognizing the claims of property, power, and convention, and taking the form
of a thought-out doctrine that could be elaborated in educated, elite circles to
refute or counterbalance more utopian, transformative doctrines.

For one thing, since at least the third century B.C. there was a major tendency to condemn as "heterodox and evil" philosophies trying to disentangle
political practicalities from absolute moral standards. Thus, Mencius' (fourth
century B.C.) outright rejection of realpolitik was usually preferred to Xun Zi's
(third century B.C.) more nuanced view (this refers to the issue of the "true
king" vs. the "hegemon"). A central consequence was the Confucian failure to
develop a clear concept of legitimate yet amoral political authority, although
such a concept can be found in the institution of the "emperor" *(huangdi)*,
which lasted from 221 B.C. to 1912 A.D., and which was partly "heterodox"
(Legalist) in origin. In Confucian theory, morality tended to be the only legitimate basis for political authority.

This reluctance to conceptualize politics in more practical terms was connected to a particularly basic idea. Already by at least the third century B.C.,
even the leading "heterodox" philosophies like Legalism, Maoism, and Taoism
shared with Confucianism the peculiar conviction that political morality depended
on the absence of "selfish" feeling. As a result, although the Confucian virtue
of empathy and compassion *(zhungshu eryi)* did allow harmonious cooperation
with people perceived as moderately "selfish," the classical philosophic framework precluded the explicit legitimation of selfish impulse as a natural aspect of
political forms.

This attitude was certainly connected to that refusal to legitimate amoral
authority noted above. It was also connected to the way both Confucius and
Mencius denounced as "hypocrites" *(xiangyuan)* those prudent, practical men
with good intentions but bruised integrity who in fact are indispensable for the
smooth functioning of any large-scale political institution.

Even today in Taiwan, despite all the sophisticated interest in American
politics, political effort is still publicly conceptualized as an effort to eliminate
"selfish interests" rather than frankly to recognize them as a starting point for

constructive negotiation. *Da gong wusi banhao xuanju* (carrying out the elections by putting aside all selfish interests and devoting ourselves to the great public good) reads a typical magazine headline referring to the elections of December 6, 1980.

From an economic standpoint too, this attitude toward "selfishness" made it difficult to develop a realistic "ethic of responsibility," to use Weber's term. Like "selfishness," private economic interests could only be tolerated, not conceptualized as a natural and proper aspect of elite political activity. Chinese intellectuals have usually regarded the pursuit of profit *(zhuili, wenshe qiutian)* as only the inevitable tendency of a vulgar populace that ought to be guided by an elite with higher ideals. "An adequate piece of permanent [private] property" *(hengchan)* was defined by Mencius only as something ordinary, uneducated people needed for their peace of mind, not as the rightful economic foundation of the elite as well. In the Confucian tradition, this elite was to be economically supported by exchanging its contribution of moral service for large, richly deserved state stipends *(lu)*, not by selfishly seeking to acquire private property. Similarly, Xun Zi patronizingly referred to *minde* (the morality of ordinary people), who "approve of respect for custom, regard wealth as precious, and think of physical well-being as their highest value" *(Ruxiao* chapter). This distinction between a vulgar and a higher morality epitomizes the Confucian reluctance fully to legitimate accommodative behavior.

Another example can be taken from the seventeenth century. As China's economic structure became larger, more complex, more monetized, and more commercialized, private property became more securely institutionalized. For many Confucian scholars, however, this process was morally suspect as based on the popular preoccupation with increasing one's family property holdings *(jiadang)*, a preoccupation connected to filial piety but perceived as bottling up that natural flow of universal moral feeling on which the true ordering of society depended. Intellectuals accommodating themselves to these administrative and economic changes were often called *xiangyuan* (hypocrites) in this period.

Similarly in modern times, an intellectually vital conservatism of the Burkean sort did not arise in China, as shown by the essays in *The Limits of Change.*[7] As illustrated by the Guomindang's ideological leaning to socialism, a vigorous defense of capitalism has been almost impossible to mount in modern China's intellectual climate. Similarly, intellectuals suggesting some shift from an "ethic of ultimate ends" to a conservative "ethic of responsibility" have risked being regarded as *xiangyuan*. A good example is the confrontation in 1958–59 in Taiwan between the great May Fourth liberal Hu Shi and Yin Haiguang, the leading intellectual liberal criticizing the Guomindang at that time. Hu accommodatively urged that intellectuals treat the Guomindang with more "tolerance" *(rongren)*. Yin, however, felt that the Guomindang's behavior was rooted in the pathologies of the traditional culture, which, he held, should be thoroughly reformed. Transformative in outlook and using the vocabulary of heroic struggle,

Yin insisted on vigorously condemning all of the Guomindang's shortcomings according to absolute, "scientific" standards of "right and wrong." Eventually, he referred in private to Hu as "a big hypocrite" *(da xiangyuan).* [8]

Whatever the complexities of this encounter, it is clear that even if Chinese have sometimes regarded Yin as wrongheaded, they have not regarded him a *xiangyuan.* On the contrary, as one who *ganjiang* (dared to speak out), he did not need to worry about his reputation for integrity. When in the summer of 1980, 11 years after his death, the popular Taiwan-based periodical *Shibao Zhoukan* reprinted some of Yin's letters, a letter to the editor signed in a most conventional way that China now more than ever had a need for such a scholar with the courage to speak "the truth" no matter what. Conversely, Hu's attempt to argue that an absolute ethic of ultimate ends cannot be directly applied to politics led many to question his integrity.

Similarly, if we look at the history of dissidence in Taiwan during the 1970s, culminating in the Gaoxiung Incident of December 10, 1979, we again can see the powerful appeal, especially among the young and the intellectuals, of an ethic of defiance and ultimate ends. In recent years, the Confucian cry *dangren burang* (in matters of moral principle there can be no yielding) has been used by President Jiang as well as the dissidents (Confucius himself said "In matters of moral principle, one should not yield to one's teacher"). But in this rhetorical interchange the government has appeared to many if not most intellectuals in Taiwan as morally compromised.

To be sure, one could enter into the facts of the government's response to the dissident demand for more democracy and conclude in some "objective" sense that, in this case, one side or the other was indeed morally compromised. Whatever the specifics, however, it is clear that in intellectual circles habitually demanding that authority be based on pure morality and "truth," an actual government, which can never live up to such a utopian standard, is often on the rhetorical defensive. Moreover, since the abolition of the emperorship *(huangdi),* the Chinese have found it difficult to conceptualize a political center which could, like the *huangdi,* demand "loyalty" while ostentatiously failing to realize moral absolutes *(wangdao).* As already suggested, this peculiar imperial institution, which all along had had an uneasy relation to Confucian ethics, did to some extent connote an "ethic of responsibility." Thus the abolition of the *huangdi* in 1912 led not just to the possibility of democracy but also to a euphoric revitalization of the Mencian "ethic of ultimate ends," according to which political authority had to be based only on absolute morality. Thus followed the various attempts of the Communists and the Guomindang to picture their respective parties as vehicles of absolute historical and moral truth.

Certainly these claims have repeatedly been regarded by many Chinese as ludicrous and tedious propaganda. This sense of contempt and alienation, however, does not mean that we should regard these official claims as culturally insignificant. On the contrary, the intertwining of these official claims with these negative reactions has formed one of the most prominent cultural patterns of modern China. This persistent pattern reflects the difficulty the Chinese have experienced in trying to erect a modern polity based on an accommodative "ethic of responsibility," as well as their tendency to judge the current government according to an absolutistic "ethic of ultimate ends." This point should also be considered when trying to explain the euphoria with which so many Chinese intellectuals were drawn at various times to Mao's vision of social transformation. For partly different reasons, many Western historians adopted a similar perspective, looking down on accommodative trends in modern China as culturally backward, psychologically pathological, politically reactionary, or historically epiphenomenal.

Thus noting this Chinese tendency to favor a defiant "ethic of ultimate ends" over a compliant "ethic of responsibility," we encounter a paradox, since Chinese culture is usually characterized as emphasizing compliance with and respect for the established structure of authority. Instead of this picture, we find not only that in this culture the symbols of defiance have been as well developed as the symbols of compliance, but even that the rhetoric of defiance has to some extent overshadowed that of compliance, to the point that compliant, accommodative behavior has often not been fully legitimated in leading intellectual circles. At the very least, one cannot refer simply to "authoritarianism" in China and should rather recognize a culturally widespread pattern in terms of which ego was filled with both a sense of awe for authority figures and a feeling of admiration for those autonomously able to defy authority. This ambivalence, as already indicated, can also be found in the Maoist vision of heroic action.

This is not to say that dependency theorists like Richard H. Solomon have been unaware of ambivalent feelings toward authority figures. The point at issue is rather the extent to which open defiance was morally legitimated in terms of tradition-rooted, culturally central symbols rather than stemming from Western values or values created by the Communist revolution. Indeed, to go back to the controversy about continuities with the past, these can be seen, I would say, not only in the history of both accommodative and transformative thinking but also in the problematik of legitimation overarching both these modes.

MORAL VISIONS AND SOCIAL STRATA

This question of legitimation, however, should not prevent us from treating accommodative thinking as a serious moral outlook and from examining the relation of accommodative as well as transformative thinking to different social strata and personality types. Little has been done on this subject, partly because of the Chinese and Western attitudes noted above, but Madsen's article is an important step forward. He beautifully describes some of the kinds of rural personalities receptive to transformative and accommodative policies, respectively, although with regard to the corresponding urban and elite types, his typology is limited to one, not necessarily dominant intellectual type.

In this connection I would emphasize the psychological transition often associated in China with entrance into the elite social stratum. Traditionally and in modern times, a member of this stratum could more easily than many others leave behind feelings of being just a "humble" fellow *(beiwei)* and could instead regard himself as one with the capability "resolutely to take the world as my responsibility" *(yiran yi tianxia wei jiren)*. This heroic self-image was logically and emotionally linked to the idea of "daring to speak out" *(ganjiang)*, which in turn was connected to the ancient tradition of *jian* (remonstrance).

Although much of the elite in fact acted accommodatively, this elite self-image lent itself easily to transformative thinking. At the same time, accommodative rhetoric was often typical of those large, lower strata the members of which had an economically settled though difficult life and a "humbler" self-image. To a significant extent, one finds in the modern history of Chinese stratification a political affinity between these lower strata and accommodative tendencies in elite circles, while there often was another political linkup between the most discontented lower strata and transformative intellectuals socially connected to elite circles.

This pattern of stratification seems connected to the contrast between the picture of modern China offered by historians and that of social scientists. Often focusing on the latter linkup between transformative intellectuals and the most discontented lower strata, historians have pictured an explosion of defiance, while the compliant members of the other strata have perhaps been predominantly represented in social science surveys.

Yet, defiant and compliant behavior have both been basic to Chinese society as an historically evolving pattern. Thus, Jerome Ch'en complains: "It is perplexing that the Westerners so often applaud the meekness of the Chinese and yet ignore the frequent riots against missionaries, boycotts, demonstrations against foreign aggression, civil wars, and rebellions against all forms of oppression."[9] What this means from our standpoint is that defiant behavior should interest social scientists as much as compliant, and, conversely, historians should study and respect accommodative trends in modern China just as they have lavished attention on transformative movements. To say that only the rebel is an authentic human being worthy of the scholar's attention is as meaningless as giving the conformist this place of honor. Indeed, to a large extent, this volume departs from the sociological custom of regarding only compliant accommodative behavior as the structural norm in China.

CHINESE MORAL LIFE AND THE CRITERIA OF
MORAL DEVELOPMENT

If, then, we want to ask about moral development in China, we have to deal with these attitudes regarding compliance and defiance, accommodation and transformation, but we also need some lucid definition of moral development. Contradicting each other, the three critiques of Chinese behavior noted above leave us with the task of rethinking what it is we mean by "moral development." In this situation, Wilson's definition of moral development is most valuable, since it would be hard, I think, to devise a list of criteria very different from his "reciprocity," "empathy," and "responsibility" or "autonomy." Moreover, Wilson is careful in arguing that despite some emphasis on the autonomy needed to defy authority figures, Chinese culture can generally be criticized in terms of these criteria. He holds that Chinese culture has encouraged too much reliance on "situational cues, especially those that are related to rules and the dictates of custom and to the pronouncements of authority figures," as well as on given, fixed moral doctrines.

Yet, if we agree with Madsen that the individual should be "anchored" in a community and a social tradition, how is the individual to distinguish between being thus properly "anchored" and excessively respecting "the dictates of social custom"? If "reciprocity" means recognizing "the claims of others," how does one distinguish between these "claims" and the "cues" of authority figures? Unless, as Wilson comes close to suggesting in his discussion of "dominance," all claims of authority are morally wrong, "reciprocity" should also be extended to other human beings who happen to be authority figures. (Interestingly, the traditional injunction to respect authority figures was phrased in terms of the central norm of *bao* [reciprocity].) Moreover, noting Wilson's point that the sense of autonomy differs from "egotistical" impulses, how can we confidently distinguish the latter from those "self-generated moral criteria" typical of autonomy?

In other words, how can we know whether a particular act of deference is based on a "responsible" decision to avoid egotism or an "irresponsible" decision to give up one's moral autonomy? Facing these doubts, should we mainly suspect defiance as the road to egotism or suspect compliance as the dissolution of autonomy?

If Wilson most fears the dissolution of autonomy, I would instead note his reference to the "ambiguities" of the moral life and suggest that morally responsible, autonomous behavior partly depends on thoughtfulness in identifying and dealing with the ambiguities of defiance and compliance. Thus, pictured as dealing with ambiguities that we in our own culture are often bewildered by, the Chinese strike me as perhaps more successful in dealing with the problem of autonomy than they do Wilson. Above all I would urge that without first dissecting our own feelings about defiance and compliance, we are in danger of judging the Chinese in the light of our own insufficiently examined standards of individualistic liberalism.

If Chinese philosophy rigidly universalizes a system of Apollonian, bourgeois morality, we need to ask whether this fallacy is more serious than that moral relativism on the brink of which individualistic skepticism dangerously teeters, as Steven Lukes also recognizes. A philosophy, perhaps, should not be judged purely in an analytical way but should also be considered as a language justifying a particular pattern of childhood socialization, education, adult sanctions, and stratification. From this standpoint, we should perhaps more comprehensively and realistically compare Chinese culture to American rather than dwelling on Chinese authoritarianism and philosophical dogmatism.

Thus, the individualistic critique of Chinese behavior is not necessarily convincing. Moreover, even apart from the ambiguities of compliance and defiance, there seems as yet to be no way of judging between the competitive definitions of moral autonomy offered by individualism and that modern defense of the Confucian ethos mentioned above.

A linked ambiguity is presented by the dichotomy between the transformative and accommodative forms of social action. I would suggest that the failure of many Chinese intellectuals to legitimate accommodative action, their failure to envisage fully what Weber called an "ethic of responsibility," has indeed prevented many of them from understanding this ambiguity and so has limited their autonomy as thoughtful persons trying to translate morality into policy. Similarly, I would agree with Madsen that when Chinese intellectuals have defined themselves as each shouldering responsibility for the whole society and in this light have insisted on a transformative "ethic of ultimate ends," they have sometimes done so at the risk of narcissism, though certainly not always.

Besides narcissism, the Manichaeanism typical of Chinese transformative thought has not necessarily enhanced the capacity for empathy. At the same time, perhaps because the traditional norm of "reciprocity" and political "loyalty" has usually been interpreted in terms of the relation between two persons, Chinese intellectuals have often, I believe, implemented their Manichaean ethic of ultimate ends in a personal way, becoming preoccupied with the *cuozhe* (humiliating setbacks) inflicted on them in particular by the state at the expense of asking whether their government has on balance promoted the well-being of their society as a whole. This personalistic definition of *cuozhe* also has some relation to the prominent issue of Chinese cliquism, since the solidarity of cliques has often been based on some shared sense of outrage, typically a reaction to the failure of a clique member to obtain advancement in the government.

Indeed, Chinese attitudes about the distribution of esteem and social rewards are exceedingly complex and little studied. Yet, it is clear that the Confucian tradition defined such distribution as purely a matter of moral choice rather than also an economic problem of finding enough room at the top for all the eligible candidates. Be that as it may, the intellectual failure fully to legitimate the accommodative option, along with Manichaeanism and cliquism, is still important today and, especially on the Mainland, serves as an obstacle to political stability, making it harder for people to react thoughtfully rather than emotionally to the inevitable frustrations of social competition, politics, and economic backwardness.

All in all, therefore, if we ask to what extent Chinese culture has facilitated an understanding of the perennial ambiguities surrounding the quest for reciprocity, empathy, and autonomy, we may conclude possibly that it has been more successful in dealing with the ambiguities of defiance and compliance than it has with those of transformation and accommodation. The mainstream of the traditional culture having fully legitimated moral autonomy and defiance, we cannot easily claim that it has failed to emphasize autonomy "enough," especially since our standard of "enough" is probably affected by our own, insufficiently examined background of individualistic liberalism. The more obvious problem, I think, has been the strong Chinese tendency to correlate moral autonomy exclusively with an "ethic of ultimate ends" instead of *also* more definitely envisioning a combination of moral autonomy with an accommodative "ethic of responsibility."

If, then, moral autonomy means not just the courage of one's convictions but also the intellectual ability to identify and reflect on these key ambiguities, this excellent volume, I think, refutes the sociological thesis that Chinese culture has traditionally precluded moral autonomy, helps us better understand to what extent the Chinese have or have not confronted these ambiguities, and should help stimulate a more comparative understanding of China's moral civilization.

Confucius once said that encountering another human being, he was often led to look into himself, evaluating himself in the light of that person's merits and shortcomings. Confucius did not suggest that he was interested only in a factual description of that person without value judgments. Today, as the interdisciplinary study of Chinese society slowly matures in the United States, we could well consider developing its methodology more in the direction of what Confucius regarded as a true human encounter.

The interdisciplinary study of societies, it seems to me, does not mean pursuing the chimera of a scientifically precise and objective discipline free of value judgments but instead means undertaking the difficult task of integrating value judgments and self-examination—in other words, establishing a serious relationship between the dissection of foreign cultures and the dissection of our own.

This returns us to the point raised by Edward Said, mentioned above, and to the whole question of the methodology needed to do justice to the moral dimension of social experience. Leo Strauss long ago warned that to thrive, the behavioral sciences must return to the question of "the good society."[10] This can be done, I would think, only if the social scientist uses all his analytical resources to combine the moral evaluation of foreign societies with the moral evaluation of his own, instead of exempting from such scrutiny those ideals regarded as most attractive in his circles and in those foreign ones fashionably defined as enlightened and progressive. Thus, the fact that many articulate, well-intentioned, and English-speaking Chinese, especially the charismatic Hu Shi, established a Chinese tradition of admiration for our "individualism" is really not enough to prove that this individualism should be regarded by us as a standard for evaluating problematic cultural patterns instead of being itself taken as a problematic cultural pattern. On the contrary, having generated one of the major critiques of Chinese civilization, our heritage of individualism should be more carefully scrutinized before we offer a final evaluation of this critique.

To be sure, any such scrutiny will itself be based on a crystallizing cultural pattern that itself will require scrutiny. Our choice, after all, is not between universal truth and culturally limited beliefs. It is only between more and less intelligent ways of constructing social science investigations within the framework of our own culturally given presuppositions. Given this choice, I believe, we should avoid the obvious shortcomings of an amoral approach and substitute an intelligent spirit of criticism and self-criticism for that syndrome of alternating condescension and adulation that has so often distorted the study of foreign societies. This volume is a significant step in this direction.

NOTES

1. Clifford Geertz, *The Interpretation of Cultures* (New York: Basic Books, 1973).

2. Leo Strauss, *Natural Right and History* (Chicago: University of Chicago Press, 1953).

3. Steven Lukes, *Individualism* (Oxford: Basil Blackwell, 1973). I here slightly distort the thrust of Luke's much more subtle and complicated discussion.

4. Tang's argument is outlined in Chapter 2 of Thomas A. Metzger, *Escape from Predicament* (New York: Columbia University Press, 1977).

5. For a discussion of Wang Ermin's views, see Thomas A. Metzger, "Author's Reply," *The Journal of Asian Studies* 39 (February 1980):282-90.

6. See an analysis of late imperial proverbs in Lu Baoqian, *Qingdai sixiangshi* (A History of Thought in the Qing Period) (Guangwen shuju youxian gongsi, 1978). For "Gu Ying's" outlook, see T.A. Metzger, "Chinese Communism and the Evolution of China's Political Culture," in *Proceedings of the Eighth Sino-American Conference on Mainland China* (Institute of International Studies, 1979), pp. 63-75; also in *Issues and Studies* (August 1979):51-63.

7. Charlotte Furth, ed., *The Limits of Change* (Cambridge, Mass.: Harvard University Press, 1976).

8. Yin Haiguang, *Yin Haiguang xuanji—diyijuan—shehui zhengzhi yenlun* (The Collected Writings of Yin Haiguang—Volume One—Social and Political Writings) (Kowloon: Youlian chubanshe youxian gongsi, 1971), pp. 419-424, 411-418, 494-498, 487-493, 499-506. *Yin Haiguang xiansheng jinianji bienweihui,* comp., *Yin Haiguang xiansheng jinianji* (Essays in Memory of Yin Haiguang) (Kowloon: Youlian shubao faxing gongsi, 1971), p. 38.

9. Jerome Ch'en, *China and the West* (Bloomington: Indiana University Press, 1979), p. 48.

10. Leo Strauss, *What Is Political Philosophy?* (Glencoe, Ill.: The Free Press, 1959), pp. 10, 18-27.

Moral Behavior in
Chinese Society

1 MORAL BEHAVIOR IN CHINESE SOCIETY: A THEORETICAL PERSPECTIVE*

Richard W. Wilson

Few societies have been as self-consciously moral as the Chinese. Scholars of both traditional and modern China are aware that Chinese speech and writings are infused with exhortation for moral behavior. The ubiquity of this characteristic seems especially pronounced when compared with the more muted way that issues regarding morality are dealt with in many other societies. Yet, moral fervor notwithstanding, the study of morals in Chinese society has not attracted widespread scholarly attention.[1] For some, perhaps, the subject may seem too broad, for others, too complex, and for still others, too difficult in terms of empirical verification. Whatever the reason, moral behavior as a framework for analysis in Chinese studies has been underutilized. Yet, as we will suggest in the papers in this volume, this is a unique focus that allows us "...to combine the capacities of heuristic formulations to illuminate large macro-systems of behavior and the scientific precision that rests with operationalizable propositions and quantitatively testable hypotheses."[2] In short, the study of moral behavior permits us to examine many facets of life in a social system, to illuminate critical values and behavior patterns, and to assess the relationship between micro- and macro-level social patterns.

This paper will begin with a discussion of definitions, after which a general model for moral development will be set forth. It will be proposed that significant differences in moral development at the individual level are related to different socialization influences. It will then be further hypothesized that the form and content of these influences reflect distinctive patterns of dominance within

*Some of the ideas presented in this paper have appeared previously in my article, "Political Socialization and Moral Development," *World Politics* 33 (January 1981).

a society. Following these initial theoretical remarks the model that has been developed will be used to analyze Chinese moral orientations.

DEFINING MORAL BEHAVIOR

Developments in a number of disciplines have aided the current search for a more precise understanding of what constitutes moral behavior. Socialization studies generally have given us more definite conceptions of the mechanisms whereby people acquire distinctive cognitive and evaluative patterns that are related to internalized controls over behavior. Political philosophers, led by scholars such as John Rawls,[3] have sparked renewed interest in the age-old quest to define the good citizen and the good society. Of the various intellectual strands, perhaps the most important are from the field of moral development, which is an area of study primarily located within the discipline of psychology; in increasing quantity and quality scholars of moral development have published literature regarding the ways whereby particular moral *judgment* capabilities are acquired.

Vigorous debate characterizes studies of moral development, championed by proponents of three schools. Those in the first group are adherents of psychoanalytic theory. Propounded initially by Freud and his followers, psychoanalytic theorists are still a major influence, especially in clinical psychology with its emphasis on the relationship between the moralistic superego and the ego and id. The work of socialization scholars represents the second school. Studies in this genre have been largely informed by social learning theories; proponents have evinced special interest in uncovering the cultural influences that are adduced as explanations for differing moral orientations. Lastly, cognitive development theorists, led by Lawrence Kohlberg and his associates, have placed special theoretical emphasis on a hypothesized relationship during the maturation process between changes in cognitive structure and corollary changes in moral judgment capabilities, the latter being said to occur sequentially in stages with age. Of the three schools, cognitive development theory currently holds pride of place in academic discourse, but its ascendancy is vigorously challenged and its propositions subjected to searching critique.

Regardless of the school of moral development, there appears to be general agreement that judgment and behavior can be categorized and ranked in accordance with explicit criteria that define mature (developed) versus immature (undeveloped) moral orientations.[4] In addition, there is also agreement that the moral stances of individuals can change over time. Evidence has also been presented that social units differ overall from one another in their degrees of adherence to various forms of morality. This suggests that social and cultural influences do have a bearing on the development of individual–level moral capability.

Morality has been defined in a number of ways. These range from Skinnerian definitions where behavior is labeled good or bad depending on the degree of positive or negative reinforcement from others[5] to sociobiological explanations that posit altruistic behavior among humans as functional for the preservation of genetic material[6] to Marxist explanations of historically relative morality based on theories of social consciousness[7] to various philosophical and sociological explanations regarding, *inter alia,* the concept of rules and respect for rules and consideration of the consequences of behavior for the welfare of others by scholars such as Kant, Durkheim, Dewey, and others.[8]

Although there are many ways in which mature and immature morality can be defined, in my own formulation mature morality has characteristics involving reciprocity, empathy, and individual responsibility. Reciprocity, from Kohlberg, is the consistent ability within diverse situations to recognize the "related claims of others"[9] Empathy is a particular form of affective relationship with others (a factor not adequately covered by cognitive development theorists) that involves the ability to take the place of another emotionally (in fact, in its highest forms, a capability for sympathetic distress).[10] Individual responsibility is the ability to accept the consequences of one's decisions. It implies a capability to form judgments and make choices that may be contrary to situational cues, most particularly those cues that reflect the influence of authority figures. Viewed from a development perspective this competence involves an increasing ability to formulate viewpoints on the basis of internalized values.

For our purposes, we may define immature morality as the reverse of the capabilities noted above. That is, immature morality is characterized by a perception of the self as the center of social activity and is noted by an inability to recognize the claims of others. There is also an inability to empathize and feel sympathy toward others and a reliance in the formulation of judgments on situational cues, especially those that are related to rules and the dictates of social custom and to the pronouncements of authority figures.

Reciprocity, empathy, and individual responsibility are related to different capabilities; they are universal human attributes that are not equally well developed in all people. Reciprocity, which involves the ability to understand the claims of others, has a strong cognitive component based on the capability to differentiate one's own goals from those of others. Involved is an awareness of the self in relation to others and an understanding of the implications of the claims that other people make. Empathy, on the other hand, involves a particular type of feeling, namely, the ability to emotionally take the place of another person. Empathy is having an echo within one's self of the feelings that others have and being able to relate sympathetically to these feelings. Individual responsibility is perhaps best characterized as ego strength, involving qualities of will and rectitude. As a capability it can be defined as autonomy, the quality of being self-governing rather than the pawn of situational influences. Individual responsibility is not "individualism," especially in the hedonistic and egotistical sense (divorced from empathy and reciprocity) that is sometimes attached to that term. It is, rather, the ability to act in terms of self-generated moral criteria; these actions may at times place one within the context of accepted group behavior, while at other times they may involve a defiance of authoritative dictates and group norms.

Taken together, the qualities of cognition in reciprocity, feeling in empathy, and autonomy in individual responsibility combine to form levels of *moral competence.* The highest forms of moral competence are an amalgam of the highest form of development of each of the constituent parts. This is an important point, for Kohlberg-oriented moral development theorists have primarily directed our attention toward age-related shifts in moral *judgment* capabilities and the relationship of these changes to cognitive growth. I grant that the development of particular cognitive capabilities, especially the ability to generalize, to relate and integrate information, and to draw logical conclusions[11] seems clearly to be a necessary (but not, I believe, sufficient) condition for the development of mature moral competence. However important though an understanding of judgmental capabilities is, I feel this focus alone is incapable of explaining moral *behavior,* where I believe our ultimate interest must be, and that behavioral explanations can be satisfactorily advanced only by reference to the full range of personality characteristics noted in the concept of moral competence.

A reliance on judgment alone to establish levels of moral competence reduces higher levels of morality to qualities related to rational thought. In Kohlberg's theory the highest levels of moral reasoning are called principled and involve logical universality and consistency. Recent data, however, suggest that in adulthood there is a regression from this form of moral orientation. Formal logic and principles of justice may seem appropriate in adolescence as the highest form of moral reasoning, but the ambiguities that are part of many events in life make such a stance unacceptable to many people later in adulthood. Compassion, tolerance, and respect modify the pure dictates of principle.[12] Such conclusions, I suggest, highlight the need for a measure of moral competence whose highest levels combine cognition with feeling and autonomy.

EXTERNAL INFLUENCES AND MORAL BEHAVIOR

Figure 1.1 is a schematic of the process whereby certain critical external socialization influences act upon internal cognitive, affective, and autonomous capabilities to develop particular types of moral competence, which, in turn, are associated with particular forms of moral behavior.[13] This behavior takes place within a social context (which can be thought of, in the largest sense, as a learning environment), and this milieu conditions the nature of feedback to the individual and also affects the form and content of the external socialization influences that act upon individual internal capabilities. Mature moral behavior, like the competence with which it is associated, is infused by reciprocity and empathy and is not unvaryingly particularistic in orientation nor directly reflective of situational cues. It develops as the result of particular kinds of training within particular social contexts. For any individual moral behavior is a set of possible outcomes that derive from the ongoing interaction of that person's judgment, feelings, and autonomous capabilities with others and that may vary to some extent from one situation to another depending upon which aspects of moral competence have been primarily engaged.

The external socialization influences set forth in Figure 1.1 can each be further differentiated in terms of characteristics that will favor or impede the

FIGURE 1.1
Moral Development Model

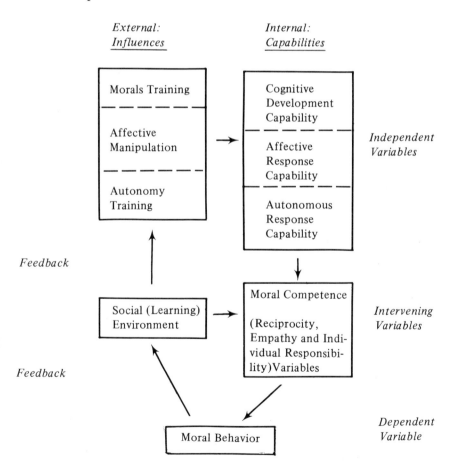

development of mature moral competence. For instance, depending upon social context, the values that are imparted during morals training may or may not place major emphasis upon reciprocity criteria. Furthermore, morals training may emphasize that values are inclusive with regard to a particular social group and are rigidly unvarying in their applicability (a framework that would be associated with an immature moral orientation). As an example, emphasis in learning may stress cooperation primarily only with other group members or unswerving loyalty to a particular leader. Many religious and political socialization influences are of this form. Conversely, and more rarely, emphasis in learning may stress the universal aspects of values and the need for experimentation regarding the application of these values involving the testing or moral alternatives and an awareness that the other person's moral stance, rather than one's own, may be the correct one.

With regard to affective manipulation, distinctive mixes of physical punishment, love withdrawal punishments, and induction training (where one is taught to empathize with the feelings that others may have as a result of one's own actions) can be noted in different social contexts.[14] There is a growing body of literature that posits that excessive amounts of physical punishment, such as spanking, slapping, or beating, induce considerable fear of authority figures; that excessive amounts of love withdrawal punishments induce guilt and shame and create fears of humiliation, ostracism, and rejection; and that either type is not conducive to the development of mature morality. Induction training, on the other hand, is said to induce mature moral orientations since from this type of training one acquires the ability to empathize with the experiences of other people.

Autonomy training refers to the development in individuals of an ability to behave in contexts that may have ambiguous characteristics without automatic reliance on cues from social rules or from other people, especially authority figures. It involves learning to act in terms of internalized notions of right and wrong and a willingness to be responsible for the consequences of such actions. One important feature of the developmental process associated with autonomy training is learning to behave as if in a secondary level context, where others are unknown, and to identify positively with the image of oneself in these contexts. A secondary level type of orientation does not mean the abrogation of strong ties with other primary group members, but it does require the acquisition of attributes that are appropriate for secondary level group membership and, ultimately, involves the capability of acting without reference to any particular group membership, primary or secondary. Such behavior is termed responsible and, hence, has attributes of moral maturity in the sense that actions manifest internalized ideals rather than demands from any particular external source. Immature moral behavior, on the other hand, is that which habitually asserts the situational needs of the self or of a particular group and which denies the possibility that behavior can be evenhanded toward others regardless of who they may be.

In childhood learning the impact of these socialization influences follows a universal format. The timing of the appearance of each influence in the development process is sequential and reflects at least partially the internal development in the child in increasingly complex cognitive structures and affective capabilities. For instance, learning social rules begins at birth, but the process accelerates and becomes more integrated after the child has mastered language. The ability to manifest empathy will not genuinely occur until individuals have a conception of their relationship to others and an ability to transcend a perception of self as the center of the social universe. Learning to behave responsibly in a manner that is appropriate for secondary level group interaction (i.e., in terms that transcend situational cues) cannot occur until one has acquired a perception of oneself that goes beyond primary group membership and has practice in behaving in terms of this perception. Clearly, for many individuals, this may not happen until adulthood, and where people have little actual experience of secondary level behavior, as was true for many individuals in primitive societies, the process may be systematically aborted throughout life.

Although our knowledge of internal capabilities is still incomplete and the precise measurement of external socialization influences still a science that is in its infancy, the limited data currently available suggest that the interaction of these variables in distinctive patterns does produce particular degrees of moral competence. For instance, comparative research involving children on Taiwan has indicated a modal moral response repertoire for Chinese that is characterized by relatively greater emphasis than for Americans on respect for authority and on the importance of fixed rules and the maintenance of the social order for its own sake (60 percent of 16-year-old Chinese adolescents in one survey responded in this way versus 35 percent of American 16-year-olds).[15] For Chinese such an orientation is considered to be highly moral,[16] yet, from the perspective of many observers this type of response pattern has other implications. Bloom, for instance, in a study of samples from Hong Kong, the United States, and France, found highly statistically significant differences between Chinese and Westerners in what he termed social principledness in which Chinese manifested "a capacity for understanding the abstract notion of socio-political responsibility at the societal level, but [were] limited to the view that socio-political responsibility consists in unanalytic adherence to the demands of existing political authority, i.e., in placing obedience to that authority above any individual intuition as to what might constitute proper action"[17] Such provocative findings impel further investigation.

MACRO-LEVEL MORAL ENVIRONMENTS

Just as there are individual level differences in moral development, so also are there modal differences in moral development between social systems. These differences reflect wide empirical variety. They can best be noted at their two limits by distinctive relationship patterns between three sets of variables—the nature of individual moral orientations, the nature of the social/political environment, and the form and content of external socialization influences (discussed above). Figure 1.2 is a schematic representation of the hypothesized interrelationships between these sets of variables, in which the open and flexible relationship pattern is assumed to be more morally mature than the closed rigid pattern.[18]

Historically closed and rigid social/political systems have overwhelmingly characterized human societies. In fact, in pure form, the open, flexible system has never occurred. The primary distinguishing characteristic of open, flexible systems is a value structure (expressed in institutional forms) that embodies commitment to personal integrity and to the belief that individuals have a right

FIGURE 1.2
Relations between Socialization Influences, Moral Orientations,
and Social and Political Environment

Rigid Closed Moral Orientation	*Closed Social and Political Environment*	*Flexible Open Moral Orientation*	*Open Social and Political Environment*
	Autonomy Training Attitudes and Identification are Sociocentric (Outcome: reliance on situational cues)		*Autonomy Training* Attitudes and Identification Transcend Sociocentricism (Outcome: reliance on internalized values)
	Morals Training Indoctrination of Group Centered Values (Outcome: ethnocentricism; rigidity regarding alternative orientations)		*Morals Training* Experimentation and Testing of Universal Values (Outcome: cosmopolitanism; admissibility of alternate orientations; reciprocity)
	Affective Manipulation Physical and Love-oriented Discipline (Outcome: fear, shame or guilt)		*Affective Manipulation* Induction Training (Outcome: empathy)
	Feedback Only one Socially Approved Channel (Outcome: strict adherence to normative prescriptions)		*Feedback* Channel not Socially Determined (Outcome: experimentation concerning modes of reciprocity

to be free from those demands of authority structures that place limits on the integrity of individuals.[19] Systems such as this, which accord preeminence to "negative rights," have begun to come into existence only in the modern period and in their emergent form are still far from the ideal, especially if one takes into account interaction patterns within groups at all levels of society.

What are the factors that predispose social/political environments and individuals toward closed and rigid moral orientations? To begin with, in any society some of the most important values are those that legitimize hierarchy. Although in macro-level analysis hierarchy can be viewed in terms of the strata of a social system, in the moral development perspective values legitimizing hierarchy are best viewed in terms of interpersonal relationships within all strata. Sociologically, the different status positions that would be noted in this type of analysis are usually referred to as superordinate and subordinate roles. However, this terminology directs attention to the positions and not to those particular patterns of feeling and behavior that are important for an understanding of moral orientations. As a consequence, I prefer to use the terms dominance and submission, which are widely used in animal studies but less so in studies of humans.

Dominant individuals exercise control over those who are submissive, while those who are submissive accord correctness and worth to dominant individuals. Although all people learn socially-approved submissive behavior patterns in childhood, which can be elicited as necessary later in life, it is the quality of dominance and its relationship to particular values that is of especial importance in moral development. Dominance involves inequality of access to important but limited resources such as wealth, force, or knowledge. In stable social systems, unequal access is justified by values that accord worth and prestige to dominant individuals. Changing these evaluative criteria is generally resisted by most people, not only because of the threat to group solidarity that a challenge poses but also because values that legitimize dominance and submission have usually been strongly acquired during childhood socialization.

Being a superordinate or subordinate is, in and of itself, morally neutral. Dominance, on the other hand, involves the assertion of an egoistic or particular group need at the expense of others and inevitably interferes with and diminishes a capacity for empathic feelings and altruistic responses. When the value criteria that justify dominance and submission become institutionalized, there develops a contradiction with mature moral orientations in the sense that these criteria legitimize differential valuations of social worth and limit the probability that moral competence can be manifested, socially or at the individual level, in an evenhanded manner.

A closed and rigid moral environment is one where individual responsibility is repressed and where reciprocity and empathy cannot be expressed except in terms of the prevailing dominance/submission criteria. In such cases equal moral treatment of others is modified so as not to disrupt the values that underlie patterns of dominance and submission. However subtly phrased, therefore, dominance values, when acted upon in such a manner as to reinforce their own legitimacy, tend to enhance rigid and closed moral orientations. When the values at the individual level that legitimize dominance are widely and strongly held, these values will be reflected in the nature of the social/political system.[20] In turn, the social/political system provides an umbrella of legitimacy for the form and content of socialization influences that help mold individual orientations regarding dominance and submission.

Mature moral orientations and the criteria that underlie dominance and submission patterns are always in a contradictory relationship. For instance, if unrestrained individualism is valued as a criterion for dominance, then political policies to equalize incomes as a way of furthering social empathy and reciprocity will directly conflict with the acquisitive quality of that individualism and hence with the prevailing dominance patterns. In fact, no effort to achieve a morally mature social order can occur without conflict with prevailing patterns of dominance and submisson. Yet, despite the pessimism of these comments it is also true that the criteria that define dominance and submission can alter to allow for more morally mature behavior, and this fact has been observed historically for many societies. The process, however, is certainly not foreordained nor, when it occurs, is it necessarily unidirectional.

These points, in my opinion, are exceptionally important, for they direct attention empirically to particular interaction contexts within a society. Among the most critical of these are those that involve social mobility at any level of the social system that is characterized by a challenge to dominance criteria (i.e., challenge to male dominance in family life, to dominance based on age in social life, to dominance based on inherited social position in political life, etc.). Examination of these "points of social mobility"[21] requires simultaneous analysis of the moral orientations of those involved and the moral nature of the social/political order and provides one means for determining degrees of social tension. It also provides clues to possible changes in the prevailing dominance system.

DOMINANCE PATTERNS AND SOCIALIZATION INFLUENCES IN CHINESE SOCIETY

In many societies dominance positions are often justified on the basis that those who occupy them have a special mandate to define and exemplify proper moral behavior I would contend that in Chinese society this kind of "sacred power" is an especially noteworthy characteristic of dominance positions, although, of course, there are other prerogatives that go with higher status within that society. However, moral excellence as a criterion for authority has, anomalously, some deleterious effects on the development of open, flexible, moral orientations, and these deserve our attention.

The basis of moral authority in Chinese society is the notion that moral knowledge is based in reason and that proper behavior is associated with proper thinking. Linked with this notion is the belief that appropriate conduct and thought are in no sense relative but have absolute features by which the social and moral worth of individuals can be measured. Since dominance characterized by moral authority is legitimized by the presumably greater capacity of the dominant individual to manifest proper thinking and behavior, it follows that all individuals can be ranked relative to each other in terms of their ability to manifest appropriate thinking and conduct and that this ranking can be noted for the members of the social group.

Within the group subordinate members are expected to emulate the behavior and thought of legitimate leaders and models, to be loyal to them, and to determine their degree of success in emulation by comparison with other members of the group. Psychologically such comparison elicits strong emotional bonds between group members and arises from mutual adherence to the values that lie behind the thinking and conduct that is expected of group members. In Chinese social life, strong identification among members of groups is an especially noteworthy characteristic, and identification in terms of the group has been remarked upon as an attribute of individuals in both traditional Chinese society and the contemporary social order.

Group orientedness is a characteristic of Chinese that has been noted by many scholars. It begins early in life with emphasis on identification with the family and on behaving in a manner that will reflect creditably both on the family as a unit and on other individual family members. In modern Chinese society, school training, the media, and associational pressures generally emphasize identification with larger groups such as brigades and communes and, of course, with society as a whole. The emphasis in training is on shifting identification to these larger secondary groups and on investing them with the same degree of commitment that traditionally was reserved for primary groups such as the family. While no firm survey evidence is currently available, it does appear that identification for younger Chinese has shifted and that new commitments have arisen.

High degrees of group identification have been referred to as "sociocentricism." Sociocentricism is related to a particular type of change in thinking during maturation. Piaget has described young children as characterized by "centration," a term that refers to an individual being fixated on one dimension of a perceptual situation.[22] In an article that has suffered some criticism from the viewpoint of developmental psychology,[23] Piaget and Weil discussed the development in children of notions of nationality.[24] Beginning with an awareness of family membership, children begin to decentrate, both logically and affectively; as they relate themselves to larger and larger groupings of people, the possibility develops of being able to pass beyond earlier self-centered egocentricity through the reciprocal development of a cognitive understanding of reciprocity as it relates to others and an affective capacity for reciprocity. The interesting and, in my opinion, still valid assertion propounded in this article is that the development with age away from self–centeredness toward group orientedness does not by itself overcome early patterns of thought that are related to egocentricity. For, unless group orientedness is itself overcome, egocentricity with its emphasis on self is merely shifted to the groups with which the child identifies but which are progressively removed from the initial self-centered focus of interest.[25] This sociocentricism, in turn, acts to block full recognition of others who are not members of the groups with whom the person identifies. In societies where right thinking and conduct rigidly define group membership, individuals who are outside of this realm of group orientation are often regarded as of lower moral worth on this account. Yet, emphasis on behavior guided by set rules of proper conduct reinforces an undeviating response to authoritative cues from the group and its leaders and thus inhibits the development of moral orientations where all others, regardless of group affiliation, have a claim to even-handed moral valuation.

High degrees of group orientedness in Chinese society appear to be related to particular forms of social sanctions that are utilized by those in dominance positions. The primary sanctions are those that arouse the ubiquitous fear of abandonment. Freud has noted how individuals are tied to group leaders and to other group members and how anxiety can be aroused by the possibility of a cessation of these emotional bonds.[26] The anxieties associated with these bonds can be manipulated in shame socialization, which involves training in comparing one's own behavior with the ideals manifested by models and perfecting one's behavior in a process of comparison and competition with other members of one's group. Shame itself encompasses the feeling that one has failed to reach an ideal, and it occurs as the result of a process that involves a subjective measurement between what an individual actually is in a given context and what he wishes he were. The development of incongruity presents a threat to the core of identity and by the revelation of inadequacy calls into question the whole self. It is a "...feeling of a crumpling or failure of the whole self...."[27] Among other characterizations, Gilligan has described shame as "feelings of inferiority, humiliation, embarrassment, inadequacy, incompetence, weakness, dishonor, disgrace, 'loss of face,' the feeling of being vulnerable to, or actually experiencing, ridicule, contempt, insult, derision, scorn, rejection, etc."[28]

Lickona has said that "...fears of humiliation, loss of face, and rejection may frequently operate as an affective impediment to moral maturity."[29] Love withdrawal punishments foster attitudes of rigid conformity to rules for their own sake and feelings of deference toward authority figures. What develops as a consequence is a kind of conformist morality.[30] In learning proper behavior and thinking, Chinese are exposed to a particular form of manipulation of affect that involves experiencing ridicule and scorn from other group members when approved conduct is not forthcoming. Of course, in most social contexts, the degree of experience of shame is relatively low; in normal conditions more or less automatic conformity to explicit rules of conduct insures that shame anxiety will be felt more as a threat than as an actuality. However, shame anxiety operates as one of the major dynamics in Chinese group interaction. Depending upon the intensity with which it is experienced, it elicits culturally specific forms of behavior including, where moral condemnation is involved, ostracism or expulsion from the group for offenders, usually as a consequence of pronouncements by those with moral authority. The range of behavior patterns for those who experience shame and for those who observe it is set forth in Figures 1.3 and 1.4 in terms of verbal scales where varying degrees of intensity of shame are associated with particular responses.[31]

FIGURE 1.3
Types of Shame and Associated Behavior Patterns for Individuals Experiencing Shame

Relationship to Generally Held Norms	*Types of Shame*		*Types of Associated Behavior*
	Chinese	*English*	
May or may not imply moral condemnation	xinli bushufu	unease	smiling, laughter, shrugging, nervousness
	buhaoyisi	embarrassment	smiling, shrugging, nervousness, evasiveness
	diulian	shame	evasiveness, blank stare, acts of regret, efforts to improve self, conformist acts, minor acts or statements of hostility
	cankui	deep shame	a. moral condemnation not implied: acts of regret, efforts to improve self, conformist acts. b. moral condemnation implied: acts or statements of hostility, cynical behavior
Implies moral condemnation	xiucan	extreme shame	acts of hostility, acts of despair, alienated behavior, cynical behavior, suicide, projection of shame onto others

Differing techniques of discipline and the particular forms of anxiety that people experience as a result are only some of the influences that affect moral development. For instance, I have already pointed out that high degrees of group orientedness in Chinese society also appear to have an important effect on the development of particular modal moral stances. The nature of the moral values that are imparted during socialization are also significant influences. In Western societies children are trained to use principled values of self–direction. In other kinds of societies, as Aronfreed has noted, "...abstract principles of conduct may be constructed around values which take a much more externalized perspec-

FIGURE 1.4

Types of Shame and Associated Behavior Patterns for Those Perceiving Shameful Behavior by Others

Relationship to Generally Held Norms	Types of Shame		Types of Associated Behavior
	Chinese	English	
May or may not imply moral condemnation	xinli bushufu	unease	concern, shrugging, nervousness, smiling
	buhaoisi	embarrassment	silence, evasiveness, concern, laughter, urging improvement
	diulian	shame	a. moral condemnation not implied: silence, evasiveness, pity, urging improvement b. moral condemnation implied: exhortation to reform, ridicule, scorn, cynicism
	cankui	deep shame	a. moral condemnation not implied: silence, evasiveness, pity, urging improvement b. moral condemnation implied: exhortation to reform, contempt, anger, cynicism, ostracism
Implies moral condemnation	wuchi [or] buyaolian	extreme shame	contempt, anger, ostracism, legal action, expulsion from group, linkage with "shameful" others, violent acts

tive on human relations...."[32] Although the *McGuffy Readers*, which were widely used in childhood learning in the United States in the latter decades of the nineteenth century, were certainly heavily infused with externalized value orientations, it is fair to say that they were mild in this regard in comparison to Chinese didactic techniques. The ubiquitous posters in Chinese classrooms, public buildings, and elsewhere stress moral virtuousness in the form of loyalty, cooperation, performance of social obligations, devotion to duty, collective solidarity, service to others, and sacrifice for the group. Of course, being true to one's principles is also emphasized, but more often than not this injunction is viewed as a means to enhance group virtue as much as to develop personal character.

One might expect an externalized value orientation to be highly congruent with the use of shaming techniques of discipline and with pressures for group orientedness; indeed, given the reinforcing nature of these influences, it would be difficult not to predict where they occur a kind of modal conformist moral outcome. The important point, of course, is that the form of these influences is not random. In the Chinese case they are translations into socialization patterns at all levels of society of a dominance system based on moral authority in which the form of each influence is connected logically to the notion that right thinking and right conduct are not relative in nature.

MORAL ORIENTATIONS IN CHINESE SOCIETY

Data from Chinese socialization tend to support the conclusion that Chinese moral values stress strong group identification, conformity to group expectations, cooperation with other group members, and loyalty to group leaders. Virtue lies in fulfilling these values, and the principled person is one who has internalized them and behaves in accordance with their dictates. That Chinese are relatively rule oriented and conformist should not, however, be equated with a low level of moral competence, for ordinary social life in China was (and is) often infused by reciprocity and empathy carried out in terms of these cultural norms. For many Chinese the ideal of conformity to social rules was frequently carried out in practice—in terms of the ambiguities of life—with prudence and good natured give-and-take rather than by dour and rigid adherence to social commandments. Of course, there has been conflict and, of course, there has been condemnation of those who are habitually deviant. But viewed in a long historical perspective Chinese society, for all its apparent conformism, has often been marked by greater tolerance than has been true of societies with a more individualistic ethic. Depending upon social status or special circumstances there has even been formal allowance made for expression of dissent from group ends and of disapproval of group leaders (although one might also posit that this formality was required in order to legitimize departures from conformist expectations). Censors had this function in traditional society, and in modern times all Chinese are expected to develop habits of criticism. That the end sought may be a more perfect group solidarity should not obscure the fact that the action itself manifests mature moral attributes.

However, to note that reciprocity and empathy can be achieved in terms of Chinese cultural norms is not to say that the dominance system that prevails in China does not modify modal patterns of moral competence, especially in the area of individual responsibility. For instance, although efforts have been made to develop a paramount identification with society as a whole rather than with primary groups such as the family, strong sociocentrism still exists and the continuing dependence on group oriented cues may impede a manifestation of mature morality toward foreigners or internal out-groups. Problems of transcending the strictures of a particular dominance system hold as true for Chinese with conformist and rule-oriented orientations as for Americans whose acquisitive behavior patterns based on values of egoistic individualism impede the fullest expression of reciprocity and empathy.

A summary of data from Chinese and American societies is presented below. Since no empirical criteria have yet been developed that can be used to compare the modal moral competence of a particular society with an ideal standard these data are inferential only. Both sets of data indicate deviations from an ideal standard, but the degree of deviation is unknown. Nor can it be definitively ascertained for either society which component of moral competence is most significant as an explanation for the variance that occurs. The usefulness of the data lies in the gross differences that can be noted between the two sets and the assumption that the findings for both societies reflect the influence of distinctive dominance systems.

FIGURE 1.5
Average Mean Percentage Values for Reliance on Internalized Rules for Behavior in Family, School, and Secondary Level Social Contexts

Group	*Context*		
	Family	*School*	*Secondary Level*
America (297)*	53	50	62
Taiwan (335)	62	74	71
Hong Kong (362)	54	63	64

*The figures in parentheses indicate the number of respondents. The respondents were children from third, fifth, and seventh grades divided approximately equally between males and females.

Figure 1.5 gives an indication of the degree to which internalized values govern behavior.[33] It was found, for instance, that Chinese tend to internalize rules regarding conduct to a greater extent than Americans. The index used here refers to behavior that is motivated not by external cues but by internalized rules and principles. Yet, although rules are internalized as guides for behavior and, thus, have this important attribute of individual responsibility, other data indicate the high degree of conformity that is also expected and the relative inability of most people to express displeasure with authority figures. In terms of whether one should conform in dress with other members of one's group, Chinese children from Taiwan and Hong Kong responded on questionnaires 92.5 percent in favor, while 41 percent of black and white American children answered in this way.[34] The two groups did not differ in their belief that an authority figure can be disagreed with.[35] When the question involved expressing anger toward authority figures, 83 percent of Chinese in interviews said they would not get angry and 50 percent of Caucasian Americans responded in this manner; in terms of being able to argue openly with leaders 80.5 percent of Chinese and 17 percent of Caucasian Americans said they could not openly argue with authority.[36] Questionnaire data indicated that group punishment was more feared than individual punishment by 77 percent of Chinese and by 60 percent of black and white American children,[37] and interviews revealed that 75 percent of children from Taiwan and Hong Kong felt they could go against their group.[38] These data lend at least partial support to assumptions that, while Chinese internalize principles regarding behavior, the modes of expression are modified by Chinese dominance patterns. The modal responses tend to be group rather than self-oriented and to be conformist in nature and deferent with regard to authority.

It is important at this point, however, to stress again that modal forms of moral orientations can vary significantly both for given individuals in different contexts and among members of a group.[39] Social role and social context, for example, are important variables. A street corner altercation is vastly different from defiance of political authority, although both may be infused with moral rhetoric and both be apparently nonconformist in nature. In the latter case, especially, the social role of the participants may be critical. In traditional and modern times, high officials in China may feel that they personally are protectors of the group's virtue and guardians of moral authority, and that open defense of the principles they hold is required regardless of pressures for conformity and for deference to authority.[40] Often such autonomous expression merely affirms what the individual deems to be more appropriate right thinking and conduct within the existing framework of social relationships. When, more rarely, such expression acts to change the very definition of dominance and sub-mission there may with time also be changes in the moral nature of the social/ political environment and of individuals themselves.

NOTES

1. The most notable exception to this, of course, is Donald J. Munro's, *The Concept of Man in Early China* (Stanford, Calif.: Stanford University Press, 1969).

2. Lucian W. Pye, "Political Culture and National Character" in *Social Psychology and Political Behavior: Problems and Prospects,* eds. Gilbert Abcarian and John W. Soule (Columbus, Ohio: Charles E. Merrill, 1971), p. 94.

3. John Rawls, *A Theory of Justice* (Cambridge, Mass.: Harvard University Press, 1971).

4. For a summary of the best known of these categorizations see Lawrence Kohlberg, "Moral Stages and Moralization: The Cognitive-Developmental Approach" in *Moral Development and Behavior: Theory, Research, and Social Issues,* ed. Thomas Lickona (New York: Holt, Rinehart and Winston, 1976), pp. 31–53.

5. B.F. Skinner, *Beyond Freedom and Dignity* (New York: Knopf, 1971).

6. Edward O. Wilson, *On Human Nature* (Cambridge, Mass.: Harvard University Press, 1978).

7. Karl Marx and Friedrich Engels, *The Communist Manifesto* (with an introduction by A.J.P. Taylor, translated from the German by Samuel Moore) (Baltimore, Md.: Penguin Books, 1967).

8. Immanuel Kant, *The Critique of Pure Reason* and *The Critique of Practical Reason* in *Great Books of the Western World,* 42 (Chicago: Encyclopedia Britannica, 1952) (Originally published 1787 and 1788 respectively); Emile Durkheim, *Moral Education* (Glencoe, Ill.: The Free Press, 1961); and John Dewey, *Moral Principles in Education* (New York: Philosophical Library, 1954).

9. Lawrence Kohlberg, "From Is to Ought: How to Commit the Naturalistic Fallacy and Get Away with It in the Study of Moral Development" in *Cognitive Development and Epistemology,* ed. Theodore Mischel (New York: Academic Press, 1971), p. 213.

10. Martin L. Hoffman, "Empathy, Role Taking, Guilt and the Development of Altruistic Motives" in Lickona, op. cit., pp. 124–143.

11. H. Weinreich, "Kohlberg and Piaget: Aspects of Their Relationship in the Field of Moral Development," *Journal of Moral Education* 4 (1975): 201–213.

12. Carol Gilligan and John M. Murphy, "From Adolescence to Adulthood: The Moral Dilemmas of Reconciliation to Reality," *Moral Education Forum* 4 (Winter 1979):3–13.

13. Derived from an earlier formulation presented in Richard W. Wilson, "A New Direction for the Study of Moral Behavior," *Journal of Moral Education* 7 (1978):127.

14. M.L. Hoffman and H.D. Saltzstein, "Parent Discipline and the Child's Moral Development," *Journal of Personality and Social Psychology* 5 (1967): 45–47.

15. Lawrence Kohlberg, "Development of Children's Orientations toward a Moral Order" in *Educational Psychology,* eds. Richard C. Sprinthall and Norman A. Sprinthall (New York: Van Nostrand-Reinhold, 1969), pp. 84–85. See also Lawrence Kohlberg, "Stage and Sequence: The Cognitive-Developmental Ap-

proach to Socialization" in *Handbook of Socialization Theory and Research,* ed. David A. Goslin (Chicago: Rand McNally, 1969), pp. 382, 384–85. There is a slight discrepancy in the results reported in these two articles.

16.   Richard W. Wilson, "Some Comments on Stage Theories of Moral Development," *Journal of Moral Education* 5 (1976):241–8.

17.   Alfred H. Bloom, "A Cognitive Dimension of Social Control: The Hong Kong Chinese in Cross-Cultural Perspective" in *Deviance and Social Control in Chinese Society,* eds. Amy Auerbacher Wilson, Sidney Leonard Greenblatt, and Richard Whittingham Wilson (New York: Praeger, 1977), pp. 69, 77.

18.   Derived from an earlier formulation presented in Richard W. Wilson, "A Moral Community of Strangers" in *Moral Development and Politics,* eds. Richard W. Wilson and Gordon J. Schochet (New York: Praeger, 1980).

19.   Isaiah Berlin, *Two Concepts of Liberty* (London: Oxford University Press, 1958) and Charles Fried, *Right and Wrong* (Cambridge, Mass.: Harvard University Press, 1978).

20.   A preliminary development of these views was first set forth in Richard W. Wilson, "Ideology, Hierarchy and Moral Behavior," paper presented at the Eighth Sino-American Conference on Mainland China held at the Institute of International Studies, University of South Carolina, Columbia, S.C., May 17–20, 1979, and subsequently published in the proceedings, *The Enduring Chinese Dimension,* (Columbia, South Carolina: Institute of International Studies, University of South Carolina, 1979), pp. 239–252.

21.   I am indebted to Mitch R. Meisner for bringing this concept to my attention.

22.   Judith V. Torney, "The Definition of Citizen Capacities and Related Psychological Research," March 1978, p. 25. Unpublished paper prepared with the assistance of Ana M. Toro as a response to "Working Definition for Citizen Education, Research for Better Schools," July 1977.

23.   Gustav Jahoda, "Children's Concepts of Nationality: A Critical Study of Piaget's Stages," *Child Development* 35 (December 1964):1081–92.

24.   Jean Piaget assisted by Anne-Marie Weil, "The Development in Children of the Idea of the Homeland and of Relations with Other Countries," *International Social Science Bulletin* 3 (Autumn 1951):561–78.

25.   Ibid., p. 562.

26.   Sigmund Freud, *Group Psychology and the Analysis of the Ego* (New York: Bantam Books, 1960), pp. 35, 37.

27.   Gerhart Piers and Milton B. Singer, *Shame and Guilt: A Psychoanalytic and a Cultural Study* (Springfield, Ill.: Charles C. Thomas, 1953), p. 52.

28.   James Gilligan, "Beyond Morality: Psychoanalytic Reflections on Shame, Guilt, and Love" in Lickona, op. cit., p. 144.

29.   Thomas Lickona, "Critical Issues in the Study of Moral Development and Behavior" in Lickona, op. cit., p. 20.

30.   Herbert D. Saltzstein, "Social Influence and Moral Development: A Perspective on the Role of Parents and Peers" in Lickona, op. cit., p. 254 (derived from Hoffman and Saltzstein, op. cit.)

31.   Richard W. Wilson, "Shame and Behavior in Chinese Society," *Asian Profile* 1 (December 1973):436–37.

32. Justin Aronfreed, "Moral Development from the Standpoint of a General Psychological Theory" in Lickona, op. cit., p. 69.

33. Richard W. Wilson, *The Moral State: A Study of the Political Socialization of Chinese and American Children* (New York: The Free Press, 1974), p. 241.

34. Ibid., p. 194.

35. Ibid., pp. 171, 174.

36. Ibid., pp. 166, 172.

37. Ibid., p. 153.

38. Ibid., p. 196.

39. James Rest, in an important modification of Kohlberg's propositions, has pointed out that moral orientations should be noted more in terms of predominant mode of usage than as invariant stage related judgments. See James R. Rest, "New Approaches in the Assessment of Moral Judgment" in Lickona, op. cit., pp. 198–218.

40. I am indebted to Thomas A. Metzger for bringing these points to my attention.

2 LANGUAGE AND THEORETICAL VS. REALITY-CENTERED MORALITY

Alfred H. Bloom

It seems reasonable to suppose, along with the Cognitive Structuralist tradition in contemporary psychology, that we as human beings impose meaningful organization on the infinitely varying world of our sense experiences by means of a highly complex and extensive repertory of cognitive schemas. On the basis of the medium of representation such schemas provide we segment the world cognitively into the types of objects, actions, properties, events, and relations we perceive to exist in it. On the basis of the medium of representation such schemas provide we construct our interpretations of the situations we encounter and define for ourselves the options we personally have available with respect to those situations. And, on the basis of the medium of representation such schemas provide we construct our evaluations of what ought to be done and what we ought to do. Our schemas serve us, in other words, as the elementary conceptual units out of which we build both our cognitive and our moral views of the world.

Some of the schemas we use are likely to be innate. Others we construct on the basis of our direct perceptual experiences, without any assistance from the language or languages we learn. But still others, and particularly those that represent highly abstract, derived categorizations of reality, we construct specifically to meet the requirements of the words and grammatical structures of the first language or any additional language, natural or technical, we learn. We are likely, for example, on the basis of our nonlinguistic, perceptual experiences to divide the world into the categories "hot," "tree," and "pain" and then to acquire the linguistic labels for these categories only after the conceptual work of category construction has already taken place. But it is exposure to the linguistic terms "GNP," "law," and "diplomatic immunity," rather than any perceptual experience, that is likely to lead us to the construction of the highly abstract and derived categorizations of the world these terms represent. And the categorizations

21

of the world we construct to meet the requirements of words take their place alongside those categorizations of the world we build without linguistic assistance as additional schemas through which we come to make sense out of and evaluate our interactions with the world. We come to think and judge in terms of "law" and "diplomatic immunity" just as we come to think and judge in terms of "hot" and "pain." So, although the words and grammatical structures of the language or languages we learn can certainly not be said to determine exclusively how we come to think, they can be said to lead us, especially in highly abstract realms of thought, to expand our repertories of thinking schemas in language-specific ways and thereby to leave their distinctive impact on the medium of representation in which we formulate both our cognitive and our moral ideas.[2]

Within this perspective let us take a look at certain specific differences between the structures of the English and Chinese language that suggest themselves as, in part at least, responsible for leading their respective speakers to develop quite distinct cognitive and related moral orientations to the world.

Chinese and English both have precise means for expressing descriptive statements such as "John went to the library and saw Mary" and for expressing straightforward implicational statements such as "If John went to the library, he saw Mary." But Chinese, unlike English and other Indo-European languages, does not have a distinct means for expressing counterfactual statements such as "If John had gone to the library, he would have seen Mary" as distinct from their descriptive and straightforward implicational alternatives. Chinese, in other words, has no way to mark distinctly that mood which, in English and other Indo-European languages, invites the reader or listener explicitly to shunt aside reality considerations and to portray a state of affairs known to be false for the express purpose of drawing implications as to what might be or might have been the case if that state of affairs were in fact true.

Certainly the simple fact that Chinese does not mark this distinction cannot be taken to imply that its speakers do not make the distinction in thought. Just because English has a single word for bank, meaning both river bank and financial institution, while French has two distinct terms for those two distinct meanings, cannot be taken to imply that English speakers think less differentiatedly about banks than French speakers do. But in the case of the Chinese counterfactual there is some evidence to suggest that the lack of a linguistic marking is not just a linguistic fact, but a linguistic fact with important consequences for the way Chinese speakers, as compared to speakers of Western languages, think in the cognitive and moral realms.

The very idea that the lack in the Chinese language of a distinct marking for the counterfactual might have cognitive consequences was first suggested by the reactions of Chinese subjects to a questionnaire administered in Hong Kong in 1973. To such questions as "If the Hong Kong government were to pass such and such a law or had passed such and such a law, how would you or would you have reacted?" the Hong Kong Chinese subjects consistently retorted "It didn't" or "It won't." Attempts to encourage them to venture into the counterfactual realm only increased the subjects' frustration and often, in fact, led to a branding of the question and the mode of thinking it involved as "unnatural," "unChinese," and sometimes even "Western." By contrast, American and French subjects, responding to translated versions of the same questionnaire, readily indulged in the counterfactual hypothesizing that the questions were designed to elicit. And with rare exceptions both monolingual Chinese speakers and native Chinese, Chinese-English bilinguals, regularly report the same observation—that counterfactual speaking and thinking is somehow unnatural to Chinese. One Chinese student at Swarthmore labeled it "evil"; a professor of English at Taiwan National University remarked, "You know, we Chinese are not used to using the counterfactual as you Americans are—when I try to speak in class this way, my students become quickly confused." Bilinguals report that they feel comfortable using counterfactual statements in English such as "If the lecture had ended earlier, Bill would have had a chance to prepare for the exam," but feel more comfortable converting such statements into descriptive alternatives such as "The lecture ended too late, so Bill did not have a chance to prepare for the exam" in order to express the same ideas naturally in Chinese. And native Chinese, Chinese-English bilinguals who were presented with matched pairs of English counterfactual and descriptive statements and asked, for each pair, if either of the pair seems closer to the way such facts are expressed in Chinese, consistently selected the descriptive form as the one and only one that "captures the way we say, think about such things in Chinese." Ironically, it is, in fact, Westerners who have had little experience in the Chinese language and culture who are usually the most reluctant to believe that the counterfactual could be unChinese, while the Chinese themselves, both monolinguals and bilinguals, just about always readily and happily acknowledge the fact.

Moreover, if the lack of a distinct marking for the counterfactual in Chinese were merely a linguistic fact, with no further cognitive consequences for speakers of Chinese, one might expect that the Chinese equivalent of the sentence "If John went to the library, he saw Mary," since it would have to carry both the implicational and counterfactual interpretations (i.e., "If he had gone, he would have ... " and "If he went, he saw ... "), would be perceived as ambiguous by Chinese subjects. Yet, the large majority of monolingual Chinese subjects interviewed did not perceive such sentences as ambiguous nor, even when the two interpretations were pointed out, was there that ready click of comprehension of the distinction that is evident among speakers of Western languages under similar circumstances. In fact, after a week of working with sample sentences, my highly intelligent, monolingual research assistant was still encountering considerable difficulty in maintaining clearly in mind the idea of a counterfactual interpretation as distinct from a negative implicational one (i.e., "If he had not gone" versus "If he didn't go"). And more generally, for the monolingual Chinese speakers interviewed, coming to understand the distinction between counterfactual and implicational sentences seemed not to be just a question of mastering new formal terms for already explicitly developed modes of categorizing experience, but rather a question of building new cognitive schemas to fit those formal terms, parallel perhaps to the predicament of the English-speaking student of logic who has to build new cognitive schemas in order to come to understand the distinctions carried by the formal labels "if-then," "if-and-only-if-then," and "only-if-then."

In addition, Chinese students of English find the counterfactual to be one of the most difficult aspects of the English language to master—an observation that has been confirmed by, among others, two professors of English from Taiwan National University, many bilinguals, and several incidents such as one that took place at a conference at Rutgers University a few years ago. While I was discussing my research at dinner, a professor from Taiwan, who had been in the United States for about three years, suddenly interrupted the discussion to exclaim "One second, what does 'would have' mean? It is the one aspect of English grammar I have been unable to grasp!"

An informal content analysis of a leading Chinese newspaper in Taiwan conducted over a three-week period uncovered only one example of the use of what one might call counterfactual argument, expressed by the circumlocution: "X is not the case; but if X then Y," and that turned out to be in a translation of a speech by Henry Kissinger.

Mao did tend to make use of counterfactual reasoning and to express it in this way even though he was not a fluent speaker of any Western languages. But he was certainly heavily influenced by Western political writings, and it is interesting to note that while Westerners find Mao's writings relatively easier to read than typical Chinese prose and his logic relatively more accessible, I have been told on repeated occasions by people with extensive experience in Mainland China that, for the Chinese, the opposite is very much the case.

Not only then does Chinese not mark the counterfactual, but Chinese speakers tend to brand the counterfactual as unChinese, tend to have difficulty in grasping the distinction between counterfactual and implicational statements, and seem relatively disinclined, by comparison to their English-speaking counterparts, to make use of counterfactual logic in responding to questionnaire queries and in writing newspaper analyses.

Yet, this evidence, suggesting a link between language and thought in the area of the counterfactual, cannot be taken to imply that the lack of a distinct marking for the counterfactual in the Chinese language reflects the absence of counterfactual thinking or even of counterfactual speaking from the Chinese psycholinguistic world. Imagine, for example, a situation in which a group of people have been waiting for John. He arrives late and they are, as a result, late for the movies. Under such circumstances, one can say in Chinese, "If John come + past earlier, they arrive at the movies on time" and mean in English, "If John had come earlier, they would have (but didn't) arrived at the movies on time." Faced with an accident of which the speaker and listener are both well aware, the speaker can say in Chinese, "If he warn + past them earlier, perhaps that accident is able to be averted" and mean in English, "If he had warned them earlier, that accident could perhaps have been averted." One can state in Chinese, "Luckily he reserved a room" and then continue "if not, [(yao) bu ran (de hua)] he slept on the street" and mean, "if he didn't, he would have slept on the street." In each case, if the presupposition were different, the identical sentence would have straightforward implicational meaning. If we do not know that John is late, the sentence "If John come + past earlier, they arrive at the movies on time." If we do not know whether the accident was in fact averted, the sentence "If he warn + past them, perhaps the accident is able to be averted" will mean "If he warned them, perhaps the accident was averted." And if we do not know whether he reserved a room, then the sentence "If not, he slept on the street" will mean "If he didn't make a reservation, he slept on the street." So, there is no linguistic marking within each sentence that signals explicitly that the sentence is to be understood as commenting on the realm of the might-have-been, but in a situational context which negates its premise, each sentence can be used to express a counterfactual thought.

We are left then with an apparent contradiction. On the one hand, Chinese certainly do think and speak counterfactually; on the other, the lack of a distinct marking for the counterfactual seems, based on the evidence presented above, to be associated with certain significant cognitive consequences. To attempt to resolve this apparent contradiction, let us return to the notion that a language, by whether it labels or does not label any specific mode of categorizing experience, while not determining whether or not its speakers will think that way, can either encourage or not encourage them to develop a labelled cognitive schema designed specifically for that mode of thought. Even if the English language did not label the notion "bachelor," English speakers could still understand the concept "bachelor" by bringing together in their minds its component elements—unmarried, never previously married, male, and adult. But the fact that the English language has a distinct label for bachelor seems to encourage its speakers to develop a schema specifically designed to categorize the world in that way and, thereby, to come to be able to: 1) make and understand references to bachelors and, in fact, to think about bachelors, without having to expend the cognitive effort necessary to integrate and keep simultaneously in mind the four dimensions—male, unmarried, never previously married and adult—2) recognize "bachelors" as one of those categories of things (in this case, individuals) into which their cognitive world is divided, 3) utilize the category "bachelor" as a mode of cognitive organization in memory to which information can be attached that is not true of adults, males, unmarried people, or never married people taken separately, and 4) make use of the category "bachelor" as a point of mental orientation for undertaking analyses in which it can serve as a convenient variable.

Analogously, that the English speaker has a distinct label for the counterfactual (i.e., "Had . . . would have") that the Chinese speaker does not share, cannot by any means be expected to bestow upon the English speaker an exclusive facility for that mode of thought, but it might be expected to encourage him or her, by contrast to his or her Chinese counterpart to develop a cognitive schema that represents an achieved integration of the idea of an implication linking two events with the idea that neither of these events constitutes a factual occurrence—of a cognitive schema specifically designed for talking and thinking about the world in a counterfactual way.

To put this general interpretation to a more objective test, the following experimental procedures were designed.

A set of stories was prepared of the form "X was not the case, but if X had been the case, then Y would have been the case, Z would have been the case, and W would have been the case, etc." (e.g., A specific Greek philosopher was unable to speak Chinese. But if he had been able to, he would have done Y, Z, W, etc.). The form was expressed in Chinese, for lack of a way to express the counterfactual directly, as "X was not the case, but if X was, then Y, then Z, then W, etc.," in other words, in the way that the counterfactual is expressed when it is expressed in Chinese outside of concrete situational contexts, as in Mao's writings or the translation of the Kissenger quote. Subjects were then asked in a variety of direct and indirect ways whether they interpreted the paragraphs as indicating that the final consequent or consequents or the series of implications presented refer to things that have happened or rather to things that have not. If the average Chinese speaker has not, as a result of the particular features of the Chinese language, been led to develop an already prepared interpretive framework designed for categorizing and thinking about the world in a counterfactual way, then he or she might be expected, upon reading the paragraphs, to have difficulty in making sense of the logical juxtaposition "X was not the case, but if X was, then" as an indication that the paragraph is about the realm of the might-have-been and/or in holding that counterfactual perspective in mind as a point of mental orientation from which to analyze the series of consequences presented. Hence, the Chinese speakers become confused as they read through them, as to whether the complex series of consequents presented do or do not refer to actual happenings. By contrast, English speakers, equipped with counterfactual schemas, might be expected upon seeing the words, "if he had . . . would have," to shift promptly into the counterfactual mode of processing and hence to understand in an almost self-evident manner that, of course, the consequents are to be interpreted as counterfactual, as considerations of what might have been but wasn't.

Chinese versions of the stories were then presented to a group of hotel workers in Taiwan as well as to a group of students at Taiwan National University, the college of highest prestige in Taiwan. English versions were presented as a control to a group of students at Swarthmore College, United States, during the fall of the same year.

The results were rather dramatic.

At Swarthmore, 25 out of the 28 or 89 percent of the students tested consistently responded that the events referred to in the last statements of the stories were false, that is, they imposed counterfactual interpretations on the paragraphs. The remaining three students gave only one inconsistent response each, which on the basis of later interviewing, turned out to be attributable to ambiguity with regard to the if versus if-and-only-if distinction, rather than to ambiguity with regard to the counterfactual distinction. Among the 54 Chinese students tested, all of whom had studied English and were frequently exposed to Western abstract modes of speech and thought, 37 or 69 percent made consistently counterfactual responses; finally, among the working class subjects, who had little exposure to English, the number of consistent counterfactual responders dropped to six out of 37 or 17 percent. In later interviewing, the Chinese subjects who had missed the counterfactual import of the paragraphs indicated either: 1) that by the time they had gotten to the last few implications in the series, they had forgotten that the philosopher could not speak Chinese and so evaluated those later implications as statements of what he in fact had done, or 2) and this was the case for the large majority of subjects, that they had remembered the philosopher could not speak Chinese but had found that fact in contradiction to the statements in the rest of the paragraph and so, in order to salvage as much as possible, had decided that what must be intended was at least that the philosopher had done X, Y, Z, and W. Otherwise, why write about it? In other words, for the majority of Chinese-speaking subjects tested, although recognition of the juxtaposition of a negative premise and implicational statements based upon it did lead to a realization that something was askew, it did not trigger, as it did in the West, a counterfactual interpretation.

Furthermore, bilingual Chinese, when responding to English versions of the paragraphs, invoked counterfactual interpretations at a significantly higher rate than when responding to the same or similar paragraphs written in their native Chinese. To the question "If all circles were large and this small triangle were a circle, would it be large?," posed in their native language, 25 percent of the 173 Chinese subjects answered yes as compared with 83 percent of the Americans. Most Chinese responded "No! How can all circles be large? How can a triangle be a circle? What do you mean?" Americans generally accepted without question both counterfactual premises and went on to reason within the counterfactual world they thus created. Their habituation to counterfactual reasoning both permitting and, as it were, legitimizing that indulgence. And again, Chinese bilinguals when responding to an English version of the question were more inclined to make use of counterfactual logic than when responding to the same question written in Chinese (43 percent versus 25 percent, $X^2_{df=1}$ 7.14, p < .01).

Moreover, the link between language and thought in the counterfactual suggested by these data becomes even more interesting when one considers that it appears to constitute only one aspect of a much more general pattern of related language and thought interconnections evident in the psycholinguistic habits of speakers of English and Chinese. The counterfactual constitutes a member of a select set of English and more generally Indo-European linguistic devices that appear to lead speakers to develop cognitive schemas specifically designed to enable and encourage them to shift from talking and thinking about the world, in terms of their baseline models of reality, to projecting and operating with theoretical extractions from those baseline models.

When we as English speakers move in speech from talking about the "dog over there" or even "all dogs" in the world, to talking about "the" dog as in "the dog is a furry animal," we move in thought from consideration of actual dogs to consideration of a generic dog, theoretically extracted from our knowledge of actual dogs. When we move in speech from talk of something being "red" or of someone being "sincere" or "honest" to talk of "redness," "sincerity," and "honesty" we are not only shifting from adjectives to nouns, but from consideration of observable properties to consideration of abstract entifications of those properties, to the construction of new theoretical entities that take their place alongside our categories for actual things in our cognitive models of the world. Similarly, when we move from "accept," "generalize," "further," and "contribute" to talk about "acceptances," "generalizations," "furtherances," and "contributions," we are not only moving from verbs to nouns, but from consideration of actions that things or people undertake to talking and thinking of those actions as things in themselves. And when we move from stating that "his attitude is or is not sincere" to talking about "the sincerity of his attitude," from stating that "That measure was or was not or will or will not be accepted" to talking about "the acceptance of that measure," from stating that "Interest rates rise or rose" to talking about "the rise of interest rates" we are not only converting sentences into noun phrases, but moving from consideration of actual events or conditions, which are occurring or which have or might occur, to considerations of the notions of those conditions or events. We can go on to say that "The acceptance of that measure resulted from X or Y," just as we can go on to say that "The acceptance of that measure will depend on X or Y," for the mere utterance of the nominalized expression—"the acceptance of that measure"— does not commit us to any event that has or might be taking place, but only to the idea of the event, to the notion of it, extracted from the world of actual or potential happenings.

And just as the Chinese language does not have any structures equivalent to the counterfactual, neither has it had, at least until very recently, any structures equivalent to these additional members of the select set of English, and more generally Indo-European, elicitors of theoretical thoughts. As in the case of the counterfactual, there are various ways by which speakers of Chinese can capture in traditionally Chinese forms roughly the same ideas as those carried by English entified forms. Rather than say "If Bier had been able to speak Chinese, he would have done X, Y, and Z," the Chinese speaker can always, for example, make use of the straightforward descriptive statement, "Bier couldn't speak Chinese and therefore he did not do X, Y, and Z." Rather than talk about "Mary's sincerity," the Chinese speaker can always say that "Mary is sincere."

Rather than state that "Mary's sincerity cannot be doubted," he can state that "Mary is so sincere, (you) cannot doubt." Rather than say, "Sincerity is a virtue" he can say "Sincere (i.e., being sincere or acting sincerely, since adjectives in this case are inseparable from verbs) is a virtue." The notion "John's discovery of that restaurant makes me happy" can be translated into the statement "John discovered that restaurant, makes me happy," and the statement "The acceptance of that measure depends on the approval of the subcommittee's report" can be translated into the statement "Whether or not that measure is accepted depends on whether or not the subcommittee's report is approved." But these substitute forms, though closely approximating the content of the corresponding English expressions, are not, cognitively speaking, equivalent to them. Talking of Mary being sincere, of acting sincerely, of John discovering a restaurant, or a measure being accepted or not being accepted, of a report being approved or not being approved, involves talking in terms of a model of the world in which things (or people) have characteristics and in which things (or people) act, rather than in terms of a model of the world in which these characteristics and happenings have become things in themselves, have gained a degree of ontological status independent of the things or people who possess them or the agents who perform them.

Significant changes have been occurring in both spoken and written Chinese as a response to the pressure of Western influence. And, as part of these changes, suffixes have begun to emerge whereby Chinese speakers can now convert certain specific adjectives into entified nominal counterparts. For example, the adjective "possible" can now be transformed into a distinct form for "possibility," the adjective "serious" into a distinct form for "seriousness," the adjective "efficient" into a distinct form for "efficiency," and the adjective "important" into a distinct form for "importance." The use of these nominalizing devices does not yet constitute a natural, freely productive aspect of Chinese grammar, and sentences employing such devices are still perceived as markedly foreign in flavor—as less aesthetic if, at times, unavoidable, alternatives to "purely" Chinese adjectival forms. But such evidence of linguistic change, however advanced, does seem to bring further confirmation to the claim that traditional Chinese linguistic structures were not suited to capturing the cognitive implications carried by English and other Indo-European entified forms, for why else would these new forms have evolved?

Furthermore, one reason, if not the principal reason, why English speakers tend to entify is that, by so doing, conditions and events can be transformed into individual conceptual units that can then be fitted, as individual components, into more general theoretical/exploratory frameworks. Contrast, for example, the typical Chinese sentences, "He is so industrious, he will certainly succeed" and "Interest rates decline, makes the housing industry grow more rapidly," with their entified English equivalents, "His industriousness insures his success" and "The decline of interest rates accelerates the growth of the housing industry."

The Chinese sentences call attention to two conditions of two events and then, in addition, stipulate relationships holding between those conditions or events, so that the hearer or reader comes to consider the individual conditions or events on their own terms as well as the interconditions or interevent relationships that link them to one another. By contrast, the entified English sentences convert the individual subject/predicate descriptions of conditions and events into individual noun phrases and then insert these noun phrases into single subject/predicate frameworks, thereby in effect subordinating the descriptions of conditions or events to the relationships that link them to one another. The hearer or reader is no longer led to consider the conditions or events on their own terms, but to consider them only as a function of the role they play in the relationships under discussion. The relationships themselves take on a reality of their own, a law-like quality, which derives from the fact that they are understood, not merely as descriptions of observable or potentially observable real-world phenomena, but as examples of a different domain of discourse altogether, as theoretical explanatory frameworks designed to provide a clarifying perspective on the world of actual conditions and events and their interrelationships, while, at the same time, maintaining a certain cognitive distance from the speaker's or hearer's baseline model of that world.

In English, the constructions "the fact that . . . " and simply "that . . . " as in "(The fact) that foreign troops line its borders leads that nation to behave conservatively" act in similar manner to signal to the listener or reader that the information being conveyed in the subordinate clause is not to be coded on its own terms, but rather in terms of its contribution to an explanatory model being projected. And, just as Chinese traditionally has had no structures equivalent to the English processes of entification of conditions and events, neither has it had structures equivalent to "the fact that . . . " or "that . . . ." So, a typical Chinese formulation of the above sentence would take the general form, "Foreign troops line its borders, makes that nation behave conservatively," in which the focus of attention falls on the description of two discrete facts as well as on their inter-relationship rather than on the fact that one fact is being used to explain the other in a projected theoretical model of explanation.

By embedding entified ascriptions of properties and descriptions of events within one another, moreover, English speakers expand their theoretical, explan-atory structures into entities of considerable complexity. Whole series of condi-tions or events can be woven into single theoretical structures with consequent shifts of focus from the component conditions or events to the roles they play in those projected explanatory frameworks. The sequencing of events in the theoretical structures becomes a function of the perspectives the structures are designed to emphasize, rather than of the logical, causal, or temporal order in which the component conditions or events have or would have actually occurred. And this further break with actuality serves to further reinforce the psychological impact of the movement away from the world of actual happenings carried by the underlying processes of entification themselves. An English speaker can, for example, take a series of events like:

1. European imperialism in Asia began to wane.
2. At the same time, the U.S. presence in Asia began to grow.
3. The two met in conflict.
4. As the conflict accelerated, Japanese leaders became increasingly concerned over protecting sources of raw materials.
5. This increasing concern contributed significantly to their decision to attack Pearl Harbor.

Then, by moving from a straightforward description of these events to an embedding of these events in a theoretical, explanatory structure, the speaker can weave the events into whatever sequence best befits the needs of his argument. He can state that:

> The uncertainties arising from the accelerating conflict between European imperialism and the growth of the U.S. presence in Asia and the increasing concern among Japanese leaders over protecting sources of raw materials contributed significantly to the Japanese decision to attack Pearl Harbor;

or, alternatively, he can state that:

> Increasing concern among Japanese leaders for protecting sources of raw materials, brought on by the uncertainties arising from the accelerating conflict between the waning of European imperialism and the growth of the U.S. presence in Asia, contributed significantly to their decision to attack Pearl Harbor;

or, alternatively, that:

> The decision by Japanese leaders to attack Pearl Harbor was significantly influenced by their increasing concern for protecting sources of raw materials, brought on, in turn, by the uncertainties arising from the accelerating conflict between the waning European imperialism and the growth of the U.S. presence in Asia.

In Chinese, by contrast, where each event is expressed individually in subject/predicate form, even in complex recountings of interevent relationships, the individual events seem to retain their individual identity more firmly than in Indo-European language, thereby leading the author to remain more closely tied to the logical, temporal, or causal sequence in which the events actually fall and precluding the free manipulation of logical, temporal, and causal order characteristic of Indo-European theoretical accounts. A typical Chinese equivalent of all three examples might, for example, take the following form:

> While European imperialism began to wane in Asia, the U.S. presence began to grow; these two phenomena met in conflict; as the conflict accelerated, Japanese leaders became increasingly concerned, how to protect sources of raw materials; strongly influenced them to decide to attack Pearl Harbor.

It is no surprise that Chinese speakers often characterize Western recountings of events, as contrasted to their own, as both highly abstracted and as "proceeding in circles" rather than straightforwardly along direct, easily accessible paths. But, from another perspective, when one considers English and, more generally, Indo-European, entification processes alongside the linguistic elicitors of the counterfactual realm, one begins to get a clearer picture of the rather imposing range of incentives the English language seems to offer for shifting in speech and thought from involvement with the world of actual things, actions, properties, events and/or conditions towards theoretical projections over that world—incentives that at least until recent date, have had few, if any, analogues in Chinese.

Even the English lexical term "theoretical" leads the thoughts of English speakers in directions quite distinct from those to which its Chinese counterpart (*lilunshang*) points. The Chinese term literally means within or from the perspective of a theory or theory in general. It is currently used in Taiwan to talk about the contents of a specific theory, to contrast what a given theory says with what is actually the case, and, by extension, to characterize any argument that smacks of a theory in being abstract, difficult to conceive, complex. "Theoretically speaking" means speaking from the perspective of a given theory, or the world of theory. A "theoretical example" is an example of fact taken from the actual world to prove a theory, and the notion "theoretical possibility," to my informants, made no sense at all. But when English speakers say that they are speaking "theoretically," they do not necessarily mean that they are speaking in terms of any given theory or theories, nor that they are necessarily speaking complexly, but rather that they are shifting from description of actual events or even from a description of a given explanation of events incorporated in a given theory to speak as if such were the case, to speak of a consciously hypothesized possible world. For English speakers, "a theoretical example" is not a fact taken from the actual world that fits the constraints of a theoretical world being projected. "A theoretical possibility" is a possibility that could occur within the constraints of that projected world. What differentiates the Chinese term for "theoretical" from its English counterpart, then, is that the meaning of the Chinese term derives principally from its link to the noun "theory," while the English term, although related to the noun "theory," derives its meaning principally from its link to a separate schema that places emphasis, not on the existing set of abstract explanations of phenomena or extensions of that set, but rather on the deliberate severing of truth commitments to the actual world that the formulation and projection of theories presuppose. For the Chinese speaker, speaking and thinking "theoretically" remains pretty much confined to the domain of the scientist, but for the English speaker, since theoretical speaking is not equivalent to theory-building, it can become a part of the speaker's everyday linguistic and cognitive activity.

Consider a final cognitive task in which American and Chinese subjects were presented with the following paragraph in their native language:

Everyone has his or her own method for teaching children to respect morality. Some people punish the child for immoral behavior, thereby leading the child to fear the consequences of such behavior. Others reward the child for moral behavior, thereby leading the child to want to behave morally. Even though both of these methods lead the child to respect morality, the first method can lead to some negative psycholog-ical consequences—it may lower the child's self-esteem.

The subjects were then asked:

According to the above paragraph, what do the two methods of child raising have in common? Please select only one answer.
A. Both methods are useless.
B. They have nothing in common because the first leads to negative psychological consequences.
C. Both methods can reach the goal of leading the child to respect morality.
D. It is better to use the second.
E. None of the above answers makes sense. (If you choose this answer, please explain.)

The American subjects consistently chose alternative C, for that is exactly in fact what the paragraph says. But nearly a majority of the Chinese subjects resisted that alternative and then went on to explain and often with great con-cern and at great length that, in their experiences, neither method works, you have to combine methods, or something to that effect. From later interviewing it was evident that Chinese subjects did notice that the paragraph states that both methods lead the child to respect morality, but they felt that choosing that alternative and leaving it at that would be misleading since, in their experience, that response was untrue. Americans, by contrast, readily accepted the question as a purely theoretical exercise, to be responded to according to the assumptions of the theoretical world it creates rather than in terms of their own experiences with the actual world.

In broader historical perspective, Joseph Needham,[3] in his major work on the history of science in China, presents an impressive array of evidence to support the claim that traditional China developed both a very rich tradition of empirical observation and an active skeptical orientation but did not develop a scientific tradition as we know it, in part because it lacked a third necessary ingredient to such a tradition, namely, a theoretical orientation, an inclination to leave the world of practical application behind in an effort to construct and test purely theoretical explanatory frameworks. Needham's[4] picture of the development of mathematics in China is strikingly similar. Whereas traditional China is shown to have developed a remarkably refined system of mathematical, problem-solving techniques for dealing with practical problems, it did not develop, or even attempt to develop, according to Needham, a theoretical system within which these various practical, mathematical, problem-solving techniques might be integrated and explained.

Neither formal logic, nor religious philosophy, nor moral philosophy, nor political philosophy, nor economics, nor sociology, nor psychology, as theoretical systems independent of each other, bearing their own internal systemic constraints and methodologies, divorced from the factual content they seek to explain, emerged in China, other than as a consequence of importation from the West.

Joseph Levenson, in *Confucian China and its Modern Fate,*[5] argues that the orientation of even the most empirical branch of the Ch'ing Confucianism should be compared to the prescientific nominalism of Abelard rather than the inductive science of Bacon. According to Levenson, Bacon and the scientific orientation he spawned, unlike Abelard or the empiricists of the Ch'ing:

> went beyond simply ascribing ultimate reality to the world of phenomena, instead of to a hypothetical realm of pure Being. He meant not merely to define the real world but to encroach upon it. It was not enough for him to banish abstractions, which can only be contemplated, in favor of tangibles, which can be observed, for observation was not enough. One had to observe with a method and purpose. Bacon's method was induction from experimentally verified 'irreducible and stubborn facts,' his purpose the eliciting of general laws for the organization of facts into science . . . . Although [according to Levenson] the Ch'ing empiricists . . . might pride themselves . . . on looking around them and "testing books with facts," they rarely asked questions systematically which might make them see the essential relevance of some orders of facts to others, they never aspired, as Bacon did, "to establish forever a true and legitimate union between the experimental and rational faculty." Though he might go as far as the Renaissance scientist in deprecating search for the universal, eternal form of particular things, the empirically-minded Ch'ing Confucianist had a temper predominantly nominalist, unembarrassing to scientific spirit, but by no means its equivalent nor its guaranteed precursor.

But Needham[6] likewise suggests that the Western proclivity for theoretical modeling, while prerequisite to certain stages of scientific advance, was, at the same time, seriously inhibitive to others. Such modeling, he argues, involves the extraction of single patterns of causal explanation from factual data that are in reality characterized by a multiplicity of internal interassociations and interrelationships and, hence, necessarily gives rise to overly simplistic and constrictive assumptions about the nature of the phenomena it seeks to describe. As Needham sees it, for Western science to have moved beyond classical mechanics to the notion of relativity, it had, in fact, to overcome the narrowing influence of its own purely theoretical perspective, and that was possible only as a result of its confrontation with the Chinese philosophical awareness of the infinite interdependence and interrelatedness of natural phenomena, first transmitted to the West, according to Needham, through the work of Leibnitz. In choosing, moreover, to view the world through one theoretical perspective rather than another, to adopt an exclusively political, social, psychological, behaviorist, or monetarist view, one easily forgets that one has adopted that perspective for the sake of analysis only and begins to perceive the world and one's knowledge of it as compartmentalized in those ways. And there is certainly an argument to be made in support of the claim advanced by the third century B.C. Confucian scholar Xun Zi that although "there is no reason why problems of hardness and whiteness . . . (as opposed to hard and white) . . . should not be investigated, . . . the superior man does not discuss them; he stops at the limit of profitable discourse."[7] The present argument is, however, not about the relative advantages or disadvantages of theoretical thoughts, but rather about the fact that an inclination to indulge in them seems to be more typical of speakers of Western languages than of speakers of Chinese.

Turning finally to the moral realm, we might interpret these cross-cultural differences in inclination to indulge in theoretical structurings of reality as offering at least a partial explanation for why Chinese moral systems in contrast to Western religions have tended to eschew reliance on formally derived and defended prescriptive theologies in favor of reliance on the development in the individual, through exposure to appropriate live and literary models, of a mature moral sense. The Confucian *junzi* decides among moral claims not on the basis of any theoretical doctrine or formalized set of laws, but on the basis of his own considered intuition. Taoism rejects theoretical system-building in favor of providing a path by which individuals might bring themselves into harmony with the rhythm of nature rather than distance themselves intellectually from it. The theoretical component of Buddhism tended to be discarded as that religion was assimilated by the Chinese and Mao responded to Marxism with a demand for integrating Marx's highly theoretical perspective with at least an equivalent stress on learning through practice.

Within Kohlberg's theory of moral development,[8] the construction of a personal moral theory based on consciously-derived and deliberately-formalized universal principles is seen as prerequisite to the attainment of the highest stage of moral thought. So, it is not surprising that Kohlberg found so few subjects in his Chinese sample who he interprets as having reached that stage. One can, however, ask whether the core of that stage should be considered the construction of such a formalized theoretical value framework, or whether it should be seen, rather, as the development of an autonomous moral orientation—of a feeling of responsibility to become one's own moral arbiter, to weigh and resolve personally the moral claims present in any given conflict situation. Under this interpretation both morality based on considered intuition and morality based on logical deduction from formalized principles would be viewed as styles of postconventional reasoning, as long as they are autonomously derived. Confucius, Mencius, Laotze, and Mao would be admitted along with Plato and Rawls into the pantheon of higher stage postconventional thinkers, and the postconventional thinkers in Chinese samples would emerge classified as such, as they did in a questionnaire survey relating to this point conducted in Hong Kong in 1973.[9]

From the Chinese point of view, a formalized theoretical approach to morality enables one too easily to separate what is morally right from what is economically, politically, or socially expedient. It enables one too easily to justify decisions and policies in terms of abstract considerations that tend to obscure the concrete effects those decisions or policies will have on individual human beings. It enables one too easily to rearrange (i.e., rationalize) one's own interpretations of those effects just as one rearranges events or conditions once entified to fit the needs of a theoretical structure being created. It enables one too easily to remain indifferent to the need for a continuing reexamination of the appropriateness of one's moral stance to changing situations at hand, and it enables one too easily to delegitimate the dictates of one's own emotional and intuitive life. In other words, as the Chinese tend to see it, the kind of thinking that leads one to accept, if only for the sake of argument, that a triangle is a circle, or that two given methods of moral training are effective even when you know they are not, is a kind of thinking that can often lead not only to an overly simplistic, but also to an alienating, a personally-debilitating, and, in fact, an amoral perspective on the world.

Certainly, from a historical point of view, if Chinese speakers at some point in the past had felt a sufficient need to venture into the realm of the counterfactual or the theoretical, the Chinese language would have evolved to accommodate that need, as it is doing today. And so, to explain historically why counterfactual and entificational speech and thought did not develop as it did in the West, one would have to look not only to the characteristics of the language but to the social and intellectual determinants of why a perceived need for such thinking did not arise. Similarly, to explain why Chinese speakers have more recently begun to construct forms to match those of Western languages and to explain why these forms once they emerge are assimilated rather than rejected, one has to look beyond the characteristics of the language to the social, political, and intellectual forces that have shaped the development of the language over the past 50 years. But the present argument is not about why the Chinese language did not traditionally develop forms of counterfactual and entificational ways of speech, or about why Western languages did, or about why the Chinese language is developing them now. Rather, it is about the distinctive impacts these languages have, through the forms they do and do not have, on the cognitive and moral lives of those who grow up within the linguistic environments they provide.

NOTES

1. The research reported in this chapter was funded during the summer of 1975 by a grant from the National Endowment for the Humanities, during the year of 1978 by a grant from the Joint Committee on Contemporary China of the Social Science Research Council and the American Council of Learned Societies, and by several grants from Swarthmore College.

2. See Alfred H. Bloom, *The Linguistic Shaping of Thought: A Study in the Impact of Language on Thinking in China and the West.* (Hillsdale, N.J.: Lawrence Erlbaum Publications, in press) and Alfred H. Bloom, "The Role of the Chinese Language in Counterfactual/Theoretical Thinking and Evaluation" in *Value Change in Chinese Society*, ed. Richard W. Wilson, Amy Auerbacher Wilson, and Sidney L. Greenblatt. (New York: Praeger, 1979), pp. 52–64.

3. Joseph Needham, *Science and Civilization in China, vol. 2.* (Cambridge: Cambridge University Press, 1956).

4. Joseph Needham, *Science and Civilization in China, vol. 3.* (Cambridge: Cambridge University Press, 1959).

5. Joseph R. Levenson, *Confucian China and Its Modern Fate: A Trilogy, vol. 1.* (Berkeley: University of California Press, 1965), pp. 8–9.

6. Needham, *Science and Civilization in China, vol. 2.*

7. Xun Zi, Chapter 2, p. 49, as cited in Joseph Needham, *Science and Civilization in China, vol. 2.* (Cambridge: Cambridge University Press, 1956), p. 202.

8. See Lawrence Kohlberg, "Stage and Sequence: The Cognitive Developmental Approach to Socialization." in *Handbook of Socialization Theory and Research*, ed. D.A. Goslin (Chicago: Rand McNally, 1969), pp. 347–380 and "From Is to Ought: How to Commit the Naturalistic Fallacy and Get Away With It in the Study of Moral Development," in *Cognitive Development and Epistemology*, ed. T. Mischel. (New York: Academic Press, 1971), pp. 151–235.

9. Cultural and societal factors may act more strongly in Chinese society than in Western societies to encourage the development of conventional as opposed to postconventional morality, but that is a different question from whether Chinese postconventional thinking comes out as such. See Alfred H. Bloom, "Two Dimensions of Moral Reasoning: Social Principledness and Social Humanism in Cross-Cultural Perspective," *Journal of Social Psychology* 101 (1977): 29–44.

3 THE CONCEPT OF JUSTICE IN PRE-IMPERIAL CHINA

Stephen B. Young

In Chinese society, as elsewhere, the concept of morality brings immediately to mind the tension-filled, dialectical relationship between an individual and his or her society. Like language, morality proceeds from social convention but is put into practice only by individuals. It is a series of abstract usages learned by individuals in the process of maturation to be applied as guides for their relationships with others in the society. Thus, moral development refers to the growth of an individual's internal capacity to distinguish right from wrong and then to pattern behavior according to such distinctions. It is the overcoming of the most crass, selfish and self-centered concerns in the subjugation of individual egoism to standards of wider applicability.

Moral distinctions are not usually made arbitrarily or randomly. To maintain a social and thereby a moral character, such distinctions when made by individuals must be consistent with a scheme of higher principles defining the ends and purposes of group activity. Another word for such a scheme is a conception of "justice." Theories of justice, therefore, establish the parameters of permissible social action. They determine what is "right" for the individual. On the one hand, they call forth from individuals dedication to duty and obligations—to do what is right—while they simultaneously shield individuals from excessive intrusion by others into those spheres of personal autonomy designated as appropriate for such individuals. Justice for individuals is always defined in terms of their place in a larger whole. To do justly is to perform one's proper role in the achievement of felicity for a relevant group: a family, a tribe, or even mankind as a whole.

Theories of justice demand definitive conclusions about the meaning of human existence. Such theories deal explicitly with natural law concepts and notions of moral purpose. Whether it is Plato's argument in *The Republic* for the functional division of labor in a totalitarian state or John Rawl's exploration of what disinterested but rational individuals would accept as the first principles of their social order,[1] theories of justice contain within themselves a conception of purpose for social life—they are teleological. While they may be used by individuals to assert claims against society, theories of justice originate in a social scheme, a tying together of different individuals into a common whole for some reason. Rawls, in attempting to discuss justice without recourse either to the premises of utilitarianism or to a leap of willful intuition, created from certain selected assumptions what he called a "workable and systematic moral conception."[2] Rawls also noted in line with my definition of a moral order that:

> An egoist is someone committed to the point of view of his own interests. His final ends are related to himself: his wealth and position, his pleasures and social prestige, and so on. Such a man may act justly, that is, do things that a just man would do; but so long as he remains an egoist, he cannot do them for the just man's reasons. Having these reasons is inconsistent with being an egoist.[3]

Plato described justice in *The Republic* only after defining the highest good to which men should be drawn. Purpose here gave rise to preferred structure. John Locke, whose treatise on civil government codified the justice of Anglo-American liberal constitutionalism, followed the same path. Having determined the purposes for which we live (life, liberty, and property), he could devise a social contract and a government obedient thereto.[4] Thomas Hobbes out of similar purposes wove a different pattern of just relationships because he viewed the nature of man more cynically than did Locke.[5] And just governments, Rousseau argued, arose from the general will that ignored the partial interests of particular persons and considered instead only what was best for their collective interest.[6] Marx and other determinist social thinkers begin with a conviction that conformity to the inevitable trend of history makes possible choices between right and wrong. Here most explicitly are individuals confined to their small economic or historic role as working parts of a larger mechanism. Thus, the Western tradition of justice from Plato to today has merely exchanged one theory for another about the purposive order in which man may be said to find himself.

Yet the principles that justify any theory of justice must be applied before that concept of justice can become part of society. Principles held by one or even a few are nothing more than a disembodied morality until they energize a judicial or a political process. One person's abstract theory is not real justice until it imposes consequences on people for their actions in particular circumstances. Unique actions encumbered with a factual setting must be judged as just or unjust, moral or immoral, right or wrong in order for the theory to have a social presence. Generally speaking, justice as theory is important because it makes possible moral distinctions, but it is justice applied through a process of formal, intentional characterization of individual actions that is of greatest moment for people in their lives. Applied justice is the basis of social order.

That the great thinkers of pre-Imperial China took the problem of social order as their central concern is a commonplace. We may infer from this that such thinkers had notions of justice for the same reasons that such notions developed in the West. Confucius, Mencius, Zhuang Zi, Shang Yang, and others, in fact, did seek to arrive at the first principles of that social condition in which they believed mankind should live. Their theories were explicitly plans for social order. They were concerned, as were Plato and the others, with a conception of justice.[7] The Chinese thinkers began with thoughts on the purpose of our human experience. They then defined the functions to be performed by the social organism in furtherance of that purpose, and from these functions finally derived the duties and obligations assigned to different individuals. In general, all these Chinese theories were based on an observed or an assumed fact that social order was made necessary by differences among men and arose from the need to coordinate the separate entities created by such differences. Such theories were organic in that society was presumed to be the sum of its constituent parts and each part had to play a defined role contributing in some small way to the overall success of the whole.

In a mechanistic fashion, Chinese theories of justice held that individuals should do no more than fulfill the roles given them, seeking neither to exceed their due lot nor to fall short of what was expected from them. Thus, we find in pre-Imperial China a notion that anyone who has met with his or her social due should have no complaint, should accept such a result as morally just, and should restrain all internal selfish impulses that might act to avoid or alter such an end.

This essay will discuss the theories of justice held by various schools of Chinese political and legal thought. It will then show that each school called upon a notion of punishment to correct and restrain individuals who could not abide by such systems of justice. Finally, the paper will indicate where different Chinese thinkers explicitly provided for the ability of individuals to judge for themselves the justice or injustice of particular actions. In particular, it will be noted that these ancient Chinese thinkers provided no legitimate role for wanton or arbitrary exercise of social position or political power.

THEORIES OF JUSTICE

The Confucians

The Confucian school, developed in pre-Imperial China by the thinkers Confucius, Mencius, and Xun Zi, drew upon the *History Classic*, the *Poetry Classic*, the *Spring and Autumn Annals*, and the *Book of Ceremony* as the texts for its social and political theory. The central concept of justice in the Confucian school was the notion of righteousness. We find a quote in the Zou Zhuan commentary to the *Spring and Autumn Annals* that: "While the people do not know righteousness, they will not live quietly."[8] Another comment in this work indicates that the righteousness of a person can be seen in the manner of his occupying his position.[9] This points out that righteousness for pre-Imperial Confucians related to the formal duties encumbent upon a position or social role—the manner in which one carried out his or her assigned function in society.

Donald Munro has noted that in the Confucian view "the social order had three components: a specific number of role positions, a hierarchical relationship between these positions, and a code of conduct governing this relationship...."[10] The *History Classic* recorded about the sage king Shun that he first "carefully set forth the beauty of the five cardinal duties."[11] The duties comprised the conduct appropriate for certain social positions arranged in relationships of superiority and inferiority.

The notion behind Confucian righteousness was the need to fulfill social obligations. Even rulers were subject to this constraint in the *Zou Zhuan*:

> Is it the business of the ruler of the people to be merely above them? The altars of the state should be his chief care....Therefore, when a ruler dies or goes into exile for the altars, the minister should die or go into exile with him. If he die or go into exile for his seeking his own ends, who, excepting his private associates, would presume to bear the consequences with him?[12]

The ruler had his proper function, so that his doing otherwise absolved his subordinates from their normal duty to obey him.

Under the scheme of righteousness, when each fulfills the function of his position, the most perfect state of order prevails. The *Zou Zhuan* noted that then, "Harmony prevails between superiors and inferiors; all movements are without insubordinate opposition; whatever the superiors require is responded to; everyone knows his duty."[13]

In perhaps his most noted statement on the functional organization of the good society, Confucius said when asked about government, that the master should master, the servant should serve, the father should father, and the son should son.[14] Here proper conduct was determined by the necessary attributes of the function or station to which a person was assigned or had achieved.[15] Correspondingly, when asked what was the first thing to be done upon the assumption of government administration, Confucius replied that it was necessary to "rectify names."[16] Because, as Confucius felt, if names were not correct, language could not accord with the reality of things and affairs could not be carried to success. This is the Confucian doctrine of "rectification of names." In other words, if proper functions ("names") were not defined for people to learn, then whatever they did would not correspond to what was correct for them to do. Under such circumstances, the interaction of people with one another could not produce a successful social order spontaneously. As Confucius went on to say:

> When affairs cannot be carried on to success, proprieties and music will not flourish. When proprieties and music do not flourish, punishments will not be properly awarded. When punishments are not properly awarded, the people do not know how to move hand or foot.[17]

Confucius also conceived of society as dependent upon hierarchical relationships of different classes and positions. Equality between positions was rejected as impossible. It was said in the *Zou Zhuan* that "equal queens, equal sons, equal powers and equal cities—all lead to disorder."[18] Confucius divided men into categories of those who are born with the possession of knowledge, those who can learn and thereby get possession of knowledge, those who are dull and stupid but yet may learn something, and, finally, those who are dull and stupid but cannot learn.[19] For himself, Confucius found persons in the roles of females and servants the most difficult people to behave with. As he said, "If you are familiar with them, they lose their humility. If you maintain a reserve toward them, they are discontented."[20] Confucius said that individual assignments to positions in the hierarchy were not immutable. Except for those who were wise and already on the top or who were of the lowest class, individuals could change their position. The amount of one's virtue (*de*) determined one's place in the hierarchy, and anyone's virtue could be increased through exercise of self-control.[21] For example, Confucius defined wisdom, an autonomous personal faculty, as giving oneself earnestly to the just obligations due other people.[22] In this way mental powers could be employed in self-restraint, which demonstrated one's virtue and so paved the way for greater things. Other personal powers were subject to control by the will and were therefore also available to increase one's virtue. Confucius said that keeping faithful and sincere while meeting the obligations of one's rightful position in society gave increased vigor to one's virtue.[23] Self-control was not the exclusive prerogative of a limited elite for Confucius but was rather an innate potential in all men: "The Commander of the forces of a large state may be carried off. But the will of even a common man cannot be taken from him."[24]

Wisdom and will could generate mobility in the Confucian social scheme, but no matter where individuals found themselves in the hierarchy, they were expected to conform to the role associated with their position. In the book the *Doctrine of the Mean* we find a simple explanation of this Confucian doctrine:

> The superior man does what is proper to the station in which he is; he does not desire to go beyond this. In a position of wealth and honor, he does what is proper to a position of wealth and honor. In a poor and low position, he does what is proper to a poor and low position. Situated among barbarous tribes, he does what is proper to a situation

among barbarous tribes. In a position of sorrow and difficulty, he does what is proper to a position of sorrow and difficulty.[25]

The Confucian theory cannot be gainsaid. If everyone behaves properly for his or her station in life, there will be order.

The difficulty for Confucians in effecting proper social relationships lay in establishing the modalities of intercourse between positions. To deal with this problem of mutual relationships, Confucius turned to the principle of reciprocity and to the notion of propriety. Confucius held out reciprocity as a word that might serve as a rule of practice for all one's life.[26] The notion of reciprocity, once again, pointed to a conception of justice as reposing in a functional allocation of hierarchical but interdependent roles. This gave rise to his formulation of the Golden Rule that one should not do unto others what one would not have others do unto oneself.

Yet, the degree of reciprocity was not to be left to the judgment of each individual. The proper way for everyone to behave was to reciprocate only the proper actions of others. Not to reciprocate such actions was to fail as a social person, but, equally, to reciprocate more than was appropriate for one's station was unnecessary. Propriety or *li*, an explicit social code of ceremonial and formal conduct, was called upon to determine the degree to which an individual in a given instance should act upon the principle of reciprocity. For Confucius even the management of the state demanded rules of propriety.[27] Confucius admonished his disciple, Yan Yuan, to "look not at what is contrary to propriety; listen not to what is contrary to propriety; speak not to what is contrary to propriety; make no movement which is contrary to propriety."[28]

For Confucius a superior person was one who considered the justice of fixed obligations, or righteousness, to be essential and who performed such obligations according to the rules of propriety, with humility and sincerity.[29] A morally superior person knew his place. For such a one propriety determined the scope of reciprocity, reciprocity arose from a sense of right hierarchy or righteousness, and righteousness could fabricate a just social order.

Mencius defined his basic contribution to Confucian social felicity as advocating the correct understanding of benevolence and righteousness.[30] Subsequently, he defined righteousness as showing respect for elders and as not taking what one has no right to.[31] He also said, "All men have some things which they will not do;—extend that feeling to the things which they do, and righteousness will be the result."[32] This thought was then developed by Mencius when he said that a man should give full development to that feeling within him that refuses to break through or jump over.[33] By giving scope to these few feelings, Mencius believed that man's sense of righteousness could easily be put into practice. Righteousness exists where an individual has a sense of being constrained, where he or she does not want to trespass beyond a certain definite social or psychic space. By stating that "without the rules of propriety and distinctions of right, the high and the low will be thrown into confusion," Mencius indicated that his conception of the social order also depended on distinctions that had to be maintained by society's participants.[34] The notion of justice for him was a scheme whereby individuals were restricted to their proper roles.

But the principle of righteousness as a scheme of justice makes little sense without reference to Mencius' other important notion of benevolence. For Mencius benevolence made man into a unique creature.[35] Human nature for him was intrinsically good because each individual had a psychological faculty that gave rise to emotionally sensitized relationships with other people.[36] Man could not be himself and not have such relationships with other people. Such relationships brought about feelings of commiseration, of self-shame and dislike, of modesty, or of approving and disapproving. For Mencius the natural fact that these feelings arose spontaneously within men indicated that man was a social being and that individuals were to be defined through their relationships with other people. Thus, to be human implied giving attention to others that, in turn, demanded acute sensitivity to the points at which the concerns and interests of others were approached. From benevolence one arrives at a need for social roles and positions that would define the points of contact between the social entities, which made each other possible through reciprocal intercourse. This arrangement of positions was righteouness or justice.

When confronted by an argument that each individual should be thoroughly self-sufficient and should not assume positions of either superiority or dependence, Mencius rejected such a philosophy as contrary to the nature of things. He stated that reciprocal dependency was even beneficial in that "getting those various articles in exchange for grain is not oppressive to the potter and the founder; and the potter and the founder, in their turn, exchanging their various articles for grain, are not oppressive to the husbandman."[37] Thus it is that "great men have their proper business and little men have their proper business."[38] For Mencius, some labor with their minds while others labor with their strength. Those who labor with their minds govern others; those who labor with their strength are governed by others. Those who are governed by others support them; those who govern others are supported by them.[39]

The Confucian writer Xun Zi put, clearly and profoundly, this central tenet of the Confucian school on righteousness as being found in a functional hierarchy of social tasks when he said that:

> Though nature produces all men, there are distinctions whereby they take different stations in life. The Emperor takes his station over the empire because his virtue and character are great, his wisdom and power of thought are very illustrious. The feudal nobles take their station over their dukedoms because their government is lawful, their calling the people up for public service is timely, their hearing of lawsuits and their judicial decisions are fair;...the officers and prefects hold their lands

and cities because their purpose and actions are cultivated; they are skilled in meeting officials; on the one hand they are willing to obey their superiors and on the other they are willing to take their responsibilities;...ordinary people get warm clothes, full stomachs, long life and plenitude of days, and escape from capital and other punishments when they show filial piety and are reverent to their elders, when they are honest, when they act carefully and toil laboriously, when they manage their affairs but do not dare to be indolent or proud.[40]

Xun Zi wrote elsewhere that:

As soon as there was Heaven and Earth, there was the distinction of above and below; when the first wise king arose, the country he occupied had the division of classes. For two nobles cannot serve each other; two commoners cannot employ each other—this is a law of nature. Were people's power and position equal and their likes and dislikes the same, there would not be sufficient goods to satisfy everybody and hence there would inevitably be strife. If there were strife, there would inevitably result general disorder; if general disorder, then general poverty. The ancient kings hated any disorder and hence established the rules of proper conduct (*li*) and justice (righteousness) to divide the people, to cause them to have the classes of poor and rich, of noble and inferior, so that everyone would be under someone's control.[41]

Xun Zi also commented that the rules of proper conduct and justice, by creating distinctions among men, would cause them to assume those duties appropriate for the age, wisdom, and ability of each. This was considered the way of living in society and yet having harmony and unity. Farmers should work the fields, merchants who knew value should manipulate wealth, and artisans with skills should use tools. This division of labor he called the Great Equitableness, saying:

Whether a man's emolument is the whole Empire, he will not think it too much for himself; whether he is gatekeeper, receiver of guests, keeper of the gate bar, or night watchman, he will not think it too little for himself.[42]

For the Confucians the purpose of righteousness and the distinctions that created social order lay in conformity with the natural order. They advised that all men should behave according to the Confucian theory of justice because to do otherwise inevitably would bring on discomfort and sorrow.

In the *Zou Zhuan* we read that men receive at birth the exact and correct principles of Heaven and Earth and that these principles are what is called their appointed nature. Rules of action, propriety, righteousness, and demeanor are used to bring out this nature.[43] Here the origin for the Confucian scheme is found in a pattern for the natural order of the cosmos. We also find the famous Zi Chan, a political leader admired by Confucius, saying with regard to proprieties that:

> Ceremonies are founded in the regular procedure of Heaven, the right phenomena of Earth and the actions of men. Heaven and Earth have their regular ways and men take these for their pattern, imitating the brilliant bodies of Heaven and according with the natural diversities of the Earth.[44]

The Confucian doctrine of the rectification of names, where language was made to conform with preexisting truth, also assumed that the truth behind such names as propriety and righteousness was determined by a natural order.

Mo Zi

Mo Zi lived after Confucius and his concept of justice reflected the same functional notions held by the Confucians. For benevolence he went farther than Mencius and called for altruistic love of everyone without regard for distinctions. Yet when asked, "What is the greatest righteousness in conduct?" Mo Zi replied:

> It is like the building of a wall. Let those who can lay the bricks lay the bricks, let those who can fill in the mortar fill in the mortar, and let those who can carry up the material carry up the material. Then the wall can be completed. To do righteousness is just like this. Let those who can argue argue, let those who can expound the doctrines expound the doctrines, and let those who can administer administer. Then righteousness is achieved.[45]

He also believed that the eminent and the wise should rule over the stupid and humble, saying that:

> Righteousness is what is right. Subordinates do not decide what is right for their superiors; it is the superiors who decide what is right for their subordinates. Therefore, the common people devote their strength to carrying out their tasks, but they cannot decide for themselves what is right. There are gentlemen to do that for them.[46]

Though Mo Zi differed from the Confucians in his emphasis on altruistic concern for others and in his objection to the music and expensive ceremonies so important to the Confucian concept of propriety, he nonetheless also envisaged a social order wherein individuals not only did what was appropriate for them but did not exceed the parameters of such roles. Thus, it was easy for Mo Zi to argue against aggressive war and to thwart the plans of those feudal princes who desired to aggrandize themselves. Once Mo Zi tried to prevent Prince Wen of Lu Yang from attacking Cheng. Prince Wen argued that the people of Cheng had murdered their lord and that Heaven was visiting them with punishment. The prince considered that by attacking he would only be helping Heaven punish Cheng. Mo Zi replied that the people of Cheng had murdered their lords for three generations, that Heaven was visiting them with punishment in the form of three unprosperous years, and that such punishment from Heaven was sufficient.[47] Additional help from man was unnecessary. Man should keep to his allotted place. Justice demanded that each part of the social scheme play its assigned role and no more.

The Legalists

The Legalist concept of justice was not called righteousness (which was a Confucian term), but it nonetheless similarly proclaimed an organic vision of the social order. The Legalists differed from the Confucians not in their view of society as necessarily organized into a hierarchy of functional positions but rather in their view as to the role of government in the creation and maintenance of that hierarchy. For Confucians government had a limited role in social life because the interaction of individuals motivated by benevolence, dedicated to righteousness, and committed to dealing with each other in accordance with propriety would see to it that maximum social tranquility and harmony would automatically prevail. There was little need for government as self-assuming social engineering. Mencius and Confucius argued for light taxes, minimal punishment, and generally mild rule. On the other hand, having a less charitable view of human nature and the potential for individuals to achieve social order on their own, the Legalists set down techniques for rulers to mobilize the full resources of all those under them for purposes of state aggrandizement. Man-made law created duties for the people in order that they could better serve the state. Justice for the Legalists was any scheme of social organization set out by the holders of political power.

For the first Legalist writer, Shang Yang, the state had only two functions: to promote agriculture and war. Shang Yang said that "a Sage, therefore, in organizing a country causes the people, in home affairs, to adhere to agriculture, and in foreign affairs, to scheme for war."[48] For him a ruler should use rewards and punishments to bring out the most martial abilities in soldiers and the best agricultural efforts of the farmers. During times of war those who did well at combat would be rewarded; those who failed would be punished. In times of peace those who produced much grain would be rewarded, and those who didn't punished. Trade and learning were to be discouraged as impediments to the flourishing of the primary social functions agriculture and war. It was the duty of the prince to set incentives for his subordinates to keep them working for the interests of the collective. Law was the tool whereby the social order was fabricated.

The *Book of Lord Shang* said, "Therefore, if law is established, rights and duties are made clear, and self-interest does not harm the law, then there is orderly government,"[49] and:

> Law is the authoritative principle for the people and is the basis for government; it is what shapes the people....That a hundred men will chase after a single hare that runs away is not for the sake of the hare, for when they are sold everywhere in the market, even a thief does not dare to take one away because their legal title is definite. Thus, if the legal title is not definite, then even men like Yao, Shun, Yu or Tang would all rush to chase after it, but if the legal title is definite, even a poor thief would not take it. Now, if laws and mandates are not clear, nor their titles definite, the men of the Empire have opportunities for discussion; in their discussions, they will differ and there will be no definiteness. If, above, the ruler of men makes laws, but below, the inferior people discuss them, the laws will not be definite and inferiors will become superiors. This may be called a condition where rights and duties are indefinite.[50]

Under such circumstances wickedness and wrongdoing would be stimulated, and the country would fall into decay to the anxious distress of its ruler. Thus, the work concludes that "the defining of everybody's rights and duties is the road that leads to orderly government."[51] Like the Confucians, the Legalists believed that the purpose of social life demanded conformity of individuals to assigned roles.

In the *Guang Zi*, another work in the Legalist tradition, we find similar sentiments:

> The shepherd of the people must bring his people under discipline. In order to achieve this, he must enforce the laws, for the laws are the foundation of government....if everyone exceeds the limits of propriety, then respect for superiors and for the government cannot be maintained....Human nature falls into types; so it can be studied and controlled; if correct observation [of men] is made,...proper duties can be assigned to men.[52]

The same secular, rational concept of positivistic social engineering appears again where it is said that:

> There is a proper science of governing the people; and a suitable technique of organizing the army; correct principles to conquer the enemy; and a proper set of principles to govern the world.[53]

Han Fei Zi, a Legalist thinker who followed Shang Yang by over a hundred years, did not follow Shang Yang's insistence that the purpose of the state was to foster agriculture and war but rather adopted certain notions of natural order from Taoism. Han Fei Zi found the obligation of government to provide for the structure of society through legal rules and manipulation of rewards and punishments to be a logical extension of the natural order into the human environment. Nonetheless, he too believed that the purpose of social order was to allow each individual to play a fixed role in a larger scheme. He wrote:

> Indeed, everything has its function; every material has its utility. When everybody works according to his special qualifications, both superior and inferior will not have to do anything. Let roosters herald the dawn and let cats watch for rats.[54]

Setting this machine in motion was the task for the ruler. Han Fei Zi said:

> The sage is the one who scrutinizes the fact of right and wrong and investigates the conditions of order and chaos. Therefore, when governing the state, he rectifies laws clearly and establishes penalties severely in order to rescue all living beings from chaos, rid all under Heaven of misfortune, prohibit the strong from exploiting the weak and the many from oppressing the few.[55]

But, in contrast to the Confucian tradition where justice worked itself out through particularistic adjustments of individuals responding freely within the code of propriety to each other's social positions, Han Fei Zi insisted that uniform principles should be applied across society by the state to determine right and wrong. Han Fei Zi argued that if order is said to follow once ruler and minister act towards each other like father and son, then it must be inferred that there are no disorderly fathers and sons. Yet, simple observation reveals that order is not always found in a family.[56] He wrote that the ancients:

> Never drew the inked string off the line and never pushed the inked string inside the line, and were neither severe beyond the boundary of law nor lenient within the boundary of law; but observed acknowledged principles and followed self-existing standards.[57]

Family connections and social status could not deflect the path of the law for Legalists as they could for Confucians. Shang Yang had even applied the law to his ruler's son. The state as embodied in its promulgated rules and decrees was supreme over all persons regardless of birth or social position. For Han Fei Zi it was the duty of the sovereign:

> To make clear the distinction between public and private interest, enact laws and statutes openly, and forbid private favors. To enforce whatever is ordered and stop whatever is prohibited is the public justice of

the lord of men. To practice personal faith to friends and not to be encouraged by any reward nor to be discouraged by any punishment, is the private righteousness of ministers. Wherever private righteousness prevails, there is disorder; wherever public justice obtains, there is order.[58]

For Legalists order was justice and justice required enactment of positive law.

The Daoists

The Daoists believed in natural justice. They rejected both the righteousness of Confucianism and the laws of Legalism as the products of social contrivance and as leading either to hypocrisy or to exploitation.[59] The Daoists sought for justice in nature alone. By creating society, they believed, man had only created evil. Lao Zi wrote that Confucian benevolence and righteousness only appear when the great Dao decays.[60] And that righteousness or justice arises only after the Dao, virtue, and benevolence, have all been lost.[61] For Daoists, social justice ran only fourth as a preferred means to organize man's life.

The Daoists asserted that, unlike Confucian gentlemen, Heaven knows not benevolence; it treats all things as straw dogs. Yet, in nature things do prosper according to a rule. No striving or contrivance is necessary for each to receive its due. This is natural justice.

Zhuang Zi elaborates on this theme of a natural order that should not be disturbed. He wrote that:

> That which is the perfectly correct path is not to lose the real character of the nature with which we are enclosed . . . . what is long should not be considered too long, nor what is short too short. A duck's legs, for instance, are short but if we try to lengthen them, it occasions pain.[62] . . . And moreover, in employing the hook and line, the compass and square, to give things their correct form you must cut away portions of what naturally belongs to them.[63] . . . Thus, it is that all in the world are produced what they are by a certain guidance while they do not know how they are produced so; and they equally attain their several ends while they do not know how it is that they do so. Anciently it was so, and it is so now; and this constitution of things should not be made of none effect.[64]

Accordingly, men should realize that there is no alternative to their acting as they do and that they should "rest" in the place where they find themselves because such a place constitutes the life that has been appointed for them. Zhuang Zi advised men to let their minds find "enjoyment in the circumstances of your position, nourish the central course which you pursue, by a reference to your unavoidable obligations."[65] Since all men receive a similar fate in being destined for some end, each man for Zhuang Zi was equally a son of Heaven.

Distinctions, other than natural ones, were sources of evil and were unjust. For Daoists, Confucian social distinctions merely brought out envy and strife, while Legalist rewards for meritorious service and punishments for infractions of man-made laws brought about competitive self-seeking and oppression of man by man. Mo Zi and the Daoists had certain similarities in their desires for simplicity and rejection of the formalism of Confucian rites and music. Mo Zi, however, still saw a role for political leadership in creating social order as a piece of human handiwork, albeit in conformity to Heaven's will.

Daoist justice consisted of only the events that would occur when men do nothing out of regard for self-selected ends. Such justice cannot really be defined other than as an organic process without beginning, end, or apparent purpose.

Regarding the state, Lao Zi advised that good government should not hurt and that the best government consists of no government or nonaction (*wuwei*).[66] If the ruler would merely collapse himself into the Dao then all would be well. "Whoever meddles with the Empire spoils it."[67] One should "rule a large country as if you were cooking small fish."[68] In other words, leave them alone. Doing otherwise ruins them.

PUNISHMENT

The Confucians

Concern for punishment, as a legitimate consequence of excess and self-indulgence, permeated the Confucian theory of society because under such theory, since social order depended on individuals fulfilling their prescribed roles, it was impermissible for persons to neglect the duties and obligations assigned to such roles. What was not permitted could therefore be punished. Thus, we find in the *Poetry Classic* songs referring to the just overthrow of the Shang Dynasty due to the inability of its last king to behave properly. One ode says:

> King Wan said, 'Alas!
> Alas, you sovereign of Yin-Shang
> It is not God that has caused this evil time,
> But it arises from Yin's not using the old ways.
> Although you have not old experienced men
> There are still the ancient statutes and laws
> But you will not listen to them,
> And so your great appointment is being overthrown.[69]

The Shang king was being punished by Heaven for his failure to carry out the prescribed pattern for kingly rule. The ode assumes that the Shang sovereign was capable of being a true king but that he did not discipline himself to be one. Thus, he brought punishment on himself.

In the *History Classic*, we also find that the just punishment of this last Shang king brought about the legitimate ascension of the Zhou Dynasty to the throne. In addressing his troops before battle, King Wu, who founded the Zhou Dynasty of Chinese sovereigns, said that he was going to administer a great correction to Shang:

> Now Shou, the king of Shang, follows only the words of his wife. In his blindness he has neglected the sacrifices which he ought to offer and makes no response for the favors that he has received....There are only the vagabonds from all quarters, loaded with crimes, whom he favors and exalts, whom he employs and trusts, making them great officers and high nobles so that they can tyrannize the people and exercise their villainies in the cities of Shang. Now, I, Fa, am simply executing respectfully the punishment appointed by Heaven.[70]

In this ancient Chinese political text, punishment came from Heaven for transgression of its orderly ways, but men acted as the agents of Heaven. Punishment was not only justified under those circumstances, it also created a basis of political legitimacy, for the two famous dynasties of Shang and Zhou both began by rebelling against a corrupt king of a previous dynasty. Legitimacy for such rebellions was found in their purpose as punishing violation of a code of proper behavior.

In a separate reference to punishment, the *History Classic* also noted that the sage king Shun had banished and punished several people during his reign, used the whip in magistrate's courts, imposed fines and banishment in place of harsher sanctions, and pardoned offenses arising out of negligence. Shun was, thus, an advocate of penal sanctions under proper circumstances. We also read in the *History Classic* that King Qi of the Xia Dynasty justified a military expedition as doing Heaven's work in punishing an offender:

> The Lord of Hu wildly wastes and despises the five elements that regulate the seasons and has idly abandoned the three acknowledged commencements of the year. On this account Heaven is about to destroy him and bring to an end his appointment to Hu. I am now reverently executing the punishment appointed by Heaven.[71]

In the *Zou Zhuan* it is recorded that the famous prime minister of Cheng, Zi Chan, said that, "It was the command of the former kings, that, wherever there was guilt, it should in every case be punished."[72]

And the *Spring and Autumn Annals* record that the feudal leaders who set themselves up as hegemons or presidents over alliances of various princes took as their solemn obligation the punishment of those states that broke the covenants whereby such combines had been formed and by which the states had agreed to let each other live in peace. Thus, here again failure to act in the manner appointed as proper and correct brought harsh consequences upon the delinquent. In this case the appropriate set of duties was voluntarily assumed through a contractual act and was not set out by Heaven. Nonetheless, responsibility for infliction of just punishment on transgressors still constituted the moral grounds upon which a claim for legitimate political supremacy could be based. In these cases valid authority was claimed by hegemons and not by kings.

While not approving of coercive regulation as the primary way to maintain social order, Confucius himself, nonetheless, admitted that punishments played a role adjunct to the attempt to achieve justice. As noted above, he said that, "When punishments are not properly awarded, the people do not know how to move hand or foot."

Confucius himself was Minister of Crime for the state of Lu.[73] And once he importuned his duke to invade the neighboring state of Chi in order to punish an usurper of that state, saying "Jen Hung has slain his sovereign. I beg that you will undertake to punish him."[74] But when his ruler refused to act and the great families also declined the mission, Confucius, as became his station, did not set out to do justice on his own. It was not his place to execute a punishment even though such punishment was well deserved.

But also he held forth the notion that if good men were to govern the country for a hundred years, they would be able to so educate the people that capital punishments could be dispensed with.[75] Punishments were necessary because people were weak and from time to time might be expected to fall into self-indulgence. For him, people, when led by virtue and not laws, would develop a sense of shame and in so doing would internalize their social obligations and spontaneously be good.[76] While this preference for virtue reveals the Confucian belief in moral education as the only basis for perfect social organization, it also indicates that under normal circumstances, punishments are necessary to deal with those individuals who have not yet learned the self-control necessary for propriety and righteousness. While superior men value righteousness, Confucius noted that mean men value gain and that the world does not consist exclusively of superior men.[77] The self-seeking of mean men required the restraint of punishments to keep them in their proper places.

Mencius made a distinction between a just use of force and an unjust use of force when he admitted that one feudal lord could attack another, and so he, too, accepted a legitimate role for punishment in his social theory. The passage from Mencius is as follows:

> The people of Chi smote Yen. Someone asked Mencius saying, "Is it really the case that you advised Chi to smite Yen?" He replied, "No. Shan Tong asked me whether Yen might be smitten and I answered him, 'It may,' They accordingly went and smote it. If he had asked— 'Who may smite it?' I would have answered him, 'He who is the minister of Heaven may smite it.' Suppose the case of a murderer, and that

one asked me, 'May this man be put to death?' I will answer him, 'He may.' If he asks me—'Who may put him to death?' I will answer him, 'The chief criminal judge may put him to death.'"[78]

This passage also illustrates the Confucian notion of appropriate allocation of functions. Punishment may be just, but it must be carried out only by those formally appointed to the task. Justice was not for vigilantes.

Mencius also provided for a right of revolution whereby subordinates could dethrone their emperor if such an emperor failed to live up to the responsibilities inherent in his role. Mencius, in this passage, makes specific reference to the seizure of power by the Shang and Zhou Dynasties through the overthrow of unscrupulous monarchs.[79]

For the Confucian Xun Zi punishment was also an important part of government. He felt that the origin of all punishment lay in the need to restrain violence and to warn against its future occurrence.[80] He wrote:

In ancient times, King Wu chastised the monarch of the Shang dynasty; he killed Chau; he cut off his head and hung it on a crimson banner. Now chastising the violent and punishing the overbearing is the summit of good government.[81]

By refusing to uphold the principles of righteousness and proper conduct, the last kings of the Shang and Zhou Dynasties had lost their right to rule. As Xun Zi put it, in point of moral fact, "They did not possess the empire" and were not legitimate rulers, so that those who rose up against them could not be accused of disloyalty or insubordination.[82] More explicitly than Mencius, Xun Zi argued for the removal of tyrannical rulers. He said:

When the country has no real prince, if there is a feudal noble who has ability, and if his virtue is illustrious and his majesty is great, none of the people of the country will be unwilling to take him for prince and leader; then if he should seek out and kill this isolated and wasteful tyrant, he would not injure anyone, he would be a blameless subject. If he put to death a prince of a tyrannous state, it would be the same as killing an ordinary individual.[83]

Those who misbehaved and ignored their social obligations could expect punishment from Confucians. Such punishment was part of the just order for Confucians, though their theory was tempered by a preference for moral education and its power to improve the wayward.

Mo Zi

Mo Zi, too, believed in punishments as a means to achieve social order. He likened them to:

the main thread binding a skein of silk or the main cord controlling a net, by which the Sage Kings bound and hauled in those among the people of the world who failed to identify with their superior.[84]

Those who knew not their lot were to be punished according to Mo Zi. His belief in universal love did not prevent him from applauding just punishments. Only, Mo Zi said, no partiality should be shown in the infliction of punishments. That insured the accommodation of altruism with social discipline. Mo Zi held that one purpose of Heaven was to punish the wicked, who were all those people hating and injuring others.

The Legalists

For the Legalists punishment was explicitly a technique for keeping in check those subservient to the government. Shang Yang said that:

> Now the idea of punishments is to restrain depravity and the idea of rewards is to support the interdicts. Shame and disgrace, labor and hardship are what the people dislike; fame and glory, ease and joy are what the people pay attention to. So punishment and executions are the means whereby wickedness is stopped and office and rank are the means whereby merit is encouraged.[85]

Shang Yang also argued that light offenses should be heavily punished. In this way no one would dare commit even minor crimes, and by such means gradually no crimes would be committed, and, ultimately, there would be no need for punishments at all: "If light offenses do not occur, serious ones have no chance of coming."[86] Laws should be strictly applied so that no one escaped because:

> If culprits often escape through the meshes, inferior people will be depraved and dissolute and will not think of the punishments as deterrents and thus they will be applied to the people in a haphazard manner. Under those conditions, the inferior people will not avoid what is prohibited and punishments will be numerous.[87]

Shang Yang had no interest in punishing per se, only in enforcing social order. As he said:

> Indeed, there is no greater benefit for the people in the Empire than order and there is no firmer order to be obtained than by establishing a prince; for establishing a prince there is no more upraising method than making law supreme; for making law supreme, there is no more urgent task than banishing villainy, and for banishing villainy, there is no deeper basis than severe punishments.[88]

For Han Fei Zi, punishment was also to prevent selfishness, because it was destructive of order. He wrote that:

> The purpose of enacting laws and decrees is to abolish selfishness. Once laws and decrees prevail, the way of selfishness collapses. Selfishness disturbs the law....Whoever tolerates selfishness finds chaos, whoever upholds law finds order. If the superior misses the correct way, astute men will use selfish phraseology, and worthies will cherish selfish motives, principals will bestow selfish favors and subordinates will pursue selfish desires. When worthy and astute men form juntas, coin terms, manipulate phrases and thereby denounce laws and decrees before the superior, then wicked men may count on rewards and accumulate wealth.[89]

Under such conditions the state would have difficulty in obtaining its necessary end of public tranquility through the functional specialization of its subjects according to established rules.

In addition, punishments served for Han Fei Zi as an admonition to those who have not yet committed any crime but who will stand in awe of the harsh consequences meted out to those who do.[90]

> Severe penalty is what the people fear, heavy punishment is what the people hate. Accordingly, the wise man promulgates what they fear in order to forbid the practice of wickedness and establishes what they hate in order to prevent villainous acts. For this reason, the state is safe and no outrage happens. From this I know very well that benevolence, righteousness, love and favor are not worth adopting, while severe penalty and heavy punishment can maintain the state in order.[91]

Punishment was one of the two handles by which a ruler could control his subordinates and so ensure that his wishes were carried into effect. The power of the ruler, for Han Fei Zi as for Shang Yang, was the guarantee of public order, and both power and order required the use of punishments.

In the *Guang Zi*, punishment was similarly looked upon as an artificial tool of government. Punishments should be imposed rigorously, we are told in this work: "When prohibitions are strictly enforced and punishments made severe, even the unruly and the lazy will conform and obey."[92] Furthermore:

> A wise sovereign closes the door (to evil), stops the path to (wrongdoing), and prevents all footprints (of crime), in order to protect the people from coming into contact with the immoral and the wrong. Consequently, the people behave well and do good as if by their nature. Criminal punishments seldom become necessary and the people live in peace.[93]

The Daoists

Rejecting any need for social order and falling back on the justice inherent in nature itself, the Daoists of this period saw no need for punishment imposed by a calculating human hand. If he who governs the empire "ought always to be without activity" as Lao Zi says, then there will be no punishment by the state.[94] Heaven is called the "Master of Killing" by Lao Zi. Of those who dare to supplant this master, "There are few who will not hurt their hands."[95] While the net of crime is described in the *Poetry Classic* as set by Heaven for men to catch those who stray from approved ways, Lao Zi responds by characterizing it as coarse, having a very wide mesh so that things can easily slip through it. Yet, such a net paradoxically still "loses nothing."[96] Natural punishment is like the gentle dew falling on the place beneath. On its own Heaven will diminish what has too much and add to what has not enough.[97] Thus, excess and deficiency are naturally compensated for. In a sense there is punishment in the Daoist theory of justice in that the creator of how things are (which is also how they should be) remedies situations where there is a departure from the norm in order to restore an appropriate balance. For the Daoists such corrective measures are best left to the author of the scheme of justice in which we live, and man himself is not such author. Zhuang Zi wrote that:

> When all men do not carry their nature beyond its normal condition, nor alter its characteristics, the good government of the world is se-cured....Therefore the superior man who feels himself constrained to engage in the administration of the world will find it his best policy to do nothing. In doing nothing he can rest in the instincts of the nature with which he is endowed.[98]

Zhuang Zi added that to govern the world one should:

> Let your mind find its enjoyment in pure simplicity; blend yourself with (the primary) ether in idle indifference; allow all things to take their natural course; and admit no personal or selfish consideration—do this and the world will be governed.[99]

One who practices the Dao, says Zhuang Zi, "does not censure men."[100]

APPLIED JUSTICE

Under the above theories—where justice is a hierarchy of different functional obligations and punishment is the means whereby such a hierarchy is main-tained—consequences accurately imposed for a failure to meet the requirements of one's position are just applications of power. However, each infliction of punishment involves a determination as to matters of fact not precisely foreseen by the theoretical design for social order. When one individual, be it ruler, minister, father, or son, trespasses beyond the bounds of his appropriate role, a judgment must be made as to the degree of that specific trespass. For example, it might be relevant to learn in such a case if there were mitigating circumstances present or if the trespass arose from simple negligence. Making such an investigation of facts in order to form a judgment is application of theory to social reality. Traditional Chinese thinkers were quite clear and insistent that such judgments on the infliction of punishment should not be made in an arbitrary fashion. Moreover, judgments incorrectly made carried no moral force. Punishments were just not merely because they were imposed by those legitimately in authority but because they accurately applied the theory of justice to the facts of the case at hand. It was therefore important for punishments to fit the crime. In addition, for Confucians and for Mo Zi individuals could openly criticize government for its failure to implement the scheme of justice correctly.

The Confucians

In one of the odes in the *Poetry Classic* we find the following lines protesting injustice:

> There is nothing settled in the country;
> Officers and people are in distress.
> Through the insects from without and from within,
> There is no peace or limit.
> The net of crime is taken up,
> And there is no peace or cure.
> Men had their ground and fields,
> But you have them now.
> Men had their people and followers,
> But you have violently taken them from them.
> Here is one who ought to be held guiltless,
> But you snared him (in the net of crime).
> There is one who ought to be held guilty,
> But you let him escape (from it).[101]

Here, the net of crime caught the wrong individuals. Punishment was visited on those who had done no wrong.

In another ode, we find the lines:

> Compassionate Heaven, arrayed in terrors,
> How is it you exercise no forethought, no care?
> Let alone the criminals:
> They have suffered for their offenses;

But those who have no crime
Are indiscriminately involved in ruin.[102]

Here, even Heaven stands accused of making a mistake.
And, in another ode we again find Heaven itself denounced as unjust:

Oh vast and distant Heaven,
Who art called our parent,
That without crime or offense,
I should suffer from disorders thus great!
The terrors of great Heaven are very excessive,
But indeed I have committed no offense.[103]

In the *History Classic*, there are numerous references to the just application of punishments, defined as a specific punishment befitting the particular facts of a case where some excess or want of duty has occurred. The Minister of Crime for the sage king Yu was praised for his restraint in adapting each punishment exactly to the facts of each offense.[104] In that same document the people of Miao were held forth as the example of how not to use punishments. Such people made the five punishments into "engines of oppression" by slaughtering the innocent, not making any distinctions among those subject to punishment, and not recognizing any mitigating factors or excuses. This document then warned against any application of punishment as long as there were still doubts as to the facts involved because the objective when imposing punishment was to gain agreement from all parties concerned that the final decision was correct or just.[105]

Another document in the *History Classic* explicitly rejected the notion of arbitrary punishment when a king instructed his younger brother not to presume that he could willfully inflict a severe punishment or death upon a man, saying, "Do not, to please yourself, punish a man or put him to death."[106] A judge's individual inclination could not therefore be relied upon as the determinant of punishment. Some objective standard had to be applied.

The Confucian concept of justice demanded that punishment could only be a causal consequence of some transgression. As transgressions properly so-called do not arise from accident so much as from a state of mind heedless of social obligations, punishing negligent and accidental wrongs was less important than punishing intentional crimes. The presence of intent indicated the existence of a will unable to remain within the confines of its social position. Thus, in the above document, we also find the king saying:

When men commit crimes which are purposed and not by chance, intentionally doing what is contrary to the laws, they must be put to death even though their crimes be small. But in the case of great crimes which are not purposed but from mischance and misfortune, accidental, you must not put them to death if the transgressors confess their guilt without reserve.[107]

In fact, Gao Yao, the great Minister of Crime to the sage king Yu, said that inadvertent faults, however great, should be pardoned, and intended crimes, however small, should be punished. Moreover, he said that, rather than put an innocent person to death, an official should instead run the risk of irregularity and error.[108]

But once punishment correctly embodied a principle of justice, it was to be acknowledged as a proper use of state power. In the *Zou Zhuan* it is recorded that Confucius approved of the justice dispensed by one who condemned his relative to death for corruption. In that case, a man, knowing that he was in the wrong, offered a bribe in order to buy a verdict in his favor. A judge accordingly sold his judgment in the dispute but another party then killed him for such corruption. All three individuals were considered by Confucius to have been properly punished even though one offender was a relative of the official who decided on capital punishment.[109]

Another part of the *Zou Zhuan* noted that:

> The skillful administration of a state is seen in rewarding without error and punishing without excess. If punishments be inflicted in excess, there is a danger in some reaching good men. If, unfortunately, mistakes cannot be avoided, it is better to err in the matter of rewards than of punishments. It is better that a bad man get an advantage than that a good man be lost.

This passage then quoted the provision from the *History Classic* cited above on freeing the guilty to prevent a miscarriage of justice.[110] And in another part of the *Zou Zhuan* we again find a comment demanding correct application of punishments noting that:

> Now, since Wang-Shuh became Chief Minister, the government has been carried on by means of bribes, and punishments have been in the hands of his favorites. His officers have become enormously rich and it is not to be wondered if we are reduced to such hovels....If the low cannot obtain right, where is what we call justice?[111]

At several points the *Zou Zhuan* recognized that similar circumstances should bring on similar punishment: "Their crime was the same and their punishment is different; you do not show an equal justice;" and "To inflict different penalties on parties guilty of the same offense is improper punishment."[112] In this sense justice had to be equal for all under Confucian theory, for if in two cases the facts were similar and the judge correctly correlated the facts of the crimes with the rule adopted for such circumstances, the results would be the same in each case. So Xun Zi said that if "punishment should not fit the crime—there is no misfortune greater than this."[113]

Neither Mencius nor Confucius discussed what might constitute improper punishment, but both permitted people to criticize the government for its mistakes. This right of remonstrance implied that governing officials must conform to a standard of righteousness other than their own will in order to be just and to deserve obedience. Confucius said that if a ruler's words were bad and no one criticized them, then the ruin of the country would result.[114] Mencius provided for revolution when rulers neglected their duties and praised Confucius for writing the *Spring and Autumn Annals* so that the deeds of princes would be fairly evaluated according to an objective standard. And for Xun Zi serving a poor prince but being able to follow the right was better than serving an unjust prince while obtaining a high position.[115] As noted above, Xun Zi approved of tyrannicide.

It was important for Confucian thinkers that application of a social rule to particular situations bring about an exact correspondence between the cognitive principles embodied in the rule and the dynamic principles found in the reality to which the rule was applied. This was the doctrine of rectification of names. It opposed arbitrary punishments and thereby gave some protection to individuals.

Mo Zi

Mo Zi also believed that just administration of punishments was necessary for a well-ordered state. He said that "punishments must fall on those who deserve them" and that laws and punishments must be "justly administered."[116]

Though Mo Zi demanded that inferiors adopt the morality of their superiors ("What the superior considers right, all shall consider right."), if the superior goes against his own standard and commits a fault, then his subordinates may remonstrate with him.[117] Mo Zi himself protested against the unjust attacks of feudal rulers against one another but agreed that some warfare could be legitimately waged if it were true punishment of an offender.

People could look to the will of Heaven to discriminate between good and bad actions and therefore decide who ought to be punished. Actions in accordance with the will of Heaven were good; those at variance were to be punished. Heaven defined what was right for the ruler as well.[118] Anyone could consult Heaven to see if a government was good or bad. For Mo Zi it was as easy and as natural as telling black from white. Mo Zi said:

> The will of Heaven is to me like a compass to a wheelwright or a square to a carpenter. The wheelwright uses his compass to test the roundness of every object in the world saying, "What matches the line of my compass I say is round. What does not match my compass I say is not round." Therefore he can tell in every case whether a thing is round or

not, because he has a standard for roundness. The carpenter uses his square to test the squareness of every object in the world, saying, "What matches my square is square. What does not match my square is not square." Therefore he can tell in every case whether a thing is square or not, because he has a standard for squareness.

In the same way Mo Zi could use

the will of Heaven to measure the government of the rulers and ministers above, and the writings and words of the multitudes below. He observes their actions, and if they obey the will of Heaven, he calls them good actions, but if they disobey the will of Heaven, he calls them bad actions.[119]

The Legalists

Interestingly enough, the Legalists, for all their emphasis on the untrammelled authority of the government and the prince to determine the terms of social intercourse for the people, did not permit in their theory arbitrary application of punishment. Manipulation of the law for self-interest by rulers, ministers, and officials was seen as a great evil by the Legalists because it deflected individuals from dedication to public purposes. Shang Yang said that:

If models and measures are abolished and private appraisal is favored, then bad ministers will let their standards be influenced by money in order to obtain emoluments, and officials of the various ranks will, in a stealthily and hidden manner, make extortions from the people. So if ministers of state vie with one another in selfishness and do not heed the people, then inferiors are estranged from superiors. When this happens, there is a fissure in the state.[120]

Shang Yang's book notes that:

Nowadays, princes and ministers of a disorderly world each, on a small scale, appropriates the profits of his own state, and each exercizes the burden of his own office for his private benefit. This is why the states are in a perilous position.[121]

Even a ruler should not act in an arbitrary manner because an intelligent ruler does not enrich and honor his ministers according to his own whims prompted by selfish interest. The ruler, too, should conform his actions to the norms specified in public law.[122]

Therefore, is an intelligent ruler cautious with regards to laws and regulations; he does not harken to words which are not in accordance with the law; he does not exalt actions which are not in accordance with the law; he does not perform deeds which are not in accordance with the law.[123]

In chapter V, paragraph 26, of the *Book of Lord Shang*, provision is made for a system of government by law and not by men. It is recommended there that the laws, once promulgated, not be changed and that authoritative copies of the laws be kept under seal. In addition, special officers should be set up who are experts on the contents of the law and who may be consulted by government officials or by the people when questions arise over interpretation of the laws or mandates. In this way, one body of officials would serve as a check against other officials.

> Thus there shall be no one among the government officials and people of the empire who does not know the law and as the officials are clearly aware that the people know the laws and mandates, they dare not treat the people contrary to law, nor dare the people transgress the law as they would come into conflict with the law officers.[124]

In this way:

> Government officials and the people of the empire, however virtuous or good, however sophisticated or sagacious they may be, cannot add one word to twist the law, nor though they may have a thousand pieces of gold, can they use one twenty-fourth of an ounce of it for such a purpose.[125]

The objective of such a formal administration was the correct application of the law according to its terms. But because law is made by man and not Heaven, the law itself, while true to the scheme of public justice created for the state, may still be oppressive to men who prefer a different scheme. Such private preferences were of no consequence for the Legalists.

Han Fei Zi said that, "Punishments equivalent to crimes are never too many; punishments not equivalent to crimes are never too few."[126] Therefore, the important point in determining whether or not there are too many punishments in a country was not the number of punishments, but their relationship to the crimes that had occurred. This emphasis on precise application of the law was again mentioned by Han Fei Zi when he said:

> Who overcompensates for an evil would inflict a big punishment for a small offense. To inflict a big punishment for a small offense is an eccentric action by the criminal court. It constitutes a worry to the court. The menace arises not from the criminals already punished, but from the number of enemies thereby made.[127]

At another passage, he made the same point by saying:

> If the crime is committed by A, but the consequent disaster befalls B, then hidden resentment will grow. In an orderly country, reward and punishment correspond with the tallies of merits and demerits.[128]

For him, allowing personal prejudice to enter into the courts of justice is a threat to the social order:

> When the ruler estimates wisdom and virtue not according to meritorious services and judges crimes and faults not through the processes of investigation and testimony, but simply listens to the words of the courtiers and attendants, then incapable men will fill up the court and stupid and corrupt magistrates will occupy all posts.[129]

Application of law should not be arbitrary but should conform to certain fixed standards.

Han Fei Zi also related a story regarding a disciple of Confucius who had been a judge in a criminal court and had cut off the feet of a certain criminal. One night, this disciple found himself pursued and hid in the presence of that criminal who was now a gatekeeper. The gatekeeper sheltered the disciple. The disciple asked, "Why are you willing to shelter me? How can I receive such a kindness from you?" The footless man replied, "I had my feet cut off as my crime deserved such punishment. Nothing could be done about it."[130] During the case the disciple as judge had interpreted the ordinance in all possible ways, being anxious to hold the gatekeeper innocent, but to no avail. Thus, the gatekeeper felt that every effort had been taken to examine the case and that, indeed, the punishment decided upon was deserved. Han Fei Zi similarly advised that "when censuring culprits, if name and fact correspond to each other, the superior should immediately enforce the censure."[131] The process of punishment was making a correlation between a set of facts and some predetermined definition of wrong, if such definition applied to the facts.

For Han Fei Zi as for Shang Yang, the ruler was not free to do as he pleased:

> If the ruler is fond of twisting laws by virtue of his wisdom, mixes public with private affairs from time to time, alters laws and prohibitions at random, and issues commands and orders frequently, then ruin (of the state) is possible.[132]

A ruler must obey the system he has imposed on the state and must achieve in the application of justice rationally correct links between stated rules of law and the relevant circumstances.

The *Guang Zi* advised that care

> Must be taken in the matter of criminal punishment. Otherwise, strict justice will not be maintained and one may execute the innocent and pardon the guilty. It will then be difficult to rid the state of prevaricating magistrates.[133]

The work warned that "If justice does not reign in higher circles, the common people will come to hate their superiors, and orders will not be obeyed."[134]

In distinction to the Confucians and Mo Zi, the Legalists did not provide an opportunity for private individuals to criticize the state. In Shang Yang's work, those who dared to tamper with the text of the laws should be put to death. Established authority should not be challenged, and special law officers should tell the people whether or not other officers have correctly applied the law.[135] Shang Yang also believed that "he who accomplishes a great work, does not take counsel with the multitude."[136] The Confucian values of benevolence and righteousness whereby citizens could evaluate their rulers were rejected by Shang Yang as creating the "Ten Evils" leading to dismemberment of a state.[137]

Han Fei Zi similarly said that "to accord with the mind of the people is to tolerate villainous deeds."[138] However, a ruler was advised to encourage his ministers to denounce one another as a means of keeping them under royal control.[139] Han Fei Zi quoted with approval the remark of King Zhao of Chin who said:

> When the people love me, I will have to alter the law and bend my will to comply with their requests. In this manner the law will not stand. If the law does not stand, it will lead to chaos and ruin.[140]

Rulers who depended on the people's approval for support left themselves exposed to danger, according to Han Fei Zi, for when they no longer pleased the people, their power and authority would erode. Only the *Guang Zi* argued for incorporating popular support into the political method of ruling a Legalist state. This work also advised rulers to follow the will of the people:

> For though one multiply punishments mightily, if the people are not loyal in their minds, orders will not be obeyed. And though the sovereign executes many, if the people are rebellious in their hearts, his position will be in danger.[141]

The work flatly states that "if the laws conform to the will of the people, they will be obeyed."[142] While Legalists and Confucians differed as to private criticism correcting government policies, both schools of thought firmly believed with Mo Zi that the law should not be arbitrarily applied if justice was to prevail.

The Daoists

Lao Zi and Zhuang Zi said little regarding avoidance of arbitrary punishment, believing it better to do away with punishment of men by men altogether. As for punishment imposed by nature, little need be said, for nature smoothly supplemented what was deficient and reduced what was excessive, leaving, for example, the duck's leg just as long as it should be.

But Zhuang Zi advised looking upon the people as right in all things and on the government as wrong.[143] Critiques of government were axiomatic for Daoists. Government was a disturbance of the natural order and should be reduced to as small a force as possible. Lao Zi said, "If he [the prince] wants to precede the people, with his personality he puts himself behind them."[144] Furthermore, government by nonaction as prescribed by the Daoists demanded that the state not interfere with the actions of the citizens but instead should merely let them be.

CONCLUSION

This rather cursory survey of Confucian, Mohist, Legalist, and Daoist theories briefly showed how each provided for a scheme of social order logically derived from views on the moral state in which mankind found itself. The summaries presented here indicate that traditional Chinese thinkers were not apologists for oriental despotism. Rather, they were concerned with the ordering of society according to principle. For them either an individual moral faculty of self-control or a person's rational ability to respond to rewards and punishments made practical application of their schemes possible. Social order was to result from the self-imposed conformity of morally autonomous individuals.

Yet, the notion of individual autonomy presented in these theories was a restricted one. Individuals were not permitted to apply in their own lives universal principles selected through whim or through reason by a unique personal free will. The free will of the individual was, instead, to be disciplined so that it might accept the limitations inherent in the role assigned to the individual by a higher authority. A person was free to challenge the behavior of others as violating a social code but not his or her own assigned lot.

Mobility was made possible for Confucians by accumulation of virtue through self-discipline, and it was possible for Mohists and Legalists through performance of the acts that the state proclaimed deserving of reward. But for all theorists the most important features of a person's life at any given moment were determined by his or her status at that moment—superior or inferior, father, wife or son—and not be a consistent self-image, which might impress upon each such status occupied by a person a unique nuance of private personality.

This preference for individuals defined by social position and not by idiosyncratic ambitions or desires is perhaps the reason why the Chinese placed such importance on sincerity. Only a sincere will could truly subordinate the ego to the obligations required to be performed as part of the externally assigned role, or, from the Daoist perspective, as inherent in the simplicity of one's natural place. Opposed to sincerity was selfishness—the drive of the ego to break out of role-related responsibilities. Selfishness, naturally enough, was the dread enemy of social order for all traditional Chinese thinkers.[145]

But even with this great emphasis on moral order in pre-Imperial China, there were other preferences at work as well. To find a challenge to the imposition of role assignments we must look to poetry, not social theory, and to a different cultural tradition in the state of Chu, which, while part of the Chinese Empire, was a state representing a less classical heritage. This approach demanded that a scheme of justice give the individual a role appropriate to the individual's sense of self-esteem. Echoes of this approach may be heard in the lives of knight-errants and in mystics who sought magic powers and a life of immortality. We cannot conclude a discussion of justice in pre-Imperial China without giving some recognition to this variant approach, more sympathetic as it is to certain Promethean drives in Western culture.

In various songs of the state of Chu we can find the desire of individuals to leave behind them a world where they are not appreciated, where their talent is not recognized. This mismatch between their abilities and their circumstances gave rise to individual protest. The social order was rejected because the role assigned did not correspond to inner evaluations of self-worth. Therefore, the individual cried out for escape from the scheme of order itself. In the poem "Li Sao" there is the stanza:

> Truly, this generation are cunning artificers
> From square and compass they turn their eyes and change
>   the true measurement,
> They disregard the ruled line to follow their crooked fancies:
> To emulate in flattery is their only rule.
> But I am sick and sad at heart and stand irresolute:
> I alone am at a loss in this generation.
> But I would rather quickly die and meet dissolution
> Before I ever would consent to ape their behavior.
> Eagles do not flock like birds of lesser species:
> So it has ever been since the olden time.
> How can the round and square ever fit together?
> How can different ways of life ever be reconciled?
> Yet humbling one's spirit and curbing one's pride,
> Bearing blame humbly and enduring insults,
> But keeping pure and spotless and dying in righteousness:
> Such conduct was greatly prized by the wise men of old.[146]

Here the strong person can take the standard of righteousness and the straight line of the proper course and use it not to accommodate himself to the ways of the world but to hold himself apart and assert his own sense of moral worth. The reasons for withdrawal here arise partly from a desire to remain true to a moral principle amidst a sinful world and partly from a need to keep one's personal honor as an exceptional individual. Yet, in response to the disjuncture of personal circumstance with personal pride and self-esteem, suicide was the only practical solution. Fate might be criticized, but not changed.

And, in another song we find the lines:

My mind is honest and my heart is true:
I keep my feet unswerving to the ink line:
I hold the balance with impartiality,
And estimate weight with unerring accuracy,
I have brushed away the dust and disorder,
Purged all unclean attachments and returned to the true.
I am clean in body and pure in substance:
My soul within is dazzling in its spotless purity.
Yet the world turns from me in disgust and will not employ me,
And so I will hide myself far away from it.[147]

The sense of being wronged is strong, but, again, the only recourse for such an individual was silence and withdrawal.

The fact that the chosen course of action was not self-assertion should not deflect us from understanding that a profound individual sensitivity is present, contrasting the reality of an individual's aspirations and abilities with circumstances conducive neither for the realization of those aspirations nor for the exercise of those abilities. This is a sense, also, in which there was, in pre-Imperial China, a concern as to how individuals might grate against a cosmic scheme of justice. Such concern could not have existed without the development of acute moral faculties concerned over the relationship of the individual to society.

NOTES

1. John Rawls, *A Theory of Justice* (Cambridge, Mass.: The Belknap Press, 1971).
2. Ibid., p. viii.
3. Ibid., p. 568.
4. John Locke, "An Essay Concerning the True Original, Extent, and End of Civil Government" in *The English Philosophers From Bacon to Mill*, ed. Burtt, Edwin Arthur (New York: Random House, 1939).
5. Thomas Hobbes, "Leviathan" in Burtt, op. cit.
6. J.J. Rousseau, *The Social Contract and Discourses*, translated by G.D.H. Cole, (New York: E.P. Dutton, 1950).
7. The point is also made by Donald Munro. Donald Munro, *The Concept of Man in Early China* (Stanford, Calif.: Stanford University Press, 1969), p. 1.
8. James Legge, *The Chinese Classics*, vol. 5. *The Ch'un Ts'ew with the Tso Chuen* (Hong Kong: Hong Kong University Press, 1960), p. 201, Duke He, year XXVII, para. 5.
9. Ibid., p. 453, Duke Seang, year XI, para. 8.
10. Munro, *Concept of Man*, p. 11.
11. Cloe Waltham, *Shu Ching* (Chicago: Henry Regnery, 1971), p. 12.

12.   Legge, *The Chinese Classics*, vol. 5, p. 514, Duke Seang, year XXV, para. 2.

13.   Legge, *The Chinese Classics*, vol. 5, p. 395, Duke Ch'ing, year XVI, para. 6.

14.   Legge, *The Chinese Classics*, vol. 1, *Confucian Analects*, p. 256, book XII, ch. XI, 2.

15.   One document in the *History Classic* had made this point even before Confucius when the minister I Yin warned his young and newly enthroned ruler that a sovereign must play the sovereign in order to be a sovereign. Legge, *The Chinese Classics*, vol. 3, *The Shoo King* (Hong Kong: Hong Kong University Press, 1960), p. 201, book V, pt. i, 3.

16.   Legge, *The Chinese Classics*, vol. 1, p. 263, book XIII, ch. III, 2.

17.   Ibid., 6.

18.   Legge, *The Chinese Classics*, vol. 5, p. 71, Duke Hwan, year XVIII, para. 3.

19.   Legge, *The Chinese Classics*, vol. 1, p. 313, book XVI, ch. IX.

20.   Ibid., p. 330, book XVII, ch. XXV.

21.   See Munro, *Concept of Man*, ch. 4, "Path to Privilege," for a similar understanding of the Confucian approach to social order.

22.   Legge, *The Chinese Classics*, vol. 1, p. 191, book VI, ch. XX.

23.   Ibid., p. 256, book XII, ch. X, 1.

24.   Ibid., p. 224, book IX, ch. XXV.

25.   Legge, *The Chinese Classics*, vol. 1, *Doctrine of the Mean*, p. 395, ch. XIV, 1, 2.

26.   Legge, *The Chinese Classics*, vol. 1, *Confucian Analects*, p. 301, book XV, ch. XXIII.

27.   Ibid., p. 249, book XI, ch. XXV, 10.

28.   Ibid., p. 250, book XII, ch. 1, 2.

29.   Ibid., p. 299, book XV, ch. XVII.

30.   Legge, *The Chinese Classics*, vol. 2, the *Works of Mencius*, p. 126, book I, pt. I, ch. I, 3.

31.   Ibid., p. 456, book VII, pt. I, ch. XV, 3, and p. 468, book VIII, pt. I, ch. XXXIII, 3.

32.   Ibid., p. 493, book VII, pt. II, ch. XXXI, 1.

33.   Ibid.

34.   Ibid., p. 483, book VII, pt. II, ch. XII, 2.

35.   Ibid., p. 485, book VII, pt. II, ch. XVI.

36.   A similar point is made by a document allegedly of the Shang Dynasty called "The Announcement of T'ang" in the *History Classic*, which said that the Heavenly judge (Shang Ti) had conferred on men a moral sense or an ability to know the Mean. Legge, *The Chinese Classics*, vol. 3, p. 185, book III, ch. II, 2.

37.   Legge, *The Chinese Classics*, vol. 2, p. 248, book III, pt. I, ch. IV, 5.

38.   Ibid., 6.

39.   Ibid.

40.   Homer H. Dubs, *The Words of Hsuntze* (London: Probsthain, 1928) p. 56, book IV.

41.   Ibid., p. 124, book IX.

42.   Ibid., p. 66, book IV.

43.   Legge, *The Chinese Classics*, vol. 5, p. 381, Duke Ch'ing, year XIII, para. 2.

44.   Ibid., p. 708, Duke Ch'aou, year XXV, para. 2.

45.   Yi-Pao Mei, *The Ethical and Political Works of Motse* (London: Probsthain, 1929), p. 213, book XI.

46.   Burton Watson, *Basic Writings of Mo Tzu, Hsun Tzu and Han Fei Tzu* (New York: Columbia University Press, 1967), p. 79.

47.   Ibid., p. 245.

48.   J.J.L. Duyvendak, *The Book of Lord Shang* (London: Probsthain, 1938), p. 185, ch. I, para. 3 and p. 219, ch. II, para. 6.

49.   Ibid., p. 260, ch. II, para. 14.

50.   Ibid., p. 331–333, ch. V, para. 26.

51.   Ibid., p. 333.

52.   Lewis Maverick, ed., *Selections from the Kuan Tzu* (New Haven, Conn.: Far Eastern Publications, 1954), p. 36–38, Essay III.

53.   Ibid., p. 53, Essay VI.

54.   W.K. Liao, *The Complete Works of Han Fei Tzu*, vol. 1 (London: Probsthain, 1959), p. 53.

55.   Ibid., p. 124.

56.   W.K. Liao, *Han Fei Tzu*, vol. 2, p. 281.

57.   Ibid., p. 278.

58.   Ibid., p. 167.

59.   See, generally, V. Rubin, *Individual and State in Ancient China* (New York: Columbia University Press, 1976), pp. 89–114.

60.   Lao Tzu, *Tao Te Ching*, ch. 18. See Edward Erkes, *Ho-Shang-Kung's Commentary on Lao Tzu* (Ascara: Atibus Asiae, 1950); Arthur Waley, *The Way and its Power* (New York: Grove Press, 1958); and James Legge, *The Texts of Taoism*, vols. 39 and 40 of *Sacred Books of the East*, ed. F. Max Muller (London: Oxford University Press, 1927).

61.   Ibid., ch. 38.

62.   Legge, *The Texts of Taoism*, p. 270, book VIII, pt. II, Sec. I, 2.

63.   Ibid., p. 271.

64.   Ibid., p. 272.

65.   Legge, *The Texts of Taoism*, p. 212, p. 214.

66.   Lao Tzu, *Tao Te Ching*, ch. 28.

67.   Ibid., ch. 29.

68.   Ibid., ch. 60.

69.   Legge, *The Chinese Classics*, vol. 4, *The She King* or *Book of Poetry* (Hong Kong: Hong Kong University Press, 1960), p. 509, pt. III, book III, odes 1, 7.

70.   Waltham, *Shu Ching*, pp. 119–120, "The Speech at Mu."

71.   Ibid., p. 56, "The Speech at K'an."

72.   Legge, *The Chinese Classics*, vol. 5, p. 516, Duke Seang, year XXV, para. 9.

73.   Ibid., note page 781.

74.   Legge, *The Chinese Classics*, vol. 1, p. 284, book XIV, ch. XXII.

75.   Ibid., p. 267, book XIII, ch. XI.

76.   Ibid., p. 146, book II, ch. III. This analysis of social order is essentially the one given by Freud when he saw civilization as based on the power of the superego or moral sense to discipline the rest of the personality. Sigmund Freud, *Civilization and its Discontents* (New York: W.W. Norton, 1962).

77.   Ibid., p. 170, book IV, ch. XVI.

78.   Legge, *The Chinese Classics*, vol. 2, p. 223, book II, pt. II, ch. VII, 2.

79.   Ibid., p. 167, book I, pt. II, ch. VIII, and p. 467, book VIII, pt. I, ch. XXXII.

80.   Dubs, *Hsuntse*, p. 194, book XVIII.

81.   Ibid., p. 195.

82.   Ibid., p. 191.

83.   Ibid., p. 190.

84.   Watson, *Basic Writings*, p. 38.

85.   Duyvendak, *Lord Shang*, p. 223, ch. II, para. 6.

86.   Ibid., p. 209, ch. II, para. 5.

87.   Ibid., p. 223, ch. II, para. 6.

88.   Ibid., p. 232, ch. II, para. 7.

89.   W.K. Liao, *Han Fei Tzu*, vol. 2, p. 235.

90.   Ibid., p. 243.

91.   W.K. Liao, *Han Fei Tzu*, vol. 1, p. 128.

92.   Maverick, *Kuan Tzu*, p. 33, essay I, sec. 3.

93.   Ibid., p. 67, essay XIII, sec. 1.

94.   Lao Tzu, *Tao Te Ching*, ch. 48.

95.   Ibid., ch. 74.

96.   Ibid., ch. 73.

97.   Ibid., ch. 77.

98.   Legge, *The Texts of Taoism*, p. 293, book XI, pt. II, sec. IV.

99.   Ibid., p. 261, book VII, pt. I, sec. VII.

100.   Ibid., pt. II, p. 33, book XX, pt. II, sec. XII.

101.   Legge, *The Chinese Classics*, vol. 4, pp. 560–561, pt. III, book III, ode 10, para. 1, 2.

102.   Ibid., p. 326, pt. II, book IV, ode 10, para. 1.

103.   Ibid., p. 340, pt. II, book IV, ode 4, para. 1.

104.   Waltham, *Shu Ching*, p. 231, "The Marquis of Lu on punishment."

105.   Ibid., p. 233, 235.

106.   Ibid., p. 149. "The Announcement to the Prince of K'ang."

107.   Ibid., p. 148. The same concept appears in the earlier document, "The Canon of Shun," on p. 14.

108.   Ibid., p. 22, "The Counsels of the Great Yu."

109.   Legge, *The Chinese Classics*, vol. 5, p. 656, Duke Ch'aou, year XIV, para. 6.

110.   Ibid., p. 526, Duke Seang, year XXVI, para. 7.

111.   Ibid., p. 449, Duke Seang, year XI, para. 11.

112.   Ibid., p. 213, Duke He, year XXVII, para. 19 and p. 428, Duke Seang, year VI, para. 2.

113. Dubs, *Hsuntze*, p. 194.
114. Legge, *The Chinese Classics*, vol. 1, p. 269, book XIII, ch. XV, para. 5.
115. Dubs, *Hsuntse*, p. 47.
116. Watson, *Basic Writings*, pp. 26 and 23.
117. Ibid., p. 35.
118. Ibid., p. 80.
119. Ibid., p. 92.
120. Duyvendak, p. 265, ch. III, para. 14.
121. Ibid., p. 264.
122. Ibid., p. 289, ch. IV, para. 18.
123. Ibid., p. 317, ch. V, para. 23.
124. Ibid., p. 331, ch. V, para. 26.
125. Ibid.
126. W.K. Liao, *Han Fei Tzu*, vol. 1, p. 158.
127. Ibid., vol. 2, p. 195.
128. Ibid., vol. 1, p. 273.
129. Ibid., vol. 1, p. 103.
130. Ibid., vol. 2, pp. 66–67.
131. Ibid., vol. 2, p. 263.
132. Ibid., vol. 1, p. 138.
133. Maverick, *Kuan Tzu*, p. 40, essay III.
134. Ibid.
135. Duyvendak, *Lord Shang*, p. 328, ch. V, para. 26.
136. Ibid., p. 169, ch. I, para. 1.
137. Ibid., p. 199, ch. I, para. 4.
138. W.K. Liao, *Han Fei Tzu*, vol. 1, p. 154.
139. Ibid., p. 290.
140. Ibid., vol. 2, p. 124.
141. Maverick, *Kuan Tzu*, p. 32, essay I, sec. 2.
142. Ibid., p. 34, essay I, sec. 3.
143. Legge, *The Texts of Taoism*, p. 123, book XXV, pt. III, sec. III.
144. Lao Tzu, *Tao Te Ching*, ch. 66.
145. See Richard H. Solomon, *Mao's Revolution and the Chinese Political Culture* (Berkeley: University of California Press, 1971) for a treatment of this issue in contemporary Chinese society.
146. David Hawkes, *Songs of the South* (Oxford: The Clarendon Press, 1959), p. 25.
147. Ibid., p. 139.

4 ON LIANG QICHAO'S DARWINIAN "MORALITY REVOLUTION," MAO ZEDONG'S "REVOLUTIONARY MORALITY," AND CHINA'S "MORAL DEVELOPMENT"

James R. Pusey

Has China had a "morality revolution?" Liang Qichao, the great revolutionary advocate of reform, cried out for a "morality revolution" in 1902.[1] He said that China could not survive without one. But what came of his cry? Was it or was it not answered in the "revolutionary morality" of Mao Zedong? And what has become of that? China survives. China seems "fitter," indeed, than it has for two centuries. But does a morality revolution lie at the heart of that fitness? Mao Zedong tried most forcefully to fit China to survive, and he tried most forcefully to revolutionize his people's morality, more forcefully, perhaps, than anyone else in history. But did he succeed? Did the efforts and exhortations of Liang Qichao, Mao Zedong, and a host of others really lead the Chinese people to a new level of "moral development."

What is "moral development?" Nobody knows, not even the scholars who pursue the new social science of moral development, a science which studies individual moral development, the moral development of societies, and the evolution of morality in general. This science of moral development is an evolutionary science. It owes its modern inspiration ultimately to Darwin, and to Spencer, Huxley, and Kropotkin. But could it also be a "revolutionary science?" Could "morality revolutions" or "revolutionary moralities" be the very stuff of moral development? Or are such things merely reflections of it? Or is all talk of morality revolutions empty talk?

This is a very difficult question. The role of ideas, of consciousness itself, either as agent or image of evolution is a very mysterious business. Psychologists with substructures and superstructures of their own construction have made child's play of those of Marx, but a thousand essays on history and the hero and, now, on the hero's or even the crowd's subconscious still have not told us who or what makes history—or evolution. So students of the history of ideas do not know what they are studying either.

Nevertheless, would-be intellectual historians must now try to deal with the science of moral development, just as students of that science must try to deal with ideas like "morality revolutions." Are "morality revolutions" possible? If there is a will for one is there a way? Or must all just wait on evolution? Liang Qichao and Mao Zedong surely each had a will for a morality revolution. Indeed, much of Liang Qichao's will seemed alive in the Chairman's. But if that is true, if even in part, Liang Qichao unwittingly willed his will to the Chairman, what came of it?

A FIT MORALITY

"You may threaten to cut me to pieces or boil me alive," said Liang Qichao (on May 22, 1902), "but I will still dare state with conviction and without fear that not every one of the moral principles in the *Four Books* and the *Six Classics* is fit for our use today . . . . We should broadly survey the direction the world is moving, quietly assess what is fitting for our race, and then invent a new morality as a way to strengthen our people, improve our people, and advance our people."[2] China needed a fit morality—and a morality that would make China fit. To survive, China needed a "morality revolution." Charles Darwin said so.

Charles Darwin, since 1896, had said a lot to Liang Qichao. By way of Yan Fu's translation of T.H. Huxley's *Evolution and Ethics* and various and sundry Japanese articles, Charles Darwin had told Liang Qichao that the world was *naturally* a world of warring states and warring races, that there was a natural struggle for existence among peoples, and that only fit peoples, or *peoples who made themselves fit*—Liang Qichao's "instinctive" revision—survived. But the Chinese people did not look fit. They faced the "White Peril," said Liang Qichao, in poor condition, and they would go down before it as had the redskins in America and the browns in India and the blacks in Africa, unless they shaped up and pulled themselves together. For it was togetherness, solidarity, he said, that was strength. Peoples who pulled together could *pull* together, and pull ahead of peoples who pulled apart. And it was morality and morality alone that could pull a people together.

That is how Darwin, still thought at the time by many in the West to be morality's mortal enemy, became in China, for Liang Qichao, at least, its champion. But what was *revolutionary* about saying that morality could lead to solidarity and thence to strength? Xun Zi had said that much in the third century B.C. Men, Xun Zi had said, in a series of remarkably Darwinesque passages, had distinguished themselves from birds and beasts, and held their own against birds and beasts, thanks to their ability to flock together—far better than birds of a feather. And they had been able to do that thanks to their *i*, their morality. But for Xun Zi that morality was something fixed. It was good for all time. As far as morality was concerned, *"Gu jin yi ye,"* "The past and the present were one." For *"Tianxia wu er dao,"* he said, "The World has not two Ways."[3]

But that, said Liang Qichao, was what Darwin had disproved. And that was why China needed a morality revolution and not just good old moral rearmament—with tried and true old weapons. For Darwin had proved that morality itself was subject to evolution and that moralities themselves had to be fit to survive. "This thing, morality," said Liang Qichao, "is half natural and half man-made and it develops and progresses according to the great law of Evolution." For "there is no escaping," he said, "the law of the survival of the fittest."[4]

Morality developed. Liang Qichao believed in moral development—of some sort. He even had a word for it, *daode fada*, coined half a century before Western behavioral scientists would deem it a fit field of study.[5] Liang Qichao, of course, was not a scientist. He had no time to sit down and slowly study moral development. He was a reformer who had to write in a hurry. He *had* to leap to conclusions. But the conclusions he leapt to clearly placed him in the company of his "Darwinian" mentors once removed, Spencer, Huxley, and eventually Kropotkin, the first modern Western believers in *evolutionary* moral development. Liang Qichao was the first—confessed—Chinese believer.

He was not, of course, the first Chinese ever to have *thought* about moral development. In one way—or actually in several—the classical philosophers had been obsessed with moral development—of individuals and of society. Confucius, after all, had plotted out his own moral development by the decade. And when he claimed that at age 70 he could finally "follow the desires of [his] heart without transgressing the rules of propriety,"[6] he even seemed to rejoice in his "internalization" of something. Xun Zi went on to ask directly where that something came from. "Whence," he asked, "did the *li* [the rules of propriety] arise?" And he gave an answer, similar to that of the *Li Yun* chapter (the evolution of the *li*) from the *Li Ji* (the *Book of Rites*). The *li* were "made up" by the sages—somehow. They did not just develop, they were developed by wise men, who somehow figured out what was "good" for mankind, a good that would help mankind to survive.[7] Mencius, of course, disagreed, but in so doing he in one sense came even closer to an evolutionary scheme of moral development. He did not dwell on how such a development could have come to pass, but he did say that we had all been somehow naturally endowed (strange phrase) with moral instincts.[8]

Mencius' and Xun Zi's famous argument over human nature and over the question of whether morality was natural or man made would have much in common with the much later argument between Huxley and Kropotkin, and it still, I think, has much in common with arguments in the field of moral development today, but there was one way in which I am sure Liang Qichao would have thought that both Mencius and Xun Zi, and Confucius himself, had missed the developmentalist's mark. Confucius, Mencius, and Xun Zi all agreed about what was moral, even if they disagreed about how they knew it. They all thought they knew what was right for mankind for ever and ever, amen. But Liang Qichao said they *had* no such right, because there was no such right. The first revolutionary thing about his cry for a morality revolution was that it was based on the premise that "morality is not something that once formed (or developed) does not change."[9] Morality had not just evolved. It was ever evolving. Liang Qichao might seem to hedge on the Mencian-Xun Zian moral development problem when he said that morality was half natural and half man-made. He might consequently get mixed up (over and over again), as we all still do, over the problem of whether the word "development" in "moral development" comes from a transitive or an intransitive verb, but he did, at least, clearly insist that "morality" changes, that "right" itself changes, that there is no everlasting Way. And so his cry did threaten to undermine "morality"—old and maybe even new.

NEW VIRTUES

Liang Qichao never presented any one, neat list of "Ten New Commandments" or "Sixteen New Maxims." The "fitting and fittening" virtues that he extolled he presented in a host of different articles and essays written and published over several years time, mostly in his two famous series, "On Liberty" and "Towards a New People." A complete list of these new virtues would be hard to assemble, but it is easy enough to draw up a list of "most important virtues," for those turned up in his essays over and over again.

All of them were Darwinian virtues, at least they were to him. Liang Qichao thought his ethics were evolutionary ethics. He thought they had to be. Therefore his first and foremost virtue was change. For evolution demanded change. It depended on change. But as all too often is the case, if we are to believe the late Chairman, one divided into two, and the virtue of change became the warring virtues of reform and revolution.

Liang Qichao, we know, was for reform. But he was also for revolution. It was he, not Zou Rong or Sun Yat-sen, who first said, that "Revolution is an inescapable law of Evolution." It was he, on December 14, 1902, who said that "Revolution is today the one and only way of saving China."[10] It was he, therefore, not Chairman Mao, who first—without Marx's help—found proof "in the nature of things" that "*Zaofan you li*" (It is justified to rebel).[11]

Liang Qichao, of course, remained a reformer—in practice. But in theory he made revolution a virtue, and to that degree at least his morality revolution was one. The word *geming*, which he made a good word, had, to be sure, been a good word for two thousand years for rebels lucky enough to win "Heaven's Mandate," but now the whole Chinese people had "Evolution's Mandate"—to rebel against their sages, their rulers, their ancestors, and their parents. There was definitely, therefore, a destructive side to Liang Qichao's first virtue of change. And indeed in Bakuninite fashion he made a virtue out of destruction itself. "The one and only inescapable rule for all nations past and present that seek progress," he told his people, ". . . is destruction."[12]

Again we know, of course, that Liang Qichao did not become a bomb thrower. But in proclaiming the virtue of change, he could sound extremely destructive:

> We must pulverize our thousands of years old brutal and filthy system of government. We must wrest our millions of tiger-like, wolf-like, locust-like, maggot-like officials from their temple-rat and wall-fox positions of security! For only then will we be able to cleanse our bowels, so that we may ascend the road to Progress![13]

On the morality front, of course, that cry threatened to destroy one of the Old Morality's two most cardinal virtues: *zhong* (loyalty). Liang Qichao's Darwinian virtues of change, revolution, and destruction would also threaten the second: *xiao* (filial piety). Before long, in 1904, a poet of sorts in Liang Qichao's journal, the *Xin min cong bao*, would write:

> Father, I tell you, do not emulate your forebears!
> Sons, on your lives, do not emulate your fathers!
> For ruthless is the drama of natural selection . . . .[14]

And 15 years later, proving that morality revolutions take time, Lu Xun would carry on the same attack:

> The [Confucian] saying, "Changing not from one's father's ways throughout the three years' mourning may indeed be called filial," of course is a misguided statement. Indeed it is the root cause of infantile underdevelopment. If in ancient times single-celled organisms had respected such instructions, they would never have dared to split in two and reproduce, and the world would never have seen mankind.[15]

We will have to ask later how destructive these attacks on loyalty and filial piety really proved to be, but surely Liang Qichao's passion for such destruction was in his own mind constructive. The destruction of old virtues was itself a virtue, he said, for it would make possible the construction of better new virtues.

These fitter new virtues, Liang Qichao's positive new virtues, fall neatly into two groups (although this time two would eventually combine into one), the virtues of *gong de* (public morality) and *si de* (private morality). Of the two, however, while they remained two, the *gong de* virtues were the most important. For "one of the things that our people most surely lack," wrote Liang Qichao, "is *gong de*. What is *gong de*? It is that which makes a *qun* (group, literally, flock or herd) a *qun*, that which makes a nation a nation. It is the morality on which *qun* and nation rely to stand."[16]

The *gong de* virtues were *tough* virtues. They were "gladiatorial virtues" of the very sort that Huxley, in *Evolution and Ethics,* had decried, because they were indeed *based* on the "gladiatorial theory of existence" that he decried.[17] They were based on *the* cardinal article of Liang Qichao's Darwinian faith—that he had ironically learned from Huxley—that China was in a worldwide arena. The *gong de* virtues, therefore, were all variants on the Darwinian moral injunction: struggle to survive.

Zheng (struggle or contention) itself was the first of the *gong de* virtues. Change, revolution, and destruction, after all, had been made virtues only by the Darwinian necessity of struggle. But struggle had (almost) always been a bad word in China. Confucius had said, 'The noble man does not contend."[18] Xun Zi had said, "Struggle (or contention) is disaster."[19] Lao Zi had preached the "virtue of non-struggle."[20] And surely if the Buddhists had ever struggled it was only not to. Not even the Legalists had ever made struggle a virtue per se (and Legalism was not a good word anyway). The "better" schools, in any case, Confucian, Maoist, Daoist, and Buddhist, had jointly frowned on struggle. They had rarely, if ever, encouraged offensive churches militant.

The virtue of struggle, therefore, was the most shocking tenet of Darwinism when it was first introduced to China. The Chinese might have no *Book of Genesis* to worry about, but they did have their sages and their Ways, and when Liang Qichao, and Yan Fu, of course, before him, said that struggle was good, they did indeed revolt against their sages. Struggle was a revolting concept.

But here we should stop ourselves short for a minute and face a simple truth that confuses things. We should face the horrible difference between people's moralities and their morality, between their notions of virtue and their virtue. Chinese history, for all its sages, has not, to put it mildly, been without contention. Many in China have eaten lotuses, but few have been lotus eaters—which is hardly surprising. It simply means that it has been just as easy for the inhabitants of China to be poor Confucianists, Daoists, and Buddhists, as it has been for the inhabitants of Christendom to be poor Christians. Against the wishes of their sages, the Chinese found it perfectly possible to struggle, a very long time before Liang Qichao or Yan Fu ever told them that Darwin said that it was meet and right so to do. So who needed Liang Qichao, or Yan Fu, or Darwin? How foreign *was* Darwin's alleged doctrine, and how much of a morality revolution *was* Liang Qichao's morality revolution?

We must put that question off a little longer, but at least one more confusing, if not surprising, thing is clear: When Liang Qichao and Yan Fu said that struggle was a virtue, many leapt at that virtue, because they *wanted* to struggle. Many Chinese wanted to fight—against intruding foreign deviltry of all sorts. And Darwin gave them a *very* good excuse.

Certainly Liang Qichao wanted Chinese to fight. Although most of his own battles were fought with words not sticks and stones, he desperately wanted China to have "a blood and iron philosophy." He wanted China to have fighting power and he wanted all China to have fighting spirit. He decried traditional prejudice against the military: "Good iron is not used for nails. Good men do not become soldiers."[21] He cursed Du Fu himself for writing sympathetic poems about Chinese soldiers who did not want to fight, and praised instead the Japanese who went marching off to war with banners that proclaimed "We pray that we may die in battle."[22] The Japanese were indeed an inspiration to him. Chinese should learn from the Japanese, he said, because the Japanese had revived their *bushido* (the Way of the Warrior), their samurai spirit. "In the 1900 expedition (against the Boxers) their army's fierce bravery and fighting strength was by far the best of all the allies. They made the white men bow their heads in shame."[23] What inspiring proof of "yellow power." Yellows were better than whites at beating up Chinese! But the whites, of course, were good enough. Liang Qichao praised "all the peoples who embrace Christianity" for their "fierce love of warfare."[24]

So it was virtue to be warlike and to like war. And it was a virtue to be aggressive and daring. Chinese were urged to be (in a for once usefully pidgin literal translation) "go-getters" and "risk takers," for "There is no standing still on this earth," said Liang Qichao. "You either savagely advance or go backward."[25] Aggression was good and good for you. "There is more than one reason why European peoples are stronger than the Chinese," he said, "but the most important reason is that they are richly endowed with a daring and aggressive spirit."[26] "Why are whites better than other races?" he asked again. "Other races love tranquility. The whites love action. Other races are addicted to peace. Whites do not avoid conflict. Other races guard what they have. Whites go out for more. Therefore other races can only produce their civilizations. The whites can propogate theirs."[27]

The "white virtues" were not just militant *defensive* virtues. They were virtues of aggressive self-assertion, and self-assertion, *ziying*, by no coincidence was the very watchword of Liang Qichao's *gong de* (public morality). But there was one huge qualification to Liang Qichao's virtue of self-assertion. One was not to assert oneself for oneself. One was to assert oneself for one's *qun*. One was to assert oneself for China. For what Liang Qichao really wanted was for China to assert *itself*. The New Morality, therefore, was for selfless self-assertion.

This is where *si de* (private morality) came in. For the *si de* virtues were all virtues of self-restraint, *ke ji, zi ying* and *ke ji*, of course, were Yan Fu's translations of Huxley's terms, self-assertion and self-restraint, from *Evolution and Ethics*. But in *Evolution and Ethics* those terms were at each other's throats, the one being the way of the "Cosmic Process" and the other of its rebellious child, the "Ethical Process." For Huxley, self-restraint, the essence of ethics, was at war with self-assertion, original sin, the sine qua non of evolution.[28] But Liang

Qichao very simply enlisted them on the same side. Self-assertion was evolution's first "moral imperative," self restraint was its corollary second. The individual's self-restraint was necessary for the group's self-assertion—in *its* struggle for survival. It was the marriage of public and private morality that Liang Qichao had in mind when he wrote, in an essay on "The Need for Private Morality," "What do we rely on to vanquish our enemies? On our ability to band together (and here he used for the first time, I think, the word that would become the classic Communist term for the "solidarity" that is strength—*tuanjie*) into a firm and powerful organism, and on nothing else.... If we want to become (such an organism), what way is there except through morality?"[29]

It was "a law of sociology," Liang Qichao proclaimed, "that only those with internal solidarity can compete externally,"[30] and internal solidarity depended on individual self-restraint, on the conquest of one's selfish desires. For selfish desires could pull a *qun* to pieces. Selfless desires, of course, were still vitally important. Liang Qichao still protested, after all, that "desire is truly the well spring of social evolution."[31] It might be confusing when he could at one point survey his countrymen and sigh, "to what depths have love and desire poisoned men,"[32] and long for more of them who could "conquer and keep down their loves and desires, so that their minds are not imprisoned by their hard shells of impure flesh,"[33] and then suddenly turn around and cry, "Alas, where can we find one who will fill our people with the infatuated love and obsessive desire of Bao Yu and Dai Yu?,"[34] but the survival of the Chinese *qun* was the one moral standard that resolved that seeming double standard. Liang Qichao wanted each and every Chinese to have an infatuated love for China and an obsessive desire for *China's* survival. All one's other desires were to be sublimated to that one—even one's desire for one's own survival.

So the virtue of self-restraint led to the virtue of self-sacrifice. Liang Qichao went to elaborate lengths to find an evolutionary moral imperative for self-sacrifice and then went to even greater lengths to find evolutionary comfort for those forced to heed it. He first enlisted the help of Benjamin Kidd, a rather justly "obscure English government clerk"[35] who had won sudden, if not undisputed, fame in Great Britain and the United States as the author of a book called *Social Evolution*. Liang Qichao maintained Kidd's help only by steadfastly ignoring Kidd's real argument, but finding what he sought, he could quote Kidd out of context to prove that "the sacrifice of the interests of the individual to those of the social organism" was an evolutionary necessity—and hence a virtue."[36] "Kidd believes," said Liang Qichao, "that the goal of natural selection is to bring the greatest number within a given race to the very fittest kind of existence. But the greatest number is not in the present but in the future. Therefore, the interests of the entire present body as a whole must all be sacrificed in order to reach this future goal."[37] For as Kidd himself put it, quoted Liang Qichao, "The meaning of evolution lies in the creation of the future...."[38] Only as it meets the needs of the future does the present have meaning and value."[39] Indeed, "It is only for the future that we have life."[40]

So surely it was good to sacrifice one's life, if need be, for the future, for the future life of one's *qun*. For "death too," said Liang Qichao, "exists as an important device for the reaching of that great goal."[41] Yea, "death," he said, "is the mother of evolution and a great event in human life. Every one benefits the race with his death, and the present race benefits the future race with its death. Is not death's function noble?"[42]

Gloria est pro patria mori was hardly a new sentiment. But to explain that glory in evolutionary terms and to so glory in evolution that one could shout, as Liang Qichao did, "Such a death! Such a duty! What ground is there for hesitation, what ground for fear, what ground for dissatisfaction?"[43] —that *was* a bit new. But it proved a powerful argument. Lu Xun would be so impressed with it that he would write 17 years later, "On the road to progressive evolution the new must always replace the old. Therefore the new should joyfully go forward, to grow up, and the old should also joyfully go forward, to die. . . . Old people, get out of the way. . . . If there are deep abysses in the road then use death to fill them up. Let the young go on."[44]

Liang Qichao, it must be admitted, had not found it *perfectly* easy *joyfully* to sing "Let my people go—over my dead body" until, in 1904, he came upon Hu Shi's theory of "social immortality"—15 years before Hu Shi did.[45] Then *mirabile dictu*, he found a way to bolster Kidd's arguments with Buddhism! In an ingeniously mixed up Darwinian secularization of several Buddhist concepts he found a way to offer a this-worldly immortality to the very fellow countrymen he was urging on to self-sacrifice. He announced the good news that everyone had a "Little I (*xiao wo*)" and a "Great I (*da wo*)" and that although one's "Little I" died, one's "Great I" lived on—or could live on—forever.

One's "Little I" was to one's "Great I" as a cell was to a body and a self was to a race. Cells died but the body lived on. Selves died and the race lived on. But cell and self also lived on in the life of the body and the race. The "Little I" lived on *after death* in the "Great I," in the immortality of its *karma*. One lived on in the effects of one's deeds. One could, indeed, have an undying influence on one's race if one's deeds helped it live. For the fittest "Great Is," that could survive, would be those with the most "Little Is" willing to die for their "Great Is," and so self-sacrificing "Little Is" in such "Great Is" would never die.

To make all this more biological, Liang Qichao threw in a karmic-Lamarkian notion of heredity, which allowed those lucky "Little Is" with offspring a double immortality through good deeds that bettered their seed and their breed.[46] The basic moral, however, was still the same, "Cheerfully give your all for your people."

So the New Morality came down to that: change, struggle, rebel, be warlike, assert yourself—for China, restrain yourself—for China, sacrifice yourself—for China. And there was one more injunction: be free—for China. For freedom surely was a virtue for Liang Qichao. Freedom was a revolutionary virtue necessary for his morality revolution because freedom, as he said over and over again, was necessary for China's survival.[47] But in that notion lay the clue to his qualification of freedom, a severe qualification, much like his qualification of self-assertion. He wanted China to be free, and he wanted Chinese to be free to work for that freedom. But he reminded all Chinese that "freedom means freedom for the group, not freedom for the individual. In the age of barbarism, individual freedom triumphed, and the group's freedom was lost. In the age of civilization, the group's freedom will be strong, and individual freedom will decline."[48]

Liang Qichao did want to liberate his people—from all sorts of bonds of the past—but he wanted to liberate them to serve the People, capital P. It was in service that he saw their perfect freedom. "Do not be slaves of the ancients," he said.[49] But he also said, "Although men must not be slaves of other men, they must be slaves of their group. For if they are not slaves to their own group, they will assuredly become slaves to some other."[50] When nations were part of "nature red in tooth and claw," it was easy to qualify the virtue of freedom—qualified anyway, of course, in the best of times. Liang Qichao so feared for China's freedom that he could easily see the virtue of both freedom and slavery, just as he—and others—would soon see the virtue both of "democracy" and of "enlightened dictatorship."[51]

THE VIRTUE OF THE NEW VIRTUES

The virtue of Liang Qichao's new virtues was that they would enable China to survive. But that simple assertion was one of the most revolutionary things about them. However new or not new the New Morality's new virtues might really be, the New Morality had a revolutionary new philosophical basis. It was unabashedly utilitarian and materialistic. "Do you know whence arose morality?," asked Liang Qichao, "morality was established to benefit (*li*) the (*qun*)."[52] Therefore, "that which is of benefit to one's *qun* is good and that which is not of benefit to one's *qun* is evil."[53]

It was that simple, or so it seemed. Liang Qichao was not very good at making clear what "of benefit" meant, but clearly he was more concerned for the social organism's body than for its soul. Although he said he did so with some fear and trembling, he introduced, also with much praise, Jeremy Bentham and Bentham's English word, "Utilitarianism," which he translated as "*lelizhuyi*" (pleasure-and-benefitism). Bentham gave him another word, therefore, "happiness," to clarify "benefit" and "good," but after pages of commendable description of Bentham's incredible attempts to measure happiness against unhappiness, the only ultimate happiness or benefit that Liang Qichao clearly identified was survival itself. His ultimate new moral standard seemed to come down quite simply to "that which is of benefit to the *qun*'s survival is good." And that standard was most utilitarian.

So too was his argument, entered into again with a professed fear and trembling, but also evident glee, that all altruism was selfish.[54] With the backing of a Japanese utilitarian evolutionist, Katō Hiroyuki, he took on love itself, the nonutilitarians' most sacred concept. "All loving of others is in the end for oneself," he said.[55] "If I do not love others, I can gain no benefit for myself and must needs join the ranks of the defeated unfit."[56] Although he started with "me-first-ism," his point, of course, was still to argue for the primacy of the group. "There has never been a system of morality or law in the world that has not been established for self-benefit,"[57] he said. But "man cannot stand in the world all by himself. Therefore there is the *qun*."[58] For "the common good and private good are one and not two."[59] "Therefore he who is good at benefiting himself must first benefit his *qun*."[60] All Liang Qichao was really telling his people was what he had told them over and over before: "If you know what's good for you fight for the good of China." But in the process "the good" became "the good for," and that had not been "the good" of traditional China—leastways not its best.

At least "the good" had not been "the good for" for Confucius. Granted there had been plenty of utilitarianism in Chinese philosophy before Liang Qichao introduced Jeremy Bentham, even in Confucianism, but I would protest that the heart of Confucianism was not utilitarian—and therefore that Liang Qichao's New Morality *was* in basis revolutionary.

The "good old religion" of the *Shu Jing* (*Book of History*) was theistically utilitarian: "The way of Heaven is to bring down blessings on the good and disaster on the wicked."[61] A utilitarian word to the wise was to be sufficient. Mo Zi echoed that word. Goodness was the will of Heaven, but "if it would not work if we used it," he said, "even I would be against it. But where is there any good that cannot be used?"[62] The Daoists had no use for "goodness," but in arguing that the world would be better off without it and in arguing for the "virtue" of "non-action" in the struggle for survival, they too were utilitarian. And the Buddhists' morality of the Eight Fold Path was a way to individual salvation—as was the morality of the Confucians a way (*the* way) to social salvation. Xun Zi, *almost* avowedly utilitarian, declared that morality had been thought up by the sages as a *means* of bringing order out of chaos.[63] And even Mencius and Confucius himself, although they would never have agreed that morality was man-made, did believe, nonetheless, that morality would *work*. Although it never seemed to work for them, they steadfastly held that right was might. They seemed to promise kings that goodness would do them good.

And yet, in the end Confucius and Mencius were not utilitarian. When goodness did not work, when it led to death, they still said, "Be good."[64] *We* might explain away that suicidal choice in utilitarian terms, Darwinian, Freudian, or Sociobiological, but they did not, and they would not have if they could have. *We* might say that Confucius' version of the Golden Rule was a ploy. We might say the same thing of Christ's. Mo Zi's version at least seemed to be. "I must first set myself to loving and profiting the parents of others," he said, "and then they will repay me by loving and profiting my parents."[65] But neither Confucius nor Christ thought that way. Their Golden Rules were not *reasons* for doing good but golden rules of thumb for people who *wanted* to do good.[66] Confucius may have been fooling himself, but he believed in the *reality* of goodness. He believed in a moral universe. He would have stood with Antigone. If he had been forced to answer the question "why be good?," he would not have said "for your own good" or "for the nation's sake," but "for goodness' sake." That would have been a nonanswer, but being a nonanswer it would have been a nonutilitarian answer, and that makes Liang Qichao's answer revolutionary.

So what? *Politically*, the answer is simple. Liang Qichao's revolutionary theory of morality was significant because it helped prepare the way—or clear the way—for Marxism. Intellectuals who were convinced by Liang Qichao's arguments that human morality was utilitarian and materialistic—materialistic because it was an evolutionary product of nature, because Liang Qichao agreed that "man, physical, intellectual, and moral," as Huxley put it, "is as much a part of nature, as purely a product of the cosmic process, as the humblest weed"[67]—at once broke away from Confucius, for better or for worse, and took two sizeable leaps toward Marx. Those convinced by Liang Qichao to leap that far could thereafter have leapt elsewhere, of course. Many did. But none who had leapt at least that far with Liang Qichao could be shocked by Marx's utilitarianism or materialism, or *very* shocked by the relativity of his class standards of morality, for classes after all were just more *qun*, struggling to survive.

But what significance did Liang Qichao's new utilitarian and materialistic theory of morality have "morally?" Did a revolution in moral philosophy change his or anyone else's moral behavior? We must try to look, in one more minute, at what happened to Liang Qichao's morality revolution, but there is one strange thing to consider first. There was one disturbing way in which Liang Qichao's new moral philosophy clashed with his new morals.

All of the New Morality's new virtues were anti-imperialist virtues. Anti-imperialism was the Darwinian raison d'être of the New Morality. And yet, the new utilitarian *basis* of the New Morality seemed to make it impossible to mount a *moral* argument against imperialism. Liang Qichao's Darwinism had led him to accept the very arguments that dyed-in-the-wool imperialists were using to justify imperialism. "If a country can strengthen itself and make itself one of the fittest," proclaimed Liang Qichao, "then even if it annihilates the unfit and the weak it can still not be said to be immoral. Why? Because that is a law of evolution."[68] For as he further explained later, "when European countries meet with other European countries they all take reason to be force, but when European countries meet non-European countries, they all use force for reason.

And so they must, because of evolution. The struggle for existence makes it natural. So what cause can there be for blame? What cause can there be for hate?"[69]

But Chinese did hate. Some did, at least. And some hated to be told that they had no right to, like the person who sent in this poem to Liang Qichao's *Qing yi bao*:

Oh, how I dread
To talk of Evolution!
For if fit flourish and unfit fail,
Then whom do we dare hate?[70]

Here was someone still seething with "moral indignation." But *was* such indignation "moral?" Was it "good" to hate "evil," or was it just "natural" to hate one's enemies ("those who hate their enemies survive")? Whose morality was more "developed," that of Liang Qichao, who saw that imperialism was "perfectly natural," or that of this poet, who saw, through his "intuition," that it was "bad?"

As Mencius said, "It is hard to say,"[71] but the theoretical problem that "moral indignation" raised for the New Morality of Liang Qichao would remain a problem for the Marxist morality of Chairman Mao. For Chairman Mao, like an Old-Testament-type prophet straight out of the *Book of History,* would cry out, "The imperialists will not live much longer—because they do nothing but evil things."[72] The imperialists were unfit to live among us—but in which sense? Perhaps Liang Qichao was wrong. Perhaps the imperialists were indeed doomed by the forces of evolution or of history to perish from the face of this earth. But fit or unfit, their fate should have been perfectly natural. There was something *unnatural* in the Chairman's conviction that they were *evil.*

THE CHAIRMAN'S NEW VIRTUES

The leap from Liang Qichao's paper cry for a morality revolution—over half a century—to Mao Zedong's flesh and blood attempt to propogate a revolutionary morality is a great leap forward indeed—in time. I do not pretend that nothing of consequence happened in between. I do not pretend that Liang Qichao was sole or even co-author of the morality of Mao Zedong (although he *was* in a way a ghost writer). But I do protest, leaping for now over all mysteries of cause and effect, that Liang Qichao's New Morality may be seen intact in the official morality of the People's Republic. Liang Qichao's New Virtues have become Chinese Communist virtues and they have remained Chinese Communist virtues, throughout even the most violent shifts of party line.

Look once again—very quickly—at Liang Qichao's list of moral imperatives:

Change. That was the watchword of Liang Qichao's first manifesto.[73] That was the watchword of Karl Marx's *Communist Manifesto*, even though his most famous expression of it came in his "Theses on Feuerbach": "The philosophers have only *interpreted* the world in various ways; the point, however, is to change it."[74] And that was the watchword of Mao Zedong's manifesto "On Practice," in which, getting into the Hegelian spirit of the thing, he made "change" not only an evolutionary necessity and, ergo, virtue, but (virtually) a "sacred task": "The development of society having reached the present period, the responsibility for correctly knowing the world and changing the world has already fallen historically on the shoulders of the Proletariat and its political party."[75]

Struggle. The *objects* of struggle (struggle, for Communist convenience, having been made into a transitive verb) have changed—often drastically—during the first three decades of the People's Republic, but struggle remains, of course, a cardinal virtue. And it is still "evolutionary necessity" that makes it a virtue. Chinese must struggle to survive; they must struggle to change themselves and their objective world; they must struggle to progress. They must struggle because the world is still a jungle, because, as the Chairman said, "Class struggle, some classes triumphing, others being annihilated—that is history,"[76] because, as he also said, "Nothing reactionary will fall unless you hit it. . . . Enemies will not annihilate themselves."[77]

Rebel. "In the last analysis," said Mao Zedong, "all the truths of Marxism can be summed up in one sentence, 'To rebel is justified.'"[78] And in Chinese the *li* (reason or principle) that was rebellion's or revolution's justification was natural, for "Revolution," as Liang Qichao had put it, "is an inescapable law of the world of evolution."[79]

Be warlike. Most of the official canon now recognized as the thought of Mao Zedong was written in war for war. Its martial rhetoric has been preserved ever since, as Chinese have been urged to make war on class enemies, the Four Pests, poisonous weeds, and a host of other things. Chinese have at times been urged to learn from the model soldier, Lei Feng, and then from the PLA, and in even more radical times they have been trained in militia units that once looked as if they might be sent against the PLA. More recently China's Vietnam war produced new heroes and new models. Today, as for 30 years, Chinese are urged to be ready for war.

Assert yourself—for China. The legendary Lei Feng (whether mythical or real), the perfect boyscout PLA man, was a radical hero deemed heroic enough to have "survived" (posthumously, of course, if he ever lived) the purge of the radicals. He asserted himself—selflessly. He did not wait for orders. He rushed in to do good deeds where he saw good deeds to be done. So did Li Shuangshuang, fictional heroine, "new style 'good type'" of the People's Communes.[80] She too asserted herself, braving, when necessary, the anger of her "comrades":

"I gathered a handful of firewood and you tried to stop me, you meddlesome busybody!"
"I'm a commune member so it's my business."[81]

"You may be the leader of the production team, but our family matters are none of your business!"
"No, it is my business: any case which is not right is my business."[82]

The movie Li Shuangshuang got herself on the radicals' banned list, perhaps through no fault of her own. But her kind of self-assertion—for the people, as long as the powers-that-be agree that it is for the people—was clearly a virtue for radicals and nonradicals alike. And it remains a virtue.

Restrain yourself—for China. Lei Feng and Li Shuangshuang both had to restrain themselves to assert themselves. Lei Feng once *almost* committed a sin. He lost control of himself for one sentence and threatened to demand to be put on active duty—to fulfill his personal ambition and reap his personal revenge. But his instructor saved him with a timely sermon on a passage from Chairman Mao. So Lei Feng reined himself in and, "after a great deal of hard study, he came to understand how to be a man and what to live for." "The function of a man in the Revolution," he concluded, "is like a screw in a machine. I want to be a rustless revolutionary screw for the rest of my life."[83] And so did Li Shuangshuang on her commune. She learned to subjugate her private emotions and desires even at the risk of her marriage:

"What's the matter?" asked her Party secretary after her husband Xiwang, not able to stomach the way she asserted herself—for the commune—had run away. "Has Xiwang left you?" Shuangshuang shook her head. "Life goes on. Even if this work—point recorder leaves me, I, as a cadre, still have work to do."[84]

Sacrifice yourself—for China. The sermon Lei Feng's instructor preached was on Mao Zedong's article, "Serve the People," written in 1944 to celebrate the accidental death of the charcoal burner, Zhang Side, one who "sacrificed his life," as Lei Feng correctly drew the moral, "for the people."[85] The people in the People's Republic have been presented a whole string of martyr-models, of all kinds, from people like Huang Jiguang and Dong Cunrui, who died in battle, to people like Zhang Side and like Lei Feng himself, who also "sacrificed his life for the public good" in the course of ordinary duties.[86] Lei Feng was struck down not by enemy bullets but by a falling telephone pole, but the manner of his death did not matter.[87] He had died in service, and so, as the Chairman said, he had "died in his proper place."[88] And that gave his death—and his life—meaning. "Sooner or later all men must die," said the Chairman, " but the significance of men's deaths is different." And then Mao Zedong fell back on a sentence from the Han historian Sima Qian, just as Liang Qichao had 42 years before him, to sweep the problem of death under the rug "once and for all": "In ancient times China had a scholar named Sima Qian, who said 'Every man has his death, but it may be weightier than Mt. Tai or lighter than swan's down. Death for the benefit of the people is even weightier than Mt. Tai.'"[89] That was all the Chairman ever said about death. That was all he thought he had to.

Be free—for China. "Liberation" has been another of *the* watchwords of the Chinese Communist Party. To liberate and to be liberated were both virtues. It was good for Chinese to be free—from imperialists, capitalists, "feudal" landlords, and "Confucian" elders. It was good for Chinese women to be free from oppressive men, and for Chinese children to be free from oppressive parents. It was good for everyone to be free from the past, free in mind from the wrong ideas of the past, from the evil selfishness of the past. But it was not good to be free from the People or from the Party. "Liberalism" was and is something to be opposed. "The source of liberalism," said the Chairman, "is in the selfishness of the petty-bourgeoisie, that puts the interest of the individual first and those of the revolution second. . . . Liberalism is one expression of opportunism, and it is in basic conflict with Marxism."[90] So the virtue of freedom was qualified. Sometimes (indeed, quite often), said the Chairman, there was virtue in dictatorship.[91] But Liang Qichao had said the same thing.[92] And so had the Republican revolutionary, Sun Yat-sen. Remember that it was he who said "China must have a revolution, because Chinese have too much freedom."[93]

At any rate, there they were, Liang Qichao's virtues in the Chairman's sermons. The Chairman's new virtues were not so new. Of course, there were other virtues in the Chairman's sermons that Liang Qichao had not stressed. Besides Liang Qichao's fighting serve-the-people virtues, there was a set of gentler serve-the-people virtues. Lei Feng, after all, helped old ladies—with the same selfless spirit with which he was ready to blow up enemies. "Serve the people" has not just meant to fight for the people, or to slave for them. It has meant also to care for them.

Now surely Chairman Mao himself, who loved the people, as we used to be told in "The East Is Red," deserves credit for the inclusion of these gentler virtues in his official New Morality. So, of course, does Marx. But so too does Lu Xun, who 30 years before the success of the Communist Revolution called for a morality revolution of his own, one which complemented but differed from that of Liang Qichao, and one which surely also influenced Mao Zedong.

Lu Xun revolted against the Old Morality not just because he feared that it was evolutionarily enfeebling. He revolted against it because he thought it was revolting. He thought his people "ate people"—all too often in the very name of virtue and morality.[94] And so in *his* morality revolution he cried out: Stop eating people. Stop selfishly oppressing people. Stop blindly, ignorantly hurting people. Care for people. Show compassion!

Liang Qichao, it seems to me, worried, as he was, about what he perceived to be a life or death Darwinian struggle between peoples, almost overlooked the struggles among his people. He almost overlooked, within China, man's ordinary, everyday, mindless inhumanity to man. But Chairman Mao did not, although he may have been selective in his looking. And so he took up Lu Xun's cry against eating people. He urged his people, indeed, to love their neighbors—as long as their neighbors were not landlords, capitalists, or counterrevolutionaries.

Here was the rub. The most important of the Chairman's new virtues not on Liang Qichao's list was "Love thy comrade." But when asked "Who is my comrade?" the Chairman gave an answer that still bore the influence of Liang Qichao—and even, alas, of Lu Xun. He first rephrased the question, "Who are our enemies, who are our friends?"[95] But the answer was the same. One's friends and one's comrades were "the people." But "the people" did not mean the people. "The people" were only some of the people, and their ranks could wax and wane (although they were supposed, of course, only to wax). "The concept of the people," said the Chairman, "in different countries and in different historical periods within a country, has different compositions. In China," he said, "all classes, strata, and social groups that support and take part in Socialist construction belong to the category of the people." All others were "enemies of the people."[96]

Strictly speaking, enemies of the people were not people and did not have to be treated as people. "We cannot love our enemies," said the Chairman, "...that is everyday common sense."[97] It was common sense if, as Liang Qichao, Yan Fu, and so many others had said, the world was a Darwinian jungle of warring states, races, or classes. Liang Qichao thought it was. Marx thought it was. Even Lu Xun sometimes seemed to think it was. If he refused to believe in a perfectly natural dog-eat-dog world, or people-eat-people world, he did believe that the worst of the people-eaters were indeed dogs, who would never learn new tricks, and so should be beaten without mercy. In his sadly popular essay, "On the Postponement of Fair Play," he said that even "dogs who have fallen in the water" should be beaten, for if allowed to climb out they would surely bite again.[98]

Liang Qichao and Lu Xun both helped Mao Zedong draw a sharp line indeed between enemies and comrades, even before Mao Zedong ever went to war. And 15 years after the war, the "War of Liberation," the line was still there. The Chairman was still teaching, through Lei Feng, these two ideals:

Be merciless to your class enemies.
Be warm as spring toward your comrades.[99]

The Chairman's new virtues had a double standard—with a vengeance.

MORAL DEVELOPMENT OR PLUS ÇA CHANGE...?

The establishment of the People's Republic was quite a development. But did it represent, or has it brought about, "moral development?" Liang Qichao, Lu Xun, and Mao Zedong all looked forward to a morality revolution, but did they start one? Has there been one? Liang Qichao hoped to make Chinese better through "mind washing." Sun Yat-sen sought to do so through "psychological reconstruction," and Mao Zedong through "brain washing" and "thought reform."[100] Lu Xun, more vaguely, just wanted somehow to "save the children," so that they could become "real people," non-people-eating people.[101] At any rate, all sought one way or another to raise the Chinese people to a "new level of consciousness"—moral consciousness. But did they?

How can we not ask that question? But how can I answer it? *Caveat lector.* I have never been in China long enough to do field work. I have gathered no data about the morality of people who work in Chinese fields. Mostly, all I have before me are official Chinese sermons, moral exhortations. And the exhorters may exhort too much. Of course, one can look, perhaps significantly, for moral development in the sermons themselves—but how can one tell how either the preachers or the members of the congregation, leaders and masses, *behave*?

A second difficulty lies with my ignorance of the developing science of moral development. The science of moral development is itself, of course, in a difficult position. It has set out to study the *development* of something that no one understands. And it has also, in the process, threatened to raise again the now unpopular spector (a rather nineteenth century spector) of "better" and "worse" peoples. It is thus a fascinating but delicate science. But I have not studied it. All I know of moral development I have learned from Richard W. Wilson's article and some of the others in this volume. Surrounded as I am by social scientists, I rather feel, therefore, that the wisest course of action would be to follow the example of Xu Shu in Cao Cao's camp and say nothing.

But it is too late. Having read Mr. Wilson's article I cannot help asking how Liang Qichao and Chairman Mao's would-be morality revolutions hold up against his definitions of moral development. I do not intend to get pulled into the question of which people, American or Chinese, are the more "morally mature." I do not want to ask whether we are holier than they or even whether the ideals we honor in the breach are more ideal than theirs. But we can ask whether or not Chinese today are any more "morally mature," in Mr. Wilson's sense, than Chinese were when Liang Qichao began his moral exhortations. For even though some may object that Mr. Wilson's sense of "moral maturity" is inescapably just that, *his sense* of "moral maturity," in many ways, I think, his sense of moral maturity would have been accepted by Liang Qichao—and indeed by the late Chairman. They did believe in a similar kind of moral development. They longed for it and worked for it. So we *have* to ask whether or not their efforts were of any effect.

Consider first "reciprocity" and "empathy," the first two of Mr. Wilson's three senses necessary for "mature moral judgment." (See chapter 1.) The last 50 years would *seem* to have brought about a great increase in feelings of reciprocity and empathy among Chinese. The word *tongbao* (literally, "womb-mates") has expanded in meaning from "sibling" to "compatriots." The word *tongzhi* (comrades) has encompassed all of "the people," which means a *lot* of people, restricted though that term, as we have seen, remains. If feelings of reciprocity and empathy have indeed spread beyond "friends and relatives" to "comrades," then there would seem to have been moral development indeed.

But, several things should give us pause before we declare the question answered. Liang Qichao and Lu Xun thought in their day that Chinese morality *was* immature. They feared it was unfit. They found Chinese brutally self-centered—or at best family and (a few) friends centered, without feelings of reciprocity and empathy, at least, for even their neighbors, much less for their people as a whole. Over and over again in Lu Xun's stories the villian is the Chinese crowd, the unfeeling, spectator Chinese crowd that gathers wherever there are Chinese suffering—to watch and do nothing.

But maybe Liang Qichao and Lu Xun had too low an opinion of their people. Their fear of *China's* weakness may have led them to exaggerate the "moral immaturity" of the Chinese. For surely it was not *just* "moral weakness" that made China weak. Even Lu Xun's crowds, which did exist—they have been photographed—may not have been as devoid of feelings of reciprocity and empathy as he thought, and as we might think. We forget about fear. "To see the right thing and not do it is to lack courage," said Confucius.[102] But those who fail to act may not fail to feel. It took courage indeed to stick one's neck out in a country that cut off heads.

Liang Qichao and Lu Xun showed feelings of reciprocity and empathy for their people when they wrote in anger about those who did not. But why did so many people like their writings? Did Liang Qichao, Lu Xun, Sun Yat-sen, and Mao Zedong raise their people's national consciousness—and public spiritedness—by "indoctrination" alone—on millions of blank slates—or did they strike chords of reciprocity and empathy waiting there to resonate?

Were there really no patriots in nineteenth and early twentieth century China? Were Liang Qichao's "new" martial, patriotic virtues really unheard of? Were the Chinese people really as pathetically selfish and spiritless as impatient *patriots* thought? How can we tell if Chinese have "advanced" or "developed" in the last 50 years if we do not know where they were?

And there is another thing. The Old Morality can be seen in theory to have been much *more* developed than the New, although in practice it *may* have been less so. Confucius preached a broader ideal of reciprocity and empathy than the Chairman did. Confucius told his disciples to "love the people," and he did not just mean "the people on our side," the people with "Confucian consciousness."[103] For he said, "All within the Four Seas are brothers," and he did not even just mean "all Chinese."[104] Confucian brotherhood was, as Confucius preached it, much more inclusive than communist comradeship, and therefore, by Mr. Wilson's standards, more developed.

But in practice, of course, Confucian feelings of reciprocity and empathy, supposed only to *start* at home, often stayed there. And so it was in revolt against "Confucianism" that the Communists preached comradeship—as a revolutionary moral development. Still Mr. Wilson is absolutely right, I think, when he says that "sociocentricism . . . [may act] to block full recognition of others who are not members of the groups with whom the person identifies." Comradeship, as we have seen above, can lead to the ruthless denial of reciprocity and empathy for noncomrades. The famous *yi ku* (remember suffering) meetings, which might seem a very "mature" form of "induction training" were the masses not so forcefully induced to attend them, are example enough of the sadly possible parallel development of empathy and enmity.

But even so, ruthless though Chinese comradeship can be, is not the scope of that comradeship wider than that of a debased Confucianism? Did not the Chairman, fatal flaw though there may be in his theory, bring Chinese in practice closer to *Confucius'* ideal? Without reams of social-scientific evidence, I would guess that he did. Without being able to believe in Lei Feng, I am ready to believe that young Chinese have tried to imitate him by the drove. I would like to believe that Chinese are more likely to treat strangers in a comradely fashion now than before.

But then, of course, there is the Great Cultural Revolution, a seeming great leap backward. Factional strife brought a terrible narrowing of reciprocity and empathy. Comradeship fell to pieces, until even the Chairman was forced to say, "Oh what a revolting development this is." And yet, within each faction, big or little, one could see a resurgence of Liang Qichao's—and the Chairman's—"gladiatorial virtues." All sorts of people were changing things, struggling, rebelling, being warlike, asserting themselves, restraining themselves, even sacrificing themselves. So what sort of development was it?

Western tail-wagging Sinophiles who saw in the Cultural Revolution the advent of the New Man have surely been caught with indelible egg on their faces, but what does that egg really mean? Did the Cultural Revolution reveal the true moral colors of the Chinese—the same old colors? Or did it represent an aberration, a lapse, a zig or a zag on the mountain road to maturity? If stages of moral development or levels of moral consciousness are not things reached by people or peoples for ever and ever amen, can people or peoples ever really grow up? Chairman Mao, before the Cultural Revolution, seemed to believe, with a hearty Mencian prejudice, in the moral perfectability of man, or at least of proletarian man. But after the Cultural Revolution, he seemed to lose faith in the very children of the Revolution that he had "raised," the Red Guards that he himself had sicced upon their elders (and his enemies). Even young workers seemed to him to have "bourgeois" feet of clay. But did they? Where had all the Lei Fengs gone?

The Cultural Revolution must have bitterly disappointed Mao Zedong. It must have bitterly disappointed him in many ways. But surely it did so not least in proving that morality revolutions are hard things to pull off. When youth "rebelled" at his bidding, his—and Liang Qichao's—rebel virtues surely seemed for a time to flourish, but all too soon those same virtues, extolled to pull the Chinese *qun* together (*behind*, of course, the Chairman) began inexorably to pull it apart. Selflessness was dedicated, all too often, only to selfish, self-righteous factions. Egocentric sociocentricism, to use Mr. Wilson's terms, acted violently "to block full recognition of others," not members of one's own special group. Famed, alleged Chinese "group orientedness" showed itself, as Liang Qichao thought it of old, to be petty group orientedness.

It is one of the many ironies of the Cultural Revolution that although the Chairman's Red Guards were first whipped into action against the "Four Olds" (old ideas, old culture, old customs, and old habits), many old modes of behavior resurfaced both during and after the Cultural Revolution, old modes of behavior that many (silly?) outsiders had long thought washed away—by brain washing—before the Red Guards ever existed. I can think of four such resurgent "olds" that should make us wonder about moral development.

One is the factionalism mentioned above. But another is *Confucian* morality, or to be more specific, at the risk of multiplying olds, the five cardinal Confucian virtues demanded in the relationships between ruler and subject, father and son, elder brother and younger brother, husband and wife, and friend and friend. These virtues may not have resurfaced in their ancient guise, but they have resurfaced.

The first cardinal virtue was twisted by the radicals, of course, into a fanatical loyalty to the Chairman, but in ironic consequence, it has proved the one Confucian virtue that has clearly suffered since the Cultural Revolution. The rest, after the fall of the Gang of Four, have dramatically reappeared, even in the pages of the *People's Daily*—in article after article written by sons, daughters, husbands, wives, and friends of *victims* of the Cultural Revolution.

Most remarkable have been the expressions of filial piety. Cries of "*baba*" and "*mama*" have echoed from the pages of *The People's Daily*. The sons of Tao Yong, Wang Shiying, Chen Zhengren, and Wu Han have all written laments for their fathers—and (usually mothers) for all too often both parents were done in by the Gang of Four.[105] Wu Han's son wrote in memory of his father, mother, and sister, he himself being his family's only survivor. Tao Zhu's daughter wrote a lament for him, a very moving lament entitled "A Letter Written at Last."[106] For she, like all of these filial sons and daughters, had had to wait for years—in her case nine—before she could publicly express her love for her parents and her hatred for her parents' enemies. Li Baohua had had to wait for 50 years before writing a piece in memory of his father, Li Dazhao, whose contributions to the cause were more easily remembered after *the* leader of the cause had died.[107] But even the leader's own children wrote a filially pious piece after he died. A son, Mao Anqing and a daughter, Shao Hua, together wrote a piece, again "at last," in celebration of their father's birthday, a piece entitled, "Dad wanted us to be Strong, Healthy and Progressive." The Great Helmsman himself became a "*baba*" in *The People's Daily*.[108]

Of course all these articles could have been written by ghost writers for all we know. Surely all were polished up by editors, but even were they fake (to me most sound in part, at least, authentic) they were still all written in the *form* of expressions of filial piety. Of course all were published in part—in large part—for political reasons, but still all *honor* filial piety, just as many more articles written by friends in memory of other victims of the Cultural Revolution honor friendship. There is something about the whole movement to restore the reputations of party leaders and intellectuals done in by the Gang of Four that goes beyond the cementing of the present power-holders' political positions. The restorers of reputations are not *just* justifying themselves thereby. Behind or besides the political messages in these articles one devines a sense of justice, a traditional, almost "feudal" sense of justice, a caring for the reputations of wronged friends. There is no caring so traditional as to shout, "my friends and relatives right or wrong." In all of these stories the friends and relatives were always "truly loyal" to the Party and to Mao Zedong. So in theory the Confucian virtues of loyalty, filial piety, and friendship were never thrown into conflict. In practice, however, all of these stories reveal that *during* the Cultural Revolution the virtues of friendship, filial piety, and loyalty *were* thrown into conflict, for when friends, parents, children, wives, and husbands stood up for each other, they were standing up—at the time—for officially outcast "enemies of the people."

But *defiant* filial piety leads us to a third resurgent "old," to the defiant, Confucian official virtues, to the "Hai Rui virtues," to the virtues for which the most illustrious victims of the Cultural Revolution now are being praised, by filial sons and daughters, loving wives and husbands, good friends—and the party leaders now in power.

There is only seeming irony in this turn of events. From 1959 to 1961, Wu Han, first victim of the Cultural Revolution, praised the virtues of the Ming official Hai Rui to protest the dismissal of Peng Dehuai, to encourage other officials to resist the Chairman's Great Leap visions, and to entreat all intellectuals to dare speak out against nonsense and injustice. Hai Rui was a Confucian official who dared speak out even against his emperor. He was an "incorruptible official" and a "good official." He "lived a life of simplicity and was upright and firm in principle. . . . Uncompromising he was not swayed by threats of violence nor intimidated by defeat."[109] Despite bad times he "steadfastly clung to his own beliefs and without bending or giving in struggled on until he died."[110]

Those, said Wu Han in 1961, were the "good virtues—worth our study today."[111] In 1979 it was *not* ironic that Chinese should be urged to study those virtues through the lives of some of the very people, now dead, whom Wu Han had hoped would study them, not ironic that they should be urged to do so by other such people who have survived. It was only fitting that the very phrase most often used to describe Hai Rui, *gang zhi bu a* (firm, upright, and uncompromising), should now be used—openly—in praise of Peng Dehuai, Tao Zhu, Chen Yi, Deng Tuo, and indeed "all good . . . revolutionary cadres and intellectuals."[112] Deng Xiaoping had good reason to respect such people.

But look again at the "Hai Rui virtues." Do they not perfectly exhibit Mr. Wilson's third characteristic of a mature morality, "individual responsibility?" "Individual responsibility," says Mr. Wilson, "is the ability to accept the consequences of one's decisions. It implies a capability to form judgments and make choices that may be contrary to situational cues, most particularly those cues that reflect the influence of authority figures." Hai Rui defied the authorities. He called them wrong. "Upright and firm in principle," not swayed by threats of violence," he "steadfastly clung to his own beliefs." And so, we are told, did his modern counterparts.

Hai Rui's modern counterparts look like people heroically capable of "mature moral judgment." They also look as if they might have been products of Liang Qichao's and the Chairman's morality revolutions, for they seem to have rebelled, struggled, asserted themselves, restrained themselves, and sacrificed themselves. Of course, their existence does not prove that most Chinese are Hai Ruis. Perhaps their standing out proves just the opposite. Still, if the "Hai Rui virtues" are now officially preached, even though not yet widely practiced, it would seem a significant development.

It would seem so, were it not for the shadow of the other hand. The "Hai Rui virtues" were the virtues of a *loyal* Confucian, of a Confucian who criticized his emperor because he thought it was his *duty* to criticize his emperor. His moral opposition was *loyal* opposition, and so, we are told, was the opposition of his modern counterparts. Chinese morality has often been called highly conformist morality and therefore, perhaps, somewhat "immature." The "Hai Rui virtues" *seem* highly *nonconformist.* But there is remarkable conformity in the nonconformity both of Hai Rui and of his modern "disciples." For all were true to their *group*'s doctrine—when *the authority's* were not. Or so, at least, we are told.

As Mr. Wilson says, "In traditional and modern times high officials in China may feel that they personally are protectors of the group's virtue, guardians of moral authority, and that open defence of the principles they hold is *required* (my italics) regardless of pressures for conformity and for deference to authority." There is conformity in conforming to that requirement, even though those who so conform may show tremendous psychological stress under their "required" nonconformity. Witness Zhou Xinfang, imprisoned, kicked out of the Communist Party, and ostracized as a counterrevolutionary after he literally acted the part of Hai Rui in his own production of the Peking opera "Hai Rui Presents a Memorial." Over and over again he is said to have said to his daughter-in-law or just to himself, "I have not opposed Chairman Mao. I have not opposed the Party. Chairman Mao and Premier Zhou both understand me .... I love Chairman Mao. I love the Party ...."[113]

Like censors of old these modern Hai Ruis suffered loyally. Theirs was not the loyalty of the radicals, the "my Chairman right or wrong" loyalty that the radicals almost, at least, demanded ("Those of Chairman Mao's instructions that we understand we must carry out; those that we do not understand we must also carry out."[114]). That kind of loyalty has now been officially repudiated. It is Hai Rui's Confucian, critical loyalty that is praised. But it is praised not as nonconformist but as conformist morality. The modern Hai Ruis are praised for conforming—at the risk of their lives—to the Party's Way.

But does that mean they were morally mature or not? They lived up to the party's principles as Hai Rui lived up to Confucius', but in doing so were they autonomous individuals clinging to their own beliefs or pathetic prisoners of indoctrination, sacrificed to superegos put into them, and over on them, by their group—or its vanguard? How can we tell? We do not know well enough what "autonomy" is.

Mr. Wilson suggests that morally mature, autonomous people make moral judgments, if need be despite "the authorities," "in terms of internalized values," or, quoting Alfred H. Bloom, in adherence to "individual intuition." But can adherence to "individual intuition" be the same as adherence to "internalized values?" If there are not any "real" values somehow "out there" to be intuited, then "intuition" is no more than a sensing of internalized values, but if values are "internalized" not after "real" intuition but only after some sort of "socialization," then the "intuition" of such internalized values is not individual at all. The "moral individual" is still slave to his society.

Mr. Wilson has evidence that suggests that Chinese are very good at internalizing rules. They quite clearly show "this important attribute of individual responsibility." But despite that fact—perhaps he should have said because of it—they appear "relatively rule oriented and conformist." And being so oriented they fall short of moral perfection. So how autonomous are the autonomous?

Consider a "classic" Western example of someone who like Hai Rui "steadfastly clung to his [or, in this case, her] beliefs and without bending or giving in struggled on until [she] died"—Antigone. Two milennia of humanists and theologions would have called Antigone autonomous and mature, for she transgressed the laws of men, clinging to her own sense of "the unwritten and unfailing laws of the gods,"[115] laws that she grasped—so we are led to believe—through her "individual intuition." But if most humanists and theologians applaud her, all social scientists might not. Freud, for one, recognizing the "religiosity of her morals, might have found them "patently infantile."[116] If Antigone's *religion* had instilled in her the fear of the gods, then maybe when her religion's laws crossed those of her state, she was dragged into a fake dilemma by her own mixed up society. Did she not give herself away when she explained herself to Creon?

> I feared not what any man might think;
> I was not about to suffer punishment
> before the gods.[117]

Sophocles did not make clear the connection between his clauses, but Freud would have said that Antigone did not this time fear man because the society of men had made her fear gods more. So Antigone's moral act may not have been a moral act. A pox on Freud.

At any rate, if Antigone's moral maturity is questionable, so is Hai Rui's. It matters not that Hai Rui may seem in speech, at least, more "secular" than Antigone. His Confucian Way was "grounded" in the Way of Heaven, and his modern counterparts' Party Way, despite the vaunted atheism of Marxism-Leninism, was most religiously grounded in a quite metaphysical Way of History. So in religiosity all may have been equally "immature." And so, although all did cling to their principles, the question remains, to what degree were their principles their own?

Secure U.S. humanists, theologians, and social scientists should all think twice, it seems to me, before labeling Chinese Communists who had died, "for principles," "unprincipled" or "immature." Nonetheless, there is no clear answer to the above question. The science of moral development is itself not mature enough yet to give us one—and I, for one, doubt it ever will be. *And yet*, even though we cannot with any confidence call Hai Rui or his modern counterparts mature or immature, we can, with Mr. Wilson's standards, call those now *preaching* "Hai Rui's virtues" immature—in at least one sense. The morality they preach, as they preach it, is decidedly not "open."

"Hai Rui's virtues" are virtues only because he was "right." His and his modern counterparts' principled nonconformity is "good" only because it conforms to the principles of the present party leaders. No followers of the Gang of Four are praised for clinging to their beliefs. Nor are any members of "The Alliance for Human Rights." Zhang Zhixin is a Hai Rui type, but Wei Jingsheng is not.[118] Nowhere in official pronouncements can I see any evidence of what Mr. Wilson calls a "commitment to personal integrity," that is, a commitment to personal integrity itself. "Correctness" is still what counts.

At the beginning of the Deng Xiaoping era, a new "openness" in China was much heralded in the West, with, within reason, good reason. The slogan "Practice is the only standard for determining the truth" seemed open indeed. It almost seemed to invite the kind of experimentation and testing of moral alternatives that Mr. Wilson declares characteristic of an "open and flexible" political system (no perfectly open and flexible system, he hastens to point out, yet exists). But none of us should have been surprised when the Wei Jingsheng

case dramatized the fact that Chinese room for experimentation is still limited—
quite severely. For all the while that the old *Bai hua qi fang* slogans flourished
in the press, another slogan was there beside them: *Tong xin tong de*. All the
while that Chinese were urged to "let a hundred flowers bloom," they were also
urged to be "of like mind and like virtue."[119]

Tong xin tong de is an old ideal. It is the same ideal, of course, as the *I xin
i de* (one mind and one virtue) of the Nationalists' national—or party—anthem.
But it is much older than that. It is an age old Confucian ideal based not only
on the age old Confucian conviction that "Heaven has not two Ways,"[120] but
also on the age old Confucian prejudice that all people can actually be gotten to
follow Heaven's *One* Way.[121]

That was the faith behind Confucian self-righteousness, a self-righteousness
not often throughout Chinese history as militant as the saddest forms of Christian
self-righteousness, but a self-righteousness that in its official form could be quite
unforgiving nonetheless. *Official* Confucianism, bureaucratic Confucianism, was
not at home with heterodoxy.

Morally, the Chinese Communists are Confucian Communists, not Daoist or
Buddhist Communists, and "knowing" now that "the Way of Heaven" is the
Way of History and indeed the Way of Evolution, they are clearly even more,
not less, self-righteous than Confucians of old. They *know* their Way is right.
And therefore they know that those who persist in being of different mind and
different virtue are wrong—cosmically wrong. This self-righteousness, this sure-
ness of the Way, is the fourth "old" that I see resurgent, after—even after—the
Cultural Revolution. It does not, I think, make easier the way of "openness."

Of course Deng Xiaoping is a more open leader than Mao Zedong. Of
course Deng Xiaoping wants more openness for China than did the Gang of Four
or Five. Many things that mattered to the Gang of Four or Five do not matter
to Deng Xiaoping. Curlers, colored clothes, *Coca Cola*—none of that matters.
Nor in many more important ways do black cats or white cats. But the cats'
task matters, and who sets them to that task matters. And when it comes to
matters that matter, even Deng Xiaoping expects unity. Even he insists that
Chinese be of "correct" mind and "correct" virtue.

So again we encounter the Great Tradition. Hai Rui's conformity and his
nonconformity, Lei Feng's love and his hate, Li Shuangshuang's collectivist
spirit and her minding of her neighbors' business, Liang Qichao's self-assertion
and his self-restraint, Mao Zedong's nationalism and his daughter's filial piety,
Deng Xiaoping's restoration of reputations and his suppression of Democracy
Wall—in the moral justifications for each and every one of these things is there
not *something* traditional? Is there anything so *untraditional* as to mark a new
level of Chinese moral development?

If there is, I do not see it. I do not see anything that new even though I
most readily admit that "the New China" does seem to exude a "new spirit."
Much of that spirit, of course, is a *renewed* spirit, but it *is*, at least, a spirit
renewed on a *new* scale. For the Chinese people have been touched by their

government as never before. They have been educated as never before. They have been *morally* educated as never before. They have been preached to as never before. And yet even so, this unprecedented propagation of the word—of any moral word—has not yet lifted the Chinese people to a new *level* of moral development. For the word is not that new, and new or not it is hard to live up to.

Perhaps social scientists will soon be able to document a quantitative and therefore qualitative leap in Chinese feelings of empathy and reciprocity. Nationalism itself should have widened the Chinese "We." So should Marxism. Comradeship and—quite literally—commune-ism, the moral ideals of Lei Feng and Li Shuangshuang, have been pursued on an unprecedented scale. *Perhaps* they have been approximated on an unprecedented scale. But they are not brand new ideals, they are no higher than the ideals of Confucius, and the notion of the primacy of the *qun*, so essential to them, seems almost quintessentially Chinese.

Finally, however forcefully the virtues of "the new style good type," new or not new, have been propogated, I can see no overwhelming evidence that good comrades come any more a dime a dozen than have good Samaritans. At least there is no evidence of any remarkable Lamarkian acquisition of inheritable comradely characteristics.

"But of course not," any readers should reply with justifiable exasperation. Even if evolution *is* up to the creation of a better human being, at evolution's pace what do you expect in 50 or 100 years? Not very much. When Li Shuangshuang's husband asked her, "Say, how long does it take before a man can finally get rid of his selfishness," she should have replied, "Longer than a lifetime."[122]

But that is the sad part of this story. Liang Qichao and Chairman Mao in their cries for a morality revolution did expect evolutionary as well as revolutionary progress—within a century. There was a strong Lamarkian streak in each of them. Liang Qichao and Chairman Mao expected the emergence of "a New People," fit for a new stage of human history, not a perfect people—that *would* take time—but a better people once and for all. Liang Qichao probably felt like a prophet in the wilderness when he first cried out for a morality revolution. He would have been overjoyed, therefore, to have heard Chairman Mao so widely preaching his virtues. But even Chairman Mao lived to be discouraged by the amount of clay on, if not in, his people's shoes.

"Plus ça change, plus c'est la meme chose." That would seem a harsh judgment for the morality revolutions of Liang Qichao and Mao Zedong were not "la meme chose" still so pregnant with possibility.

NOTES

1.   Liang Qichao, *Xin min shuo* (Taibei: Zhunghua Shuju, 1959), p. 15. Many of the ideas and a fair amount of the writing in the sections on Liang

Qichao that follow come from my unpublished Ph.D. dissertation: James R. Pusey, "China and Charles Darwin," Harvard University, 1977, now being readied for publication at the Harvard East Asian Research Center.

2. Ibid.

3. Liang Qixiong, ed., *Xun Zi jian shi* (Taibei: Shangwu yin shu guan, 1969), 5, p. 51; 21, p. 290.

4. Liang, *Xin min shuo*, p. 15.

5. Ibid.

6. Yang Bojun, ed., *Lunyu yi zhu* (Beijing: Zhunghua Shuju, 1965), 2.4, p. 13.

7. Liang, ed., *Xun Zi*, 19, p. 257; 9, p. 100, 108–109.

8. *Meng Zi yi chu* team of the Lanzhou University Chinese Department, ed., *Meng Zi yi chu* (Hong Kong: Wenyan Shuju, n.d.), 3.6, pp. 79–80.

9. Liang, *Xin min shuo*, p. 15.

10. Liang Qichao, *Yin bing shi wen ji* (Hereafter YBS) (Taipei: Zhunghua shuju, 1960), 4.9: 41, 42.

11. I cannot find where Mao Zedong first said this, but see Richard Solomon, *Mao's Revolution and the Chinese Political Culture* (Berkeley: University of California Press, 1971), p. 474.

12. Liang, *Xin min shuo*, p. 60.

13. Ibid., pp. 64–65.

14. *Xin min cong bao* (Hereafter XMCB) (Taibei: photolithograph, 17 vols., 1966), 10.52:91.

15. Lu Xun, *Fen* (Hong Kong: Jindai tushu gongsi, 1964), pp. 99–100.

16. Liang, *Xin min shuo*, p. 12.

17. T.H. Huxley and Julian Huxley, *Evolution and Ethics, 1893–1943* (London: Pilot Press, 1947), p. 82.

18. Yang, ed., *Lunyu*, 3.7, p. 27.

19. Liang, ed., *Xun Zi*, 10, p. 119.

20. *Lao Zi dao de jing* (Shanghai: Shangwu yin shu goan, 1935), 68, 2: 19 a–b.

21. Liang, *Xin min shuo*, p. 108.

22. Liang Qichao, *Ziyou shu* (Taibei: Zhunghua shuju, 1960) p. 37.

23. Liang, *Xin min shuo*, pp. 109–110.

24. Ibid., p. 10.

25. Ibid., p. 23.

26. Ibid.

27. Ibid., p. 10.

28. Huxley, *Evolution*, pp. 31, 44, 81–82.

29. Liang, *Xin min shuo*, pp. 130–131.

30. Ibid., p. 130.

31. XMCB, 10.50:1.

32. Liang, *Xin min shuo*, p. 49.

33. Ibid., p. 50.

34. Liang, *Ziyou*, p. 75.

35. Richard Hofstadter, *Social Darwinism in American Thought* (Boston: Beacon Press, 1955), p. 99.

36. Benjamin Kidd, *Social Evolution* (New York: MacMillan, 1844), p. 293.

37. Liang, YBS, 5-12:81.

38. Ibid., 5-12:84.

39. Ibid., 5-12:86; 5-12:82.

40. Ibid., 5-12:81.

41. Ibid.

42. Ibid., 5-12:82.

43. Ibid., 5-12:83.

44. Lu Xun, *Re feng* (Hong Kong: Jin dai tushu gongsi, 1964), p. 44.

45. See Hu Shi, *Hu Shi wen xuan* (Taibei: Yuan Dong tushu gongsi, 1962), p. 78; YBS 6-17:1-2; Pusey, *op. cit.,* pp. 385-406.

46. Pusey, *op. cit.,* pp. 389-405.

47. See Liang, *Ziyou,* p. 1.

48. Liang, *Xin min shuo,* pp. 44-45.

49. Ibid., p. 47.

50. Ibid., p. 78.

51. Pusey, *op. cit.,* pp. 447-452; YBS 6-17:77.

52. Liang, *Xin min shuo,* p. 14.

53. Ibid., p. 15.

54. Pusey, *op. cit.,* pp. 326-327.

55. Liang, YBS, 2-5:49.

56. Ibid., 5-13:39.

57. Ibid., 2-5:48.

58. Ibid., 2-5:49.

59. Ibid., 5-13:32.

60. Ibid., 2-5:49.

61. My translations from the Chinese text given in James Legge, *The Chinese Classics*, vol. 3, *The Shoo King* (Taibei: reprint, 1963), pt. IV, bk. III, chap. II, 3, p. 186.

62. Sun Yirang, ed., *Mo Zi jiengu* (Taibei: Shijie shuju, 1970), 16, pp. 72-73.

63. Liang, ed., *Xun Zi,* 9, p. 100.

64. See Yang, ed., *Lunyu,* 15-18, p. 238, and *Meng Zi,* 11-10, p. 265.

65. Sun, *Mo Zi,* 16, p. 78.

66. Yang, ed., *Lunyu,* 12-2, p. 187.

67. Huxley, *Evolution,* p. 11.

68. XMCB, 1-1:6.

69. Liang, YBS, 3-6:39.

70. *Qing yi bao* (Taibei: photolithograph, 12 vols., 1967) 12:65, 64.

71. *Meng Zi,* 3-2, p. 62.

72. Mao Zedong, *Mao Zhuxi yu lu* (Beijing: Xinhua shuju, 1967), p. 70.

73. See Liang, YBS, 1-1:1.

74. Lewis S. Feuer, ed., *Marx & Engels: Basic Writings on Politics and Philosophy* (Magnolia, Mass.: Peter Smith, 1974), p. 245.

75. Mao Zedong, "Shijian lun," in *Mao Zedong xuanji* (Beijing: Renmin chuban she, 1969), 1:272.

76. Mao, *Yu lu,* p. 8.

77. Ibid., p. 10.

78. See note 11.
79. See note 10.
80. Endymion Wilkinson, translator, *The People's Comic Book* (New York: Doubleday, 1973), p. 133.
81. Ibid., p. 89.
82. Ibid., p. 124.
83. Ibid., pp. 216, 220.
84. Ibid., p. 117.
85. Ibid., p. 218.
86. Ibid., p. 250.
87. Stanley Karnow, *Mao and China* (New York: Viking, 1973), p. 138.
88. Mao Zedong, "Wei renmin fu-wu," in *Xuanji,* 3:905.
89. Ibid., p. 906.
90. Mao Zedong, "Fandui ziyuzhuyi," in *Xuanji,* 2:331, 332.
91. Mao Zedong, "Lun renmin minzhu zhuanjeng," in *Xuanji,* 4:1357–1370.
92. See Pusey, *op. cit.,* pp. 447–448, and Liang Qichao, "Kaiming zhuanzhi lun," in YBS, 6–17:13.
93. Xu Wenshan, ed., *San min zhuyi zong ji* (Taibei: Zhunghua shuju, 1960), p. 227.
94. Lu Xun, *Kuangren ri ji,* in *Lu Xun xiaoshuo ji* (Hong Kong: Jindai tushu gongsi, 1964), p. 15.
95. Mao, *Yu lu,* p. 11.
96. Mao Zedong, "Guanyu zhengque chuli renmin neibu maodun de wenti," in *Xuanji,* 5:365.
97. Mao Zedong, "Zai Yan'an wenyi zuotan hui shang de jianghua," in *Xuanji,* 3:829.
98. Lu Xun, *Fen,* pp. 200–202.
99. Lucien Pye, *China: An Introduction* (Boston: Little, Brown, 1972), p. 254.
100. Pusey, *op. cit.,* p. 602.
101. Lu Xun, *Kuangren,* pp. 25, 22.
102. Yang, ed., *Lunyu,* 2–24, p. 24.
103. Ibid., 1–6, p. 5.
104. Ibid., 12–5, p. 132.
105. See *Renmin Ribao,* February 8, September 24, November 22, 1979; and *Bei Mei Ribao,* February 22, 1979.
106. *Renmin Ribao,* December 10, 1978.
107. Ibid., October 29, 1979.
108. Ibid., December 13, 1978.
109. James Pusey, *Wu Han: Attacking the Present through the Past* (Cambridge, Mass.: East Asian Research Center, Harvard University, 1969), p. 30.
110. Ibid., p. 20.
111. Ibid., p. 35.
112. See *Renmin Ribao,* March 15, 1979, December 10, 1978, January 6, 1979, February 27, 1979.

113. *Renmin Ribao,* November 19, 1978.

114. *Han ying cihui shouce* (Bibliographic information torn out), p. 2.

115. Sophocles, *Antigone* (Cambridge: The University Press, 1953), p. 18.

116. Sigmund Freud, *Civilization and its Discontents* (New York: Norton, 1962), p. 21.

117. Sophocles, *Antigone,* p. 18.

118. Zhang Zhixin was a young woman executed supposedly for speaking out against the yet unlabeled Gang of Four. Wei Jingsheng was more recently sentenced to 15 years, after criticizing China's more recent authorities. See, as examples, articles in *Renmin Ribao,* June 11, 1979 and November 8, 1979.

119. See for example *Renmin Ribao,* June 18, 1979 or September 12, 1979.

120. See note 3.

121. See Yang, ed., *Lunyu,* 2.3, pp. 12–13; 8.9, p. 87; 12.19, p. 137.

122. Wilkinson, *The People's Comic Book,* p. 131.

5 IN SEARCH OF JUSTICE: LAW AND MORALITY IN THREE CHINESE DRAMAS

Peter Li

Confucius said: "Lead the people by laws and regulate them by punishments, and the people will try to avoid wrongdoing but will have no sense of shame. Lead the people by virtue and regulate them by the rules of propriety, and the people will have a sense of shame, and moreover will become good."

Analects, II, 3

It is better to die of starvation than to become a thief; it is better to be vexed to death than to bring a lawsuit.

Chinese Proverb

The administration of justice in traditional Chinese society has been somewhat of a puzzle to Western students. To the Western scholar who has been brought up on the ideas of due process, trial by a jury of one's peers, assumption of innocence until proven guilty, and access to legal counsel, the Chinese judicial system in which the procedure was inquisitional, the plaintiff or petitioner could be punished the same as the accused, the magistrate acted as the judge and prosecutor, guilt was based on confession by the suspect, and the use of torture was permitted to extract confession, seemed a travesty of justice.[1]

Nevertheless, in the opinion of many, the legal system worked quite well. Sir Chaloner Alabaster observed: "As regards then the criminal law of the Chinese, although the allowance of torture in the examination of prisoners is a blot which cannot be overlooked, although the punishment for treason and patricide is monstrous, and the punishment of the wooden collar or portable pillory is not to be defended, yet the [Penal] Code—when its procedure is understood—is infinitely more exact and satisfactory than our own system, and very far from being the barbarous cruel abomination it is generally supposed to be."[2]

Before one can fairly evaluate the institutions of another civilization one must first understand the ground rules and history of that civilization. Otherwise, it is the height of ethnocentricism to judge the traditional Chinese legal system by American standards. The Chinese legal-cum-administrative system is closely linked to religious/ethical values, the political/administrative system, and the associated bureaucratic ethos. The ground rules are the ideas of Confucianism and Legalism both in their pristine forms and later ideological and political developments; the Chinese conception of the family and state and their interrelationships; the place of the individual in the family, state, and society; and popular beliefs and customs in these areas. To criticize a legal system as being a "barbarous cruel abomination" or as being just, fair, and humane depends on the standards one chooses in making the judgment, and these standards must be clearly stated.

The purpose of this essay is to examine the relationship between law and morality in Chinese society as exemplified in three popular dramas. One may ask, in what way can literature contribute to our understanding of moral behavior and society? A literary work, such as a drama, gives insight into the dynamic relations between an individual and social institutions. The drama, in particular, presents the ideas and beliefs of a given situation in terms that most closely reflect popular sentiment since the play is performed in front of a live audience, thus, in a sense, capturing public feeling. One must, of course, be cautious not to generalize beyond the data presented in imaginative or literary form. But literary data do have the advantage of presenting material from times gone by that are no longer accessible to the usual methods of the social scientist.

The focus of this study is on three popular dramas that depict serious miscarriages of justice and show how redress is brought about. Moreover, because they were popular dramas, we might assume that they reflected popular conceptions of justice and morality rather than elite formulations. The method will be to look closely at the plot, actions, characters, language, and social and ideological background of these dramas. Finally, we will generalize from the insights that have been gained.

The first of the three works to be analyzed is the Yuan drama *Dou O Yuan* (*Injustice to Dou O*), by the famous thirteenth-century playwright Guan Hanqing (ca. 1210–ca. 1298).[3] The other two dramas are Qing Dynasty works, probably of the late nineteenth or early twentieth century, *Liang Tianlai* and *Yang Naiwu yu Xiaobaicai*.[4] These three works are classic examples of "judgment reversal dramas"[5] (*pingfan gonganju*) in which there are at least two court judgments, the latter overturning the former and in which there is a long arduous struggle to get the judgment reversed. *Injustice to Dou O* (hereafter simply *Dou O*) may be considered to be the archetypal judgment reversal drama since it is the earliest, most powerful, and artistically the most refined, whereas the other two, following the judgment reversal pattern, are variations on the same theme but possibly reflect a slightly changed view of law and morality. Although the three dramas are not of equal artistic achievement, they have as their common theme a persistent search for justice. What is of further interest is that they are enjoyed on the stage in China today.

INJUSTICE TO DOU O

> The human heart cannot be deceived for long; injustice escapes not the eyes of Heaven and Earth. (*Injustice to Dou O*)

Guan Hanqing was a versatile playwright who wrote over 60 plays during his lifetime. Only about 17 or 18 of his plays are extant, "ranging from courtroom dramas and domestic comedies to re-creations of historical events on stage."[6] Guan was a man of many talents; he led a carefree life, associated with courtesan-actresses, and acted in plays himself. These activities might have been a form of escape for a scholar living during a time of political and social turmoil. He abandoned himself to the world of the senses, and his literary talents were channeled into the theater.

Plot Summary

Dou O is one of the masterpieces of Chinese drama, noted for its forceful and artistic use of language and dramatic intensity. It is a Yuan *zaju* (variety play) in four acts with a prologue.

The tragic heroine of the story is Dou O, who is born into a destitute scholarly family. At the age of three, she loses her mother. At seven her father Dou Tianzhang, unable to pay back 40 taels of silver that he owes the moneylender Granny Cai, gives his young daughter to Granny Cai to eventually become the old woman's daughter-in-law and goes off to the capital to take the examinations. At the age of 17, Dou O marries Granny Cai's son, but two years later he dies. So at the young age of 19 Dou O becomes a widow.

Now, another one of Granny Cai's debtors, an apothecary named Dr. Lu, instead of repaying the money he owes, decides to murder her. But his plot is foiled by two rogues, Donkey Zhang and his father Old Zhang, who suddenly appear on the scene. Grateful for saving her life, Granny Cai invites them to her house to reward them. But once there, the pair refuses to leave and insists that the two widows marry them. Granny Cai appears willing, but Dou O refuses. Donkey Zhang then tries to poison Granny Cai and subsequently to take Dou O by force. But as fate would have it, his own father accidentally drinks the poison instead and dies.

Taking advantage of this turn of events, Donkey Zhang threatens Dou O with the proposition of either marrying him or taking her to court and accusing her of poisoning his father. Dou O prefers the latter course of action, and so she is then brought to court where she is questioned and tortured to extract a confession by a muddleheaded, corrupt magistrate named Tao Wu. But even under severe torture Dou O refuses to confess until the judge threatens to torture her mother-in-law, Granny Cai. Being a dutiful daughter-in-law, she then gives in and confesses and, as a consequence, is sentenced to death.

But before her execution she swears to Heaven and Earth that she is innocent and makes three prophecies that will bear out her innocence. First, during her beheading, not one drop of blood will be spilled on the ground. Instead, her blood will flow up a pure white banner twelve feet long. Second, after her execution, three feet of snow will fall to cover her body even though it is the middle of summer. Third, there will be a three-year drought following her death. All three prophecies come to pass.

Three years later Dou O's father, having succeeded in the examinations, comes to Chujou as an Imperial Commissioner. Dou O's spirit appears to him in a dream and reveals to him the wrong that has been done her. He reopens the case, the culprits are brought to justice, and the sentenced is reversed. As his punishment Donkey Zhang is to be led through the streets and publicly disgraced, then quartered, and finally beheaded. Prefect Tao Wu, the corrupt judge, is to be given a hundred strokes and forbidden to hold office for the rest of his life. Apothecary Lu is to be banished forever to the frontier as a soldier.

Characters

Dou O is the classic innocent victim of a miscarriage of justice. Although poor, she embodies the virtues of the traditional educated elite either as the result of being very precocious since leaving her father at the age of seven, or from an inborn moral sense. She is unswerving in her dedication to the Confucian values of society. She is a dutiful daughter-in-law and later strictly follows the vows of widowhood; moreover, she is a guardian of her mother-in-law's virtue. There is never any doubt in her mind as to what she must do. The principles of her behavior are very clear. And the irony is that it is precisely because of her singleminded devotion to duty that she suffers great injustice. But at the same time, it is her purity and innocence that can move Heaven and Earth.

Granny Cai, on the other hand, lives on a lower, more practical moral plane. Her principles are more flexible. She is a moneylender who must collect her debts herself. She has to mingle with all classes; therefore, she cannot afford the high principles of Dou O. But basically she is a kindhearted woman; she promises Dou Tianzhang that she will take care of Dou O as if she were her own child, and there are no indications that she did not live up to her promise. The values that she lives by differ considerably from those of Dou O. When she is faced with remarriage, she is willing to accept the offer. On the other hand, Dou O's uncompromising answer is "If you want a husband, you go ahead, mother. I certainly have no wish for one." But then she gives her moral reproach: "I worry that you, in waning spirit, cannot swallow the wedding wine; I worry that you, with failing vision, cannot tie the same-heart knot; I worry that you, sleepy and feeling dim, cannot rest secure under the flowerquilt."[7] Granny Cai also lacks the courage to stand up and defend her daughter-in-law in court.

Donkey Zhang, Old Zhang, and Dr. Lu are totally unprincipled. They lie, cheat, rob, and kill. Their greed knows no limits. Because his proposal to Dou O is rejected, Donkey Zhang is more determined than ever to get his way. He swears that he will make Dou O his wife, even if it means plotting murder. Donkey Zhang is, thus, the classic villain.

Somewhat unlike Donkey Zhang, Dr. Lu has but moments of moral weakness. In the second act he is suddenly struck by the thought that "a man's life is the concern of Heaven and Earth, how can I treat it as though it were a speck of dust on the wall! From now on I'll change my profession and atone for my sins."[8] But this pang of conscience comes too late; Donkey Zhang arrives and forces him to sell poison, and his career of crime continues.

Prefect Tao Wu, who is supposed to be a man of justice, a man of the educated elite, appears in the drama as a caricature. He is the butt of jokes and satire. He becomes the symbol of official corruption and a chief obstacle to justice. He is the stereotyped incompetent magistrate. His opening lines in the drama are "I am a magistrate, the best on the bench. My coffers are filled from the cases I hear. When any inspector comes to check my files, I am to be found at home too sick to appear."[9] When the plaintiff kneels to present his case in court, the magistrate respectfully kneels in return, explaining that his livelihood depends on the money his plaintiff brings. In the confrontation between the arbiter of justice and the accused, we find that the accused is the most virtuous and worthy, where the arbiter of justice is the most despicable—an ironic juxtaposition.

Dou Tianzhang is an upright official, an Imperial Commissioner who travels around the country examining records, uncovering corrupt officials and punishing them. He is the epitome of integrity, unswerving in his impartiality. He sternly reprimands the ghost of Dou O when he finds out that she has been accused of poisoning her alleged father-in-law:

> Say no more, wretch!...You have committed one of the ten most atrocious crimes and suffered the penalty. When I gave you to be married into their family I charged you to observe the Three Duties and the Four Virtues. You did nothing of the kind. For three generations not one male member of the Dou family has violated the law, and for five generations not one female has married again. But now you have disgraced your ancestors and endangered my reputation.[10]

As if this were not enough, he threatens to send her "where you will never be born a human being again but will remain forever condemned to be a hungry ghost on the Mountain of Shadows" if she does not tell the whole truth of the matter. After 14 years of separation his first concern is whether or not his daughter violated the Confucian codes of behavior. If she did not conduct herself in accordance with the Three Duties and Four Virtues, then she would bring disgrace (*ru* or *rumo*) upon her ancestors and damage her father's reputation. Here the precepts of the Great Tradition are clearly stated. Father and daughter both know that these are the codes that they must live by.

Dou Tianzhang and his daughter know exactly what their roles in society are, and they act accordingly. Donkey Zhang and his father would violate all the rules to get what they want. Granny Cai's livelihood as the moneylender does not permit her to live according to the values of the elite. Her existence is a precarious one.

Concept of Justice

The supreme irony and tragedy of the drama are that this paragon of virtue should be so unjustly condemned and executed. But Dou O is by no means the passive victim that one might imagine. She is filled with righteous indignation, but the restraints of society prevent her from crying out. However, as a ghost, she is freer to express her feelings. She says to her father, "If the villain were cut into ten thousand pieces, it were not revenge enough to satisfy my soul."[11] She thirsts for retribution.

It is important to point out here that many scholars have cited the supernatural phenomena in this drama as an example of the Chinese conception of cosmic harmony or balance. The theory is that a crime disrupts the balance between man and nature. Therefore, redress is immediately needed in order to restore the balance. But this, in fact, is not quite correct, for the crime itself, in this case, does not cause disharmony as much as does the miscarriage of justice of the legal system. Donkey Zhang's murder of his father does not cause cosmic disturbances, but Dou O's unjust execution does. It is not the crime, but the punishment imposed by negligent officials, who are supposed to be agents of justice, that causes cosmic disruption.[12]

When Dou O calls out "I cry injustice! Let Earth be moved, let Heaven quake!" she shares the common belief of the people that "all deeds of injustice are known to Heaven and Earth."

LIANG TIANLAI

"Even if Heaven has eyes, these eyes must not have pupils." (*Liang Tianlai*)

This unusual story involving nine deaths comes from a notorious legal case that became the basis for several novels, a play, and a ballad in the southern style (*muyu shu*).[13] The incidents of the story occurred in 1728 or 1729 during the reign of Emperor Yongzheng.

Plot Summary

The story is about a feud between two cousins, Liang Tianlai and Ling Guixing, that results in the death of eight members of the Liang family. The Liangs and Lings used to be business partners, but after the death of the fathers, the sons decide to end the partnership. Ling Guixing chooses to become a scholar/official, and Liang Tianlai, not as well off, continues in business and becomes a sugar merchant.

Because of a setback in the examination, Ling Guixing consults a geomancer to find out what is causing him bad luck. The geomancer points to the Liang's stonecellar which he claims blocks the propitious flow of wind and water over the land (*feng-shui*). Therefore, the stonecellar must be removed.

Ling Guixing first tries to buy the property, but Liang Tianlai refuses to sell it. Desperate to improve his fortune, Ling Guixing, egged on by his uncle Ling Zongkong, hires thugs to dig up the Liangs' burial ground nearby, hoping to force the Liangs to move. But this also fails.

Next Ling Guixing and his uncle fabricate a deed that claims that Liang's father owes the Lings 3,000 ounces of silver. When Liang denies this, he is publicly beaten by Ling's hired hands. But Liang still refuses to sell his house.

These successive failures drive the Lings to try to kill Liang Tianlai and his brother. However, this plan is discovered by the beggar, Zhang Feng, who informs the two Liang brothers. The two brothers subsequently leave the house but leave behind the women, children, and servants, who hide in the stonecellar. When Ling Guixing and his gang break into the house and discover that the Liang brothers are gone, they set fire around the stonecellar and asphyxiate seven women and one unborn child.

When the Liang brothers return and discover the tragedy, Liang Tianlai, the elder brother, immediately brings his case to the district magistrate. But the magistrate, who has already been bribed by the Lings, dismisses the case. Then, the elder Liang appeals to the provincial judge, the prefectual magistrate, who also dismisses the case.

After having exhausted all the legal channels in the province, Liang Tianlai goes to Beijing to seek justice. Ling Guixing tries to stop him but fails. In his long search for justice Liang enlists the help of various stalwarts, such as Shi Zhibo, a retired legal clerk, Zhang Feng, the beggar, the monk Donglai, Donglai's friend and a high official Kong Dapeng, and the tea merchant Qu Ming. Also Heaven comes to the aid of Liang Tianlai when he is about to be discovered hiding in a tea chest. Just as the guard at the pass is about to plunge his sword into the chest to check its contents, there is a sudden peal of thunder, followed by severe wind and rain; rocks and stones fly through the air. As the guards flee for cover, the tea merchant hurries Liang Tianlai through.

Once in Beijing, Liang Tianlai finds Kong Dapeng again, the Govenor General who tried to help Liang earlier in the province but was called away. This time Kong completes the investigation and arrests Ling Guixing, his collaborators, and all the corrupt officials involved. The officials admit to having accepted bribes and are to be punished accordingly. Confronted with all the evidence, Ling Guixing finally confesses to the crime, and he is sentenced to be quartered and then beheaded. His property is to be confiscated, and the 40,000 ounces of silver of bribery money are to be used for famine and flood relief; Ling's collaborators are to be flogged and then released.

Characters

Compared to *Dou O, Liang Tianlai* has a relatively large cast of characters. Besides the two protagonists Liang Tianlai and Ling Guixing, there are the seven murdered women, four corrupt officials who dismiss Liang's case, and the upright Kong Dapeng who redresses the wrong. There are also four peripheral figures, Zhang Feng (the beggar), Shi Zhibo (the plaint writer), Donglai (the Buddhist monk), and Qu Ming (the tea merchant). These last four characters are of special interest because they are clearly subsidiary characters, and, yet, without them Liang Tianlai would not have been able to continue his search for justice. They each in their own way help Liang Tianlai at great risk to themselves even though they have no vested interest in him.

Liang Tianlai is a rather passive figure but kindhearted and a filial son to his widowed mother. Although he is a member of the merchant class and not a member of the educated elite, he is a man of great integrity, compassion, and kindness. He is incredulous when Zhang Feng informs him of Ling Guixing's plot to kill him and shows great compassion when he sees Zhang Feng tortured to death in court on his account. Liang Tianlai is the epitome of goodness and moral courage and is single-minded in his determination to avenge the eight murders committed against his family and the death of the innocent Zhang Feng.

Ling Guixing, on the other hand, is the archetypal villain. A new member of the gentry, he has not yet acquired the values of that class. He belongs to the unprincipled *nouveau riche*. The confrontation between him and Liang Tianlai also becomes a confrontation between the rich and poor, the "scholar" and the merchant. Ling Guixing says to Liang: "The poor do not oppose the rich, and the rich do not contend with the officials."[14] Furthermore, he completely disregards his kinship ties with Liang Tianlai, his first cousin. Family bonds are of no concern to him.

In the long process of his search for justice, however, Liang Tianlai changes from a person of great compassion to a bitter and hardened man. When Ling Guixing begs for forgiveness in the final scene of the play, Liang says, "My enmity is like the sea, my injustice is like the sea. My anguish I shall not forget even when I die....You have brought death to my house and dispersed my family. A debt of blood must be repaid with blood. With this anguish and hatred in my heart, how can you ask me to forgive you!"[15]

By far the most interesting characters in the drama are the four peripheral figures mentioned above. They really have no stake in the case, and, yet, they volunteer their help. Zhang Feng, the homeless beggar, at first thinks that he should just mind his own business. But on second thought he argues that if he does not help the Liang brothers, who will? Furthermore, the Liang brothers are good, and Ling Guixing is evil. "If I don't help the good, then I will have obliterated my Heaven-given conscience (*tian liang*)."[16] And once he has decided to help, he goes all the way. He becomes Liang Tianlai's only witness and is tortured to death. As he is about to die he tells Liang not to be disheartened on account of his death. Zhang Feng is guided in his conduct by his belief in a Heaven-given conscience.

Shi Zhibo is not just a retired law clerk but also a man of cultivation with a strong sense of righteousness. Liang Tianlai's case arouses his sense of indignation, and he is determined to help Liang fight the case to the end. He assumes personal responsibility for drawing up the plaints. When he dies before the case is won, he is deeply shamed. He is ashamed because his pen was not powerful enough to free Liang Tianlai; furthermore, his plaints brought about the death of an innocent man, Zhang Feng. Because of these failures, he feels that he can no longer face the world and has failed as a Confucian scholar.

Before his death Shi Zhibo advises Liang to seek his good friend, the Buddhist monk Donglai, for help. Donglai was a scholar and once took part in the state examinations before joining the priesthood. The monk helps Liang Tianlai meet Kong Dapeng, an incorruptible high official, who ultimately redresses Liang's wrong. Although he has already abandoned the mundane world for the priesthood, Donglai cannot help but be moved by Liang Tianlai's case. He even puts aside his sutras to help. Donglai is guided by the Buddhist's "merciful heart" (*cibeixin*). He says, "When a man of the cloth encounters gross injustice of this kind, how can his merciful heart not be moved?"[17] Again, later he says that "if this case should sink to the bottom of the ocean, even Buddha himself would weep."[18]

Liang Tianlai meets his fourth and final rescuer, Qu Ming the tea merchant, after he finds himself trapped on the border trying to leave Guangdong province. Qu Ming helps Liang out of the fearless sense of righteousness of an adventurer (*jianghu yiqi*).[19] He offers to hide Liang Tianlai in one of his tea chests and thus smuggles him out.

These four characters are from different walks of life and reflect different social values: the lowly beggar who acts because of his Heaven-given conscience, the other-worldly Buddhist monk who acts out of a Buddhist sense of mercy, the Confucian legal clerk who acts because of a Confucian sense of responsibility, and the tea merchant who acts out of the fearless righteousness of an adventurer. Yet they all share the sense of responsibility to redress wrongdoing.

We finally come to Kong Dapeng, the only incorruptible good official in the entire drama. He is the idealized Confucian official, a poet and scholar, upright and conscientious, and sensitive to popular opinion. It is through the popular rhymes of street children that he learns of the rampant corruption in the two provinces under his jurisdiction, Guangdong and Guangxi, and the case of the nine murders.

Canton City, Canton City
Good officials she has none.
The high officials demand gold and silver,

The lowly ones want cash.
While the rich have no fear of the law,
The case of the nine innocent lives
Sinks to the bottom of the sea.[20]

The fact that corruption is revealed through children's rhymes is significant because it is believed that since ancient times the playful verses of children often reflect the true condition of the state. These words, then, are not to be taken lightly. Kong immediately asks for more details of the case.

At the second meeting in Beijing, Kong Dapeng demonstrates his uprightness by refusing a large bribe from Ling Guixing. At first he pretends to accept the bribe in order not to upset the applecart and then summons Ling Guixing and all the officials involved to court and brings the case to a close.

Concept of Justice

Here again we have a clear case of the innocent suffering gross injustice. Since the actual victims have all died, Liang Tianlai becomes the surrogate victim who must seek revenge for the others. He makes four unsuccessful appeals on the local and provincial level; then with no alternative, he brings the case to Beijing. Because of the deep injustice, friends and total strangers offer Liang Tianlai their help. Also, the children's verses become an instrument of justice, and, finally, Heaven itself intervenes.

Several times, after having suffered greatly, Liang Tianlai looks askance at Heaven. He argues that if Heaven can let the treacherous go free and let the "deep injustice" (*chenyuan*) sink to the bottom of the ocean then "even if Heaven has eyes, these eyes must not have pupils."[21]

Before he departs for Beijing, after all his trials and tribulations, Liang Tianlai prays earnestly to Heaven and Earth to protect him on his journey, to help the virtuous and punish the evil. The final lines of his prayer read:

I beseech you Heaven, I beseech you Earth,
Do not let the evildoer go free.
If Heaven wishes man to do good,
Then he should help the virtuous and good
    and stop the evil.
Heaven, Heaven, Heaven!
Heaven, Heaven, Heaven!
O Heaven, please do not close your eyes again![22]

This time Heaven and Earth respond. When Liang's life is in grave danger, Heaven and Earth intervene with a sudden storm and save Liang's life so that he can complete his mission.

Here once more the underlying concept is that of an all-powerful Heaven that sees everything.

YANG NAIWU YU XIAOBAICAI

> My grudge is against the corrupt officials who gang together to further their power. There is only the force of the powerful and little justice; if you have money you can get away with anything.
>
> *Yang Naiwu*

Yang Naiwu is an early twentieth-century drama in 16 scenes.[23] The story, based on actual incidents, took place in the 1880s. It is a melodrama that makes a vicious attack on the corruption in Zhejiang province during the last years of the Qing Dynasty (1644-1911).

Plot Summary

Four years prior to her marriage, an attractive young woman named Bi Xiugu, nicknamed Xiaobaicai or "Little Cabbage" by her admirers, has an affair with Yang Naiwu, a promising young scholar and physician. After her marriage to Ge Xiaoda, who is an impecunious beancake maker, Xiaobaicai tries to turn over a new leaf and lead a straight life. Unfortunately, she catches the fancy of the wayward district magistrate's son Liu Zihe, who then seduces her by drugging her drink. Unsatisfied with only an affair, Liu Zihe poisons Ge Xiaoda and wants to take Xiaobaicai as his wife.

When the case of Ge Xiaoda's murder is brought to court and the district magistrate (Liu Xitong) learns that the accused is his one and only son, the only one who can continue the family line, he calls on his private secretary Qian Ruming to help save his son. Qian plots to throw the blame on Yang Naiwu. In scenes four and five, Xiaobaicai, who has also been persuaded to go along with the plot, accuses Yang Naiwu. Yang is imprisoned, stripped of his rank, and then beaten until he confesses to the charge of *moufu duofu* (murdering the husband in order to take the wife).

The next scene takes place two years later, but in the meantime Yang and Xiaobaicai have both been in prison, and Yang Naiwu has made dozens of appeals without success. His uncle and sister-in-law have also made appeals for him, but all end up in prison.

At this point in the story an imperial directive has come from Beijing ordering a reexamination of the case. This is brought about by a signed public petition (*lianming gongsu*) submitted by Yang Naiwu's classmates. But the official in charge of the reexamination, Governor Yang Changjun, and others realize that if the case is overturned on reexamination, then more than a hundred officials in Zhejiang province will be implicated. Conversely, it would not be wise for them to return the verdict unchanged. Therefore, they change the accusation from "murdering the husband to get the wife" to *tongjian mouming* (murdering and adultery) and persuade Xiaobaicai to agree with the charge.

After this turn of events Yang Naiwu's twin sister Yang Shuying steps in and appeals directly to the Board of Punishments in Beijing. To appeal to the Board of Punishments is not an easy matter, for the plaintiff must roll on a board of nails (*gundingban*) to indicate his earnestness. In scene 11, one of the highlights of the drama, Yang Shuying rolls on the board of nails and then takes her case to the Board.

In scene 13, a reexamination of the case takes place, but unknown to the presiding official, Sang Chunrong, even the underlings at the Board of Punishments have been bribed by the Liu family. Not having taken the proper precautions, the previous conviction is upheld. The officials all know that Yang Naiwu is innocent, but they need a confession from Xiaobaicai.

In scene 15 the three officials of the Board of Punishments make an ingenious plan to trick Xiaobaicai into telling the truth. They make plans for Yang Naiwu and Xiaobaicai to have their last dinner together before their execution. During this melodramatic meeting Xiaobaicai tells everything—all the times that she has been deceived, all the false statements that she has been forced to make, and she names all the real culprits. At this point, the officials step out of hiding and get the testimony. The case is then brought to a close, and just punishment is meted out to the parties involved.

Characters

Yang Naiwu comes from a poor scholarly family. Both his parents die early, so Yang Naiwu and his twin sister Yang Shuying must manage on their own. While Yang Naiwu is talented and succeeds in becoming a *juren* (a Second Degree holder), his sister must earn her living as an embroideress. Yang Naiwu is quick-witted, sharp-tongued, and good in argument. He has earned the nickname Yang Daobi (Yang the litigation instigator). However, an indiscretion during his student days—his affair with Xiaobaicai—brings him to ruin. But true to his name, "daobi," he is relentless in his tirades against corrupt officials and tireless in his search for justice throughout his trial. Even when he is forced to sign a confession under torture, he shows his rebellious spirit by writing a message in a cryptic script stating that he is innocent. In a second confession he writes the character *pin*, which is written with three "mouths" (*kou*), and he uses this to lash out at the three people who have brought about his fate: the presiding official, the pharmacist who testifies against him, and Xiaobaicai.

Xiaobaicai is an attractive but unfortunate young woman who believes that she is destined to a life of hardship. She has no family background to speak of. Xiaobaicai was raised by an adopted mother who married her off to the latter's own son when Xiaobaicai came of age. However, even before her marriage she has already had relations with Yang Naiwu. Then her relations with Liu Zihe after marriage bring her more serious trouble. She tries to lead a good life, but the long absences of her husband from home because of work make her vulnerable. At the end of the story she becomes a nun in a Buddhist monastery to atone for her sins.

Xiaobaicai is not at all a vicious person, but not having received any education, and lacking a good family upbringing, and possessing natural attractiveness, she becomes an easy prey to wayward young men, and she becomes an easy object of the ploys of officials and yamen clerks. Throughout the trial Xiaobaicai has meant well, but when the time comes for her to tell the truth, either through intimidation or deception she changes her testimony. When her errors are finally pointed out to her, she only blames herself for not being able to distinguish good from bad (*haohuai bufenbian*). Her basically benevolent nature is revealed as she leaves for the nunnery; her last worldly concern is that her half-witted sister-in-law will be taken care of.

Liu Zihe and his parents are members of the powerful local gentry. As soon as Liu Xitong hears about the murder committed by his son, he reproaches him, "You have been an official's son in vain; you have dared to trifle with the laws of the state. Man's life is linked to Heaven and not the plaything of a child. Now even my post as a district magistrate is endangered."[24] Liu Zihe is a wastrel, a ne'er-do-well, but as he is the only son, the family is willing to pay a high price to save his life. But this is merely a beginning; the amount soon escalates into the hundreds of thousands of ounces of silver. When the Imperial Commissioner Wang Xin goes to Zhejiang to investigate the case, the provincial officials try to buy him off with 300,000 ounces of silver. Governor Yang Changjun received 270,000 ounces in an earlier reexamination of the case. Hu Ruilan, the provincial director of education, also has been bribed. Furthermore, Yang Changjun and Hu Ruilan received special treatment because they are favorite disciples of powerful officials.

Lower down on the scale of rogues, there is Qian Ruming, Liu Xiton's legal secretary. The characters of his name, "qian ruming," mean literally "to regard money as dear as life." He is Liu's unscrupulous strategist who plans and executes all his moves and is totally without any sense of right or wrong.

Finally, there is the group of high-level officials at the board of Punishments who are caught between the lower corrupt provincial officials and the still higher officials in the Grand Council. Xia Tongshan, Vice-President of the Board of Punishments, Prince Chun, Wang Xin, and Sang Chunrong are members of this group. They have a strong sense of justice but need prodding to take action. Xia Tongshan must be reprimanded by his mother before making the effort. Quoted below is his mother's cross-examination. It illustrates a mother's role in the moral training of an official.

Mother:	Do you mean to say Yang Naiwu deserves to die?
Xia:	No, he has been framed by Liu Xitong. Liu is using this as a pretext for settling a personal grudge.
Mother:	Then Yang Naiwu has been wronged?
Xia:	Yes.
Mother:	Since he is wronged, then why are you not redressing the wrong?
Xia:	Well...
Mother:	Tell me, why are you not helping him?

Xia:	Your son does not have the ability.
Mother:	No ability? Do you remember what I have taught you at home? I wanted you to be an upright and incorruptible official. Have you forgotten?
Xia:	Mother, your son does not dare to forget your instruction.
Mother:	Since you have not forgotten, then why do you sit and do nothing when Yang Naiwu is going to die?
Xia:	Your child has thought long and hard about this matter.
Mother:	Ha, you are a senior official on the Board of Punishments. It is your duty to be loyal to the emperor and help the common people. Now as the case of Yang Naiwu sinks to the bottom of the sea and you are unable to do anything, how are you going to face your friends and relatives when you go home?
Xia:	Uh...uh
Mother:	All right! If you can't help Yang Naiwu, then you might as well forget about your work and go home.[25]

Embarrassed by his mother's reprimand, Xia Tongshan makes arrangements for Yang Shuying to appeal directly to the Board of Punishments. Then with the aid of other high officials on the Board, Sang Chunrong, Prince Chun, and Wang Xin, the case is brought to a successful conclusion.

Another minor character who plays an important role in the play is Yang Naiwu's twin sister Yang Shuying. Her unswerving loyalty to her brother and the fact that only her brother can continue the family line motivate her to risk her own life to make the appeal to the Board of Punishments.

Concept of Justice

Compared to the other two dramas, *Yang Naiwu* has no supernatural elements at all. It is a factual, detailed depiction, with few stereotyped characters. Indeed, one of the most interesting aspects of this play is that the characters are not unambiguously black and white. No character is perfect, and all are reduced to human size. Yang Naiwu is not a totally innocent young scholar who suffers all sorts of injustice, but he is, nevertheless, finally redeemed. Yang has a weakness for a pretty face and gets involved in an affair. He also has an acid tongue and is vicious in litigations. Xiaobaicai is not a wicked woman who wants to do Yang Naiwu in. She tries to be a good woman, but her natural attractiveness and weak character invite trouble, and her impecunious husband's frequent absences from home make her vulnerable. Xiaobaicai does not have the iron will of Dou O; nor is Yang Naiwu a selfless, kindhearted Liang Tianlai.

Under these circumstances reliance on Heaven as the overseer of justice is diminished in this drama. Since he does not have the moral purity of Dou O or Liang Tianlai, Yang Naiwu does not appeal to Heaven nor does he blame Heaven for his fate. First of all, he realizes that he has done something he shouldn't have:

"I regret that I ever had this affair with Xiaobaicai.... Now disaster has sprung up from these very roots, and I cannot bear to look back at the error I have committed in the past."[26] But in his moment of greatest desperation he calls on Xiao He (third century B.C.), the lawmaker under the first emperor of the Han Dynasty. Unable to sleep because of the beatings he has suffered, Yang Naiwu crawls over to the Hall of Xiao He, struggles to his feet, and sings:

> Prince Xiao, Prince Xiao! Xiao He, Xiao He!
> You made the laws that were promulgated throughout the land,
> For the purpose of punishing the evil and quelling the violent.
> But now the sword is used to behead the innocent,
> And the good are put in prison.
> My grudge is against the corrupt officials,
> Who gang together to further their power.
> There is only the force of the powerful and little justice,
> If you have money you can get away with anything.[27]

There is definitely a legalist conception of law and justice here as opposed to the distinctly Confucian interpretation in the two previous works. Instead of appealing to Heaven, Yang Naiwu appeals to Xiao He, the lawmaker. Instead of holding a grudge against Xiaobaicai or Liu Zihe, he is embittered against the corrupt officials who judge his case, Liu Xitong, Yang Changjun, and Hu Ruilan.

LAW, MORALITY, AND THE SUPERNATURAL

> When laws are just, Heaven's heart's in accord; with ethical purity comes an unblemished world. My brush exalts sons loyal and true, and my sword beheads the guilty. (*The Ghost of the Pot*)

The Chinese judicial system is extremely punitive. Chinese law, which is designed to enforce the precepts of Confucianism and which emphasizes the primacy of the Chinese family system, is especially severe in dealing with unfilial acts, acts that may result in the injury or death of parents or parents-in-law, even if accidental. Also, the courtroom procedures aim to extract confessions. The accused, the plaintiff, and even the witness may be beaten. As Prefect Tao Wu reprimands Dou O, expressing the official view toward the populace, "People are mean worms. If you don't beat them, they do not confess."[28]

For this and various other reasons, there has never been great respect for the law in Chinese society, only fear. The popular view is that law is unsympathetic, a necessary evil to maintain order and not an instrument for the protection of the individual. Historically, Chinese law did not come into being as a result of divine action. It had no divine origin, as contrasted with the law of Hammurabi, Moses, or the Greeks in the West, all of which were given by the gods, or God. It is believed that Chinese law came to be written down in the sixth century B.C. as the result of the moral decline of society.[29]

Specifically with regard to the taking of a human life, a Chinese proverb said it all: "As the debtor pays his debt, so a murderer pays with his life." Not only was the taking of human life a serious matter, even the conferring of the death penalty by the judge needed confirmation by the Board of Punishments and, in some cases, the emperor himself.[30] High regard for human life is expressed by some of the characters in the dramas in this way. For instance, the apothecary Dr. Lu says, after his attempt to kill Granny Cai fails, "Now I know that human life is tied to Heaven and Earth. How can one treat it like mere dust on the wall?" Liang Tianlai never expects that his cousin Ling Guixing will resort to murder to achieve his aim since his cousin is from a rich and cultivated family and must realize that the law of the state requires that "a life taken must be replaced with another." And Liu Xitong sternly reprimands his son, "You dared to trifle with the law of the state. Man's life is linked to Heaven. It is not a child's game." But the motivations for the crime outweigh the moral injunctions. For Donkey Zhang and Liu Zihe it is desire and lust for a woman; for Ling Guixing it is a feud over family property.

In the eyes of the villains money is all-powerful; with money they can "get away with anything." Expressions such as *"zhi yao you qian, wanshi wushang"* (If you have money, there will be no harm.) or *"you qian keyi tong tianxia"* (With money you can do anything) convey this general sentiment.[31] The villains are irredeemable; they experience no sense of shame. And from the point of view of the villains, the officials, from legal clerks, magistrates, prefects up to the governors and governor generals, are all corruptible. The villains have full confidence that the whole legal-cum-administrative system can be circumvented with gold and silver.

However, as cases reach higher and higher levels, the villains also find that the price increases and that influence is more difficult to obtain. Once cases get beyond the province to the capital, villains find themselves in trouble. Thus, the Board of Punishments and, ultimately, the emperor himself at the capital, in the eyes of the villains, become symbols of righteousness and incorruptibility. And, conversely, for the innocent victims, the capital is their bastion of justice and righteousness.

Shame Ethics

In the three dramas that we have examined, the concept of shame does not appear very frequently. The villains seldom express a sense of shame, or regret. They only fear the prospect of pain or punishment. In fact, their behavior is marked by a blatant lack of shame.

Dou O is the only protagonist who speaks of shame with any degree of frequency and that is to reprimand her mother-in-law for wishing to remarry. Dou O tells her that trying to remarry at 60 "... you make people split their mouths with laughter";[32] or "Won't that make people talk;"[33] when her mother-in-law keeps Donkey Zhang and Old Zhang in her own house; or on her own refusal to marry, "It is not that I am contrary; only I fear what others may say."[34]

Liang Tianlai feels that he would not be able to face up to (*nandui*) Zhang Feng, who dies for him as a witness. The legal clerk Shi Zhibo, as a Confucian scholar, feels shame (*cankui*) when his plaints do not help Liang Tianlai at the hearing and cause Zhang Feng to be killed in the process.

In *Yang Naiwu*, Xia Tongshan, the Vice-President of the Board of Punishments is shamed by his mother when he claims that he cannot help Yang Naiwu.

In all these cases the feeling of shame is associated with the behavior of the educated elite or the ethos of that group. As pointed out by Wolfram Eberhard, the idea of shame came into play only when members of the upper classes performed acts that were "contrary to the behavior expected of a person of high social status or rank."[35] The sense of shame, frequently referred to as "loss of face," involved a violation of codes of conduct of a class that not only affected the individual but were a reflection on his class as a whole. This sense of shame in Chinese society is like the loss of honor "in the aristocratic societies of the Near East, Central Asia, and Old Europe"; it is the idea of "noblesse oblige."[36] The Confucian gentleman feels the sense of shame when he believes that he has not been able to live up to the obligations of his class, as in the case of Shi Zhibo, Dou O, and Xia Tongshan. The other characters in the plays do not exhibit these sentiments.

In Chinese society the sense of shame far from being "an effective impediment to moral maturity"[37] is, in fact, an indication of morally "mature" behavior, as shown in these three dramas. Indeed, to be without a sense of shame would be the height of immorality, whether mature or not.

The idea of shame ethics and its effects on behavior have been a topic of interest for some time. In this volume Richard W. Wilson has once more raised this question under the guise of the cognitive/developmental theory of moral development. I do not wish to comment much on the theory here except to say that the assumptions underlying the theory need closer examination, and it should be noted that as an individual moves "higher" up on the hierarchical scale of moral development his behavior does not necessarily become better. As Mancuso and Sarbin put it, "while we might yearn to see a society of persons who understand rules within a morality of reciprocity, the fact that this kind of morality develops later in the course of psychological growth does not show that once we have achieved it, we are farther along the road to 'ultimate goodness.'"[38]

The Supernatural and the Moral Order

When justice cannot be obtained within the existing legal system, the victims of injustice appeal to *tianli* (principles of Heaven, or the Heavenly order), *gongli* (generally accepted principles), *zhengyi* (righteousness), *zhengfa* (following the laws), *guofa* (laws of the state), *wangfa* (kingly laws), or *xingming* (the fitting of punishment to the crime). We see that the appeals extend from the supernatural, to ethical principles, and to punishments. Although in Chinese law (*lüli*) itself there is no specific reference to supernatural phenomena such as ghosts, spirits, gods, ordeals, curses, or intervention by Heaven and Earth in the functional operation of the administration of justice and in maintaining the social order, supernatural phenomena do play an important role. In Chinese society, as in many other societies, the supernatural is employed as a means of encouraging desired forms of behavior and deterring undesired forms. Also, since the administration of justice can never be perfect in practice, the belief in the supernatural provides the victims of injustice with a last appeal to vent their anguish and relieve their tensions.

Up to this point we have not discussed Chinese religion and its relationship to law and morality. But frequent mention of the supernatural in the dramas makes it necessary for us to take a look at religion in Chinese society. In Chinese society *tian* or Heaven is not considered a totally separate and distinct entity apart from the human world and possessing its own set of transcendental laws. *Tian* is closely associated with man and society. Heaven upholds and gives supernatural sanction to the existing moral order; it does not impose on society an order of its own. But neither is Heaven "mute and silent"; there is an interaction between Heaven and man. Heaven expresses its approval of good and disapproval of evil by bringing about extraordinary phenomena such as droughts, floods, storms, and eclipses.[39] The Chinese religiosity is one of immanence rather than transcendence. Therefore the "li" of *tianli* or *gongli* is not a transcendental law or an abstract principle of the Neo-Confucian type, but more like a natural order. The term *tianli* appears in such early texts as the *Shiji* (*Records of the Grand Historian*), *Hanshu* (*History of the Han Dynasty*), and the *Zhuangzi* (*The Writings of Zhuangzi*) before the writings of the Neo-Confucian philosophers of the Sung Dynasty (960-1279).[40] Unfortunately, it is not possible to discuss further the use of the term here.

Heaven not only gives supernatural sanction to the existing order, but it is also believed that an evildoer's actions, even if not exposed in public, cannot escape the "eyes of Heaven." Moreover, not only does Heaven "see" but it also responds. This is reflected in Dou O's statement to her executioner: "You say that Heaven cannot be counted on/ It has no sympathy for the human heart/ You don't know Heaven *does* answer man's prayer."[41] This belief in a fair and just Heaven by the common man is one of the major rationales that legitimize the Chinese legal system with all its imperfections. As the *Administrative Statutes of the Qing Dynasty* (*Da Qing huidian*) states "The mind should embrace *tianli* and *renqing* (human sentiments). If the mind dwells within these principles and sentiments, then he will not be entrapped by laws and regulations."[42]

On the other hand, the place of supernatural forces should not be overemphasized. Even if Heaven knows who the evildoer is and demonstrates to the public through extraordinary phenomena that an injustice has occurred, redress of the wrong must still be demonstrated in court. As Dou O says, "not appealing to the court, only appealing to Heaven, the wronged-feeling in my heart is difficult to express."[43] She must have her name cleared in court. Therefore, during the retrial of her case, Dou O's spirit is called forward to make the charge against Donkey Zhang; she even beats him to vent her anger. As her name is cleared and the true criminal punished, her *yuanhun* (wronged spirit) is appeased and departs. Finally, it should not be ruled out that the appeal to Heaven may also be an emotional outburst, a cry for an intuitive sense of justice, or poetic justice. These characters are afterall not actual types, but literary projections.

From these three dramas, it appears that the deaths of the actual victims of the crimes (poisonings and a burning) do not draw any response from Heaven, but the miscarriages of justice will "startle Heaven and move Earth." It is not known from our sample whether a dastardly crime in itself will cause a response from Heaven if the evildoer goes unpunished. In any event, the concern of these dramas and their focal point is the vindication of the innocent victims of the miscarriages of justice.

These dramas have also shown that law, morality, and the supernatural are closely intertwined, mutually supportive, and complementary. The ethical concepts of Confucianism form the basis of the moral system, laws and regulations are the instruments for enforcing these moral precepts, and supernatural forces provide an overall structure that sanctions the existing moral system. The following speech that a magistrate delivers on the occasion of the annual sacrifice to the spirits illustrates most clearly this mutually supportive and complementary relationship among law, morality, and the supernatural. Note here that an intermediary agent, the God of the City, has been introduced, and the prefecture has become a microcosm of the larger universe.

> All the people within the territory of my prefecture who are obstinate and unfilial to their parents, who are disrespectful to their relatives ... will be reported by the spirits to the God of the City, thus causing their crimes to be disclosed and punished by the government ... If their crimes are not disclosed, they will receive supernatural punishment.
>
> Those good and upright persons who are filial to their parents, who are in harmony with their relatives ... will be reported by the spirits to the God of the City and will be protected and blessed secretly ....
>
> We, all the officials in the prefecture, who deceive the court, who are unfair to the good people, who are greedy for money and practice fraud ... the spirits will not be partial to us and will exact retribution in the same amount.[44]

This passage indicates that the evildoer, the good, and the officials will all be watched over by the spirits and treated accordingly.

CONCLUSION

This essay has examined the relationship between law and morality in Chinese society as revealed in three Chinese dramas that are characterized by a persistent search for justice. In the process we have seen that supernatural forces play an important part in the functional administration of justice; that moral norms vary in accordance with social standing; that the idea of shame or "loss of face" does not arise frequently and, when it does occur, is associated with the behavior of the educated elite; that the concepts of justice and morality exists primarily as this-worldly and human, although reinforced by popular religious ideas. The power and appeal of these dramas are focused on the victims of the miscarriage of justice rather than the victims of the crimes themselves.

These miscarriages of justices do not seem to undermine the moral and legal system; the people continue to have faith and confidence in the system and their goal is to seek "imperial justice" (*guofa* or *wangfa*) within the system. This imperial justice is more readily found in the capital than in the outlying regions of the empire. But imperial justice is carried to the outer regions by emissaries from the capital in the person of the Imperial Commissioner.

The traditional administrative-cum-legal system in China seems to be legitimized by the belief in a benevolent Heaven that gives supernatural support to the existing system. Even though crimes and injustices may not always be exposed by the officials, they do not escape the notice of Heaven. Heaven can always to called upon to make the final judgment and will indicate its approval or disapproval with extraordinary phenomena. We might conclude that while a crime is an offense against society, a miscarriage of justice is a crime against the "cosmic order."

NOTES

1.   Shuzo Shiga, "Some Remarks on the Judicial System in China: Historical Development and Characteristics," in *Traditional and Modern Legal Institutions in Asia and Africa,* ed. David C. Buxbaum (Leiden: E.J. Brill, 1967), p. 47.

2.   Sir Chaloner Alabaster, *Notes and Commentaries on Chinese Criminal Law* (London, 1899). Quoted in Robert van Gulik, translator, *Celebrated Cases of Judge Dee* (New York: Dover, 1976), p. xix.

3.   For the Chinese edition, see Guan Hanqing, *Dou O yuan* (Hong Kong: Shanghai shuju, 1967), with annotations and two analytical essays. There are several English translations of the play. The most authoritative is Shi Chung-wen's translation, *Injustice to Tou O* (Cambridge: Cambridge University Press, 1972). Another translation consulted is Liu Jung-en's translation *Injustice Done to Tou Ngo,* in his *Six Yüan Plays* (Baltimore, Md.: Penguin Books, 1972), pp. 115-158.

4. The most recent versions of these dramas, the ones used in this study, are contained in the 13-volume collection of Chinese drama entitled *Zhongguo difong xiqu jicheng* (A Collection of Chinese Regional Dramas) (Beijing: Zhongguo xiju chubanshe, 1958–1964). For *Liang Tianlai*, see the volume on Guangdong province (*Guangdongsheng juan*), vol. 1, pp. 95–152. For *Yang Naiwu yu Xiaobaicai*, see the volume on Shanghai (*Shanghaishi juan*), pp. 39–138. Other versions will be discussed later.

5. Ching-hsi Perng, *Double Jeopardy: A Critique of Seven Yüan Courtroom Dramas* (Ann Arbor: Center for Chinese Studies, University of Michigan, 1979), p. 1.

6. Chung-wen Shih, *The Golden Age of Chinese Drama: Yuan Tsa-chü* (Princeton, N.J.: Princeton University Press, 1976), p. 210. This brief characterization of Guan's life is also based on Shih.

7. Shih, *Injustice to Tou O* (Cambridge: Cambridge University Press, 1972), pp. 99, 101.

8. Liu, *Six Yüan Plays*, p. 129.

9. Ibid., p. 135.

10. Ibid., p. 149.

11. Ibid., p. 151.

12. For a discussion of this general problem, see Hsü Daulin, "Crime and Cosmic Order," *Harvard Journal of Asiatic Studies* 30(1970): 111–125.

13. Aside from the play there is a novel by the late Qing writer Wu Wo-yao (1867–1910), *Jiuming qiyuan* (The Strange Case of the Nine Murders) (Taibei: Shijie shuju, 1968 reprint), which is based on an earlier story called *Jingfu xinshu* (A New Book to Warn the Rich). There is also a southern-style ballad text (*muyushu*) entitled *Liang Tianlai gao yuzhuang* (Liang Tianlai Brings a Case to the Emperor) (Hong Kong: Wu Guitang, n.d.).

14. *Liang Tianlai*, in *Complete Dramas*, p. 135.

15. Ibid., pp. 151–152.

16. Ibid., p. 102.

17. Ibid., p. 125.

18. Ibid., p. 126.

19. Ibid., p. 143.

20. Ibid., pp. 127–128.

21. Ibid., p. 135.

22. Ibid., p. 139.

23. Soon after the incident took place, there appeared a ballad of the coastal Yangzi River region, called a *tanci*, which described the event. This became the basis for a novel called *Yang Naiwu yu Xiaobaicai* by Jiang Xiaodie (Hong Kong: Shanghai yinshu guan, 1952). This case is also written up in *Qingbei leichao* (Minor Cases of the Qing Dynasty) (Taibei: Shangwu yinshuguan, 1966 reprint), pp. 227–229.

24. *Yang Naiwu*, in *Complete Dramas*, p. 58.

25. Ibid., pp. 100–101.

26. Ibid., p. 95.

27. Ibid., p. 94.

28. Shih, *Injustice*, pp. 175, 177.

29.   For a general discussion, see Ch'u T'ung-tsu, *Law and Society in Traditional China* (Paris: Mouton, 1961), p. 207; and Derk Bodde and Clarence Morris, *Law in Imperial China* (Cambridge, Mass.: Harvard University Press, 1967), p. 49.

30.   Bodde and Morris, *Law in Imperial China*, pp. 131–134.

31.   *Yang Naiwu*, in *Complete Dramas*, p. 94 and *Liang Tianlai*, in *Complete Dramas*, p. 137, respectively.

32.   Shih, *Injustice*, p. 95.

33.   Ibid., pp. 131, 133.

34.   Ibid., p. 151.

35.   Wolfram Eberhard, *Guilt and Sin in Traditional China* (Berkeley: University of California Press, 1967), pp. 122–123.

36.   Ibid., pp. 123–124.

37.   Thomas Lickona, "Critical Issues in the Study of Moral Development and Behavior" in *Moral Development and Behavior*, ed. Thomas Lickona (New York: Holt, Rinehart and Winston, 1976), p. 20; quoted in Richard W. Wilson, "Moral Behavior in Chinese Society: A Theoretical Perspective," p. 54.

38.   James C. Mancuso and Theodore R. Sarbin, "A Paradigmatic Analysis of Psychological Issues at the Interface of Jurisprudence and Moral Conduct" in Lickona, op. cit., p. 333.

39.   C.K. Yang, *Religion in Chinese Society* (Berkeley: University of California Press, 1961), pp. 278–93. In Chapter XI Yang gives an excellent discussion of the relation between Chinese religion and the moral order.

40.   *Zhongwendacidian* (Dictionary of Chinese Words and Phrases) (Taibei: Zhongguowenhua yanjiusuo, 1963), Vol. 8, p. 316.

41.   Shih, *Injustice*, p. 219.

42.   *Zhongwendacidian*, vol. 8, p. 316.

43.   Shih, *Injustice*, p. 273.

44.   Ch'u *Law and Society*, p. 211.

6 RADICAL IDEOLOGY AND CHINESE POLITICAL CULTURE: AN ANALYSIS OF THE REVOLUTIONARY YANGBANXI

Lowell Dittmer

I had not been particularly looking forward to this ballet, but after a few minutes I was impressed by its dazzling technical and theatrical virtuosity. Chiang Ch'ing had been undeniably successful in her attempt to create a consciously propagandistic theatre piece that would both entertain and inspire its audience.

—Richard Nixon[1]

Though often included among the limited available sources with something to say about Chinese political life, literary materials have in fact rarely been systematically utilized by political scientists.[2] Merle Goldman's work is to some extent an exception to this rule, but her primary interest has been in the political impact upon the literary scene, regarding the latter as a dependent variable; even when literary figures have a direct impact on politics by publishing such Aesopian commentaries as the *Hai Jui* plays or Three-family Village series, she tends to consider them only as spokesmen for more powerful political forces.[3] Perhaps the principal reason for the neglect of literature as a political resource base is its ambiguity. No one would deny that literature can reveal a great deal about the fantasy life, values, and everyday life of its author, audience, or subject matter, but the difficulty has been in deciding what is fact, fantasy, or value and whether it relates to the author, audience, or subject matter—this is the stuff of which critical wars are waged. Thus, most social scientists have opted to focus on more straightforward accounts of political and social life, such as Chinese media reportage or refugee accounts, even though these too are unevenly informative and sometimes quite misleading.

Yet, I wish to argue here that this neglect should no longer be tolerated. The reason has to do with the crucial importance of the cultural realm in the unfolding of the socialist revolutionary process. All successful socialist revolutions seem to go through a more or less determinate sequence of developmental stages, beginning with an early emphasis on cutting all ties with preexisting elites and political structures (the "revolutionary breakthrough"), proceeding through the transformation of ownership relationships and the consolidation of a "proletarian dictatorship" as functional substitute for the old ruling class ("socialization of the means of production"), and culminating in an attempt to transform culture and thereby also change human nature.[4] Socialist redefinition of rights of citizenship and participation during early stages in the construction of a class dictatorship help to ensure that the cultural sphere will displace an increasingly nominal electoral politics during this third stage and emerge as a significant new political arena. Writers and artists come to function as a key link between political elites and the broader population. But the evolution of cultural policy in the Soviet and East European socialist states indicates that the intellectuals are by no means fully reliable intermediaries for the Party leadership. Nor could they really be expected to be: their function requires that they reintroduce the social totality—the needs, sentiments, and demands of the larger population—into the rather abstract ideological tenets of the elites in order to create at least an entertaining and perhaps even an aesthetically stimulating work of art. Some conflict between ideological orthodoxy and artistic integrity seems almost inevitable.

The Chinese have long prided themselves on their culture, usually identifying themselves by common cultural attributes rather than by ethnic stereotype or geographic boundaries. So it was perhaps to be expected that the cultural dimension of the Chinese revolution would be even more focal that in other socialist revolutions. And so it has been, from the May fourteenth movement through the Cultural Revolution to the April fifth "movement" that ensued from the Tiananmen Incident. Certainly during the ten-year period from 1966 to 1976 it was a central concern (and indeed a very divisive one) in Chinese politics, and although one might expect it to recede in importance with the recent emphasis on the "four modernizations," the rapprochement with the West seems to have brought its own "cultural revolution" in train, and it seems likely that culture will remain politicized for the foreseeable future. However that may be, in order to understand radical politics during its heyday it is absolutely essential to understand the work on which its practitioners lavished their attentions. Certainly the centerpiece of the radical opus was the "ten great revolutionary productions" that were revised or created during this decade under their immediate supervision: the Beijing Operas *Hong Deng Ji* (*Red Lantern*), *Shajiabang* (Shajiabang is a place name in eastern China), *Hai Gang* (*On the Docks*), *Long Jiang Song* (*Song of the Dragon River*), *Ping Yuan Zuo Zhan* (*Fighting on the Plain*), *Dujuan Shan* (*Azalea Mountain*), *Zhichu Weihushan* (*Taking Tiger Mountain by Strategy*), *Qixi Baihutuan* (*Raid on White Tiger Regiment*), and *Panshi Wan* (*Boulder Bay*); and the revolutionary ballet *Hongsi Niangzi Zhun* (*Red Detachment of Women*).

The radicals set great store in these works: based on the idealism implicit in late Maoist thought, they believed that they could change human nature by revolutionizing the "cultural superstructure": Because your thoughts were scattered (*sanle*), your wheat was also scattered," the proletarian hero in one of the dramas admonishes a derelict stevedore. "Because your ideas had gone wrong (*cuole*), your sack went wrong, too."[5] The "revolutionary model theatrical works" (*yangbanxi*) were almost universally performed, and indeed it would probably be impossible to find a Chinese who lived through this period without seeing these dramas at least once. They have by and large escaped the attentions of students of Chinese literature due to their rather modest aesthetic attainments,[6] yet, in the analysis of popular culture the most useful texts have proven not to be those of highest artistic quality but those that have most thoroughly penetrated the popular psyche.[7] And despite evidence of some boredom upon seeing the same productions again and again, there seems little doubt that the Chinese masses were quite profoundly moved by these stories at the time, singing songs from the librettos and incorporating certain characters and episodes in their everyday vernacular. The peasant audiences became so emotionally involved in the performances, according to Lois Wheeler Snow, that although on the whole they were quite hospitable to the travelling drama troupes who performed them they could not suffer the actors who played the villains: "Sometimes the peasants don't even want to feed them."[8]

The "method" I employ to analyze these scores partakes of certain elements of phenomenology, structuralism, and the sociology of knowledge. It is phenomenological in the sense that I attempt to bracket my own point of view and recover as faithfully as possible the meaning/contexts of the characters involved, which entails *inter alia* the copious use of direct quotations. It is structural in the sense that meanings thus extracted from all ten of the plays are then arrayed and examined with respect to their logical and analogical relationships to one another without respect for their order to the original time sequence. The sociology of knowledge aspect lies in the attempt to relate these intrinsic and imputed patterns of meaning to the political culture of the millions of Chinese who enjoyed them. In the first portion of the paper I look at the structure of role relationships, in the second at themes and plots, in the third at internal contradictions and dilemmas.

ROLES AND RELATIONSHIPS

The role structure of these plays was extremely simple, and the impact of the drama reform of the early 1960s was to simplify it still more drastically. These are morality plays, and the roles can most easily be grouped according to their moral status: there are good characters and bad characters, and any deviation from these positions is unstable and transitional. Unlike the somewhat more complex CCP conception of the international system (according to which there are "three worlds") the role structure in these plays is one of Manichaean dualism.

The most salient virtues of the positive characters are those of martial heroism. The heroic proletariat are oppressed and exploited but inherently stronger than their oppressors; in fact, like Antaeas, abasement makes them stronger. Their underdog position justifies retribution, while their inherent strength ensures that they will ultimately prevail. Though technologically inferior (members of CCP-affiliated guerrilla bands are typically shown attacking the enemy with red-tassled spears, tridents, swords, nets, etc.), the heroes of the proletariat are dauntless and indomitable. "Now is the time to prove our worth to the Party," announces Hong Changqing of *Red Detachment of Women* after they have run out of ammunition. "When our bullets are gone, we'll still have our swords and rocks. We must defend the position with our blood and lives!"[9] Because the hero strives mightily but must fail most of the time (this is part of what it means to be "oppressed"), heroism is defined less by an efficacious outcome than by valiant efforts. Such is the valor of the heroic character that he (or she) is often moved to make gestures of defiant resistance from a position that would have to be considered untenable from any "realistic" perspective (i.e., realistic in terms of offering any prospect to inflict damage on the enemy). Captives, such as *Red Lantern's* Li Yuhe, are given to grand but futile gestures:

> Though heavy chains shackle me hand and foot, they cannot fetter my spirit that storms the heaven [*suobuju wo xiongxin zhuangzhichong yun tian*]. My bones are broken, my flesh is torn, but my will is firmer than ever....Brought up by the Party to be a man of steel, I fight the foe and never give ground. I am not afraid to have every bone in my body broken. I'm not afraid to be locked up until I wear through the floor of my cell.[10]

And *Tiger Mountain's* Li Yongqi is so enflamed by the sight of the enemy that he essays a single-handed attack on several fully-armed soldiers in his parlor: "What do I fear? I can fight it out with them with this," he cries, stabbing a dagger into the table.[11]

Balancing the martial virtues of courage and valor are the more benign qualities of love for fellow members of the proletariat. Class love is the inverse corollary of class hatred, and the two are mutually reinforcing. The metaphor most frequently used to represent the relationship among members of the proletariat is the *extended family*. "Auntie, your love for us is like a mother's," as the grateful Zhao puts it in *Fighting on the Plain*. "You have given yourself heart and soul to the Resistance [*wei kangzhan xianchule huolie di xinchang*] ; each grain of maize in our rations was raised with sweat, our homespun uniforms were woven with love."[12] In *Red Lantern*, young Tiemei is taught to refer to her father's Party contacts as "uncles": "I've more uncles than I can count; they only come when there's important business. Though we call them relatives, we never met before, yet they are closer to us than our own relative....They're all like my dad, men with red, loyal hearts [*hongliang dixin*] ."[13] "Family members" typically include a "granny," who functions to express nurturance and the affective aspects of motivation to good behavior, a devoted and usually selfless spouse, and a pubescent child, symbolizing hope for the postrevolutionary future.

What binds the new revolutionary extended family together and provides a basis for the recruitment of new members is a sense of *shared deprivation*. The efficacy of shared grief in binding primary group members together is nowhere more graphically dramatized than in *Red Lantern*, in which Tiemei discovers halfway through that those whom she had taken to be her father and grandmother were "not of the same family." When Tiemei's true father and Granny Li's husband were both killed in a strike against Wu Peifu in the 1923 Beijing-Hangzhou Railway strike, the noble Li Yongqi announced: "Auntie, from now on I am your son and this child is your own granddaughter."[14]

The proletariat resembles a family not only with respect to its communal solidarity, but with regard to its internal organization. There is no collective heroization of the "masses" as in Hauptmann's *The Weavers* and some other early twentieth century leftist dramas, but a clear chain of command and hierarchy of excellence. At the pinnacle of this hierarchy is a "primary hero," who is to command the limelight as a model of revolutionary virtue. Not only are heroes to be given more attention than villains (thereby reversing the emphasis of traditional Beijing Opera), but the primary hero is to be given "a heroic image towering above the ordinary positive characters."

> We must follow the principle of giving prominence to the principal hero by using negative characters as a foil, by setting off the principal hero with other positive characters, and by a judicious use of environment and atmosphere.[15]

Thus, the role of Yang Zerong, primary hero of *Taking Tiger Mountain*, is highlighted by the use of light, music, scenery, and costumes:

> In the original script before Yang Zerong went into the mountains, whenever the commander and fighters of the pursuit detachment appeared, the stage was invariably decorated with drooping branches and twisted tree trunks, which created a bleak and melancholy atmosphere utterly out of tune with the vigor, heroic spirit and fighting mood of Yang Zerong and his comrades-in-arms. The stage setting we see now is complete different.... A forest of giant cloud-touching pines pierced by shafts of sunlight and echoing with resounding songs expressively and vigorously reflect the dashing and firm, staunch and fearless, heroic personality of Yang Zerong.... Yang Zerong now stands upright like a green pine in the snow on a majestic and precipitous mountain-top against a background of undalating hills and bright blue clouds and there rolls out that magnificent aria. When he reaches the line, "standing in the bitter cold and melting the ice and snow, I have the morning sun in my heart," the sun-rays burst through the multicolored clouds like a thousand spears and crimson the towering peaks.[16]

The supporting characters—spouse, children, aunts, grandparents (usually fe-male)—are organizationally subordinate and morally inferior in some respect, thereby serving to "set off" the primary hero. Although the relationship among all positive characters is one of solidarity and mutual aid, when sacrifice is called for (as it quite frequently is in these plots), it is usually rendered *by those lower on the moral hierarchy on behalf of those above them.* Thus Li Yongqi of *Taking Tiger Mountain* leaps forward to shield Party representative Ko Xiang and gets shot in the arm. In *Fighting on the Plain*, Auntie Zhang covers Li with her body and is shot dead. Thus, the pattern of sacrifice generally follows the chain of command and the hierarchy of moral excellence, providing ample grounds for moral indignation but still leaving those figures integral to the plot structure in-tact. If morally significant figures are sacrificed, this usually comes late in the plot and acquires central symbolic significance.

Villainous characters in the *yangbanxi* are portrayed as being "pitch black without a trace of light" ' in accord with the customs of Beijing Opera, their vil-lainy is indicated by their costumes and makeup, their faces usually being painted a greenish-yellow hue. The "essence of the class enemy," we are told, is "cruel-ty, trickery, foolishness and decadence." They seem to commit their outrages as a natural expression of their self-indulgent and sadistic personalities rather than as a part of some overall strategy, and their misdeeds are thus often counter-productive from any but the most short-term perspective. The villains engage in immoral behavior not on behalf of opposing principles, but simply in pursuit of immediate pleasure. The villains eat and drink to excess (e.g., the Vulture spon-sors banquets where he and his men can "eat and drink our fill. Get good and drunk [*yi zui fang xiu*] .") while positive characters endure deprivation.[17] Inflict-ing gratuitous pain or death seems to be immensely enjoyable to the villains. Listening to praise is a pleasure that they indulge to excess as well, exhibiting a naive optimism about the future and an equally naive trust in flattering strangers (who often turn out to be Communist spies).

Although their values and personalities, thus, represent the antithesis of Communist heroism, in certain respects the villains *resemble* the positive char-acters. The internal organization of the enemy is also hierarchical, with a primary villain and a staff of supporting characters, but usually lacking a broader retinue ("masses"). The enemy group also comprises a cohesive bloc; appearances to the contrary notwithstanding, the Kuomintang, the Japanese, the Americans, and domestic bandits are all shown to be in intimate collusion. Their organization as-pires to the same internal solidarity as that of the positive characters, also rein-forced by fictive kinship ties. But closer scrutiny reveals that the pattern of sacri-fice does not always follow the chain of command as it does among positive characters, but seems often to be reversed. Thus, the captured platoon leader in *Raid on White Tiger Regiment* immediately confesses all in hopes of clemency; Ding of *Boulder Bay* in the end betrays Hai to save his skin. These plots teem with instances in which lesser villains, rather than sacrificing themselves to save their superiors, betray their superiors to save themselves. The reason for this pattern of treachery seems to be that the negative characters are motivated not by an ideology but by greed and ambition, so that whenever the pleasure/pain calculus shifts against their own leadership they can be induced to desert.

The emotional relationship between the two sides in these plays is not one of tolerance (in fact, tolerance is a minor crime), but one of bitter, relentless hatred. *Red Lantern's* Tiemei reaches evocative heights in this aria:

> Repressing my rage I grind my teeth [*qiangren chouhen yaosui ya*] ....
> Biting my hate, chewing my rage, I force them down my throat [*jiaosui chouhen qiang yan xia*], let them sprout in my heart. I'll never yield, I'll never retreat, no tears shall wet my cheeks, let them flow into my heart to nourish the bursting seeds to hatred. Flames of rage, ten leagues high, will burn away this reign of the forces of darkness.[18]

This hatred for the enemy seems at root to be animated by a desire to reciprocate previous deprivations, i.e., vengeance, *lex talionis*. Inasmuch as the function of catastrophic loss and injury is to justify vengeance, it recurs rather frequently. Qinghua, of *Red Detachment*, lost both parents and is cruelly oppressed by the local landlord. Han Xiaojiang, the wayward young stevedore in *On the Docks*, lost his father to a "dog of a foreman."

The initial reaction to such traumatic loss is sorrow, but the soul's chemistry can transform sorrow into potent rage. Thus the music in the *Yellow River* piano concerto was revised to express "indignation": "when sorrow is transformed into strength, then it expressed itself in the form of indignation, which means resistance and struggle."[19] Among Li Yongqi's last words before proceeding to his martyrdom are: "My only regret if I die today is the 'account' I have not settled [*zhi shi nemman "zhangmu" weihai chi ti xin bu an*]."[20] Indeed, the memory of suffering is so central to the new meaning in life that the revolutionary has found that he or she is apt to cherish the memory, even using various memonic devices to refresh it. In *On the Docks* the carrying pole used by pre-Liberation dockers as a work tool and occasional weapon is endowed with such sacred significance that when young Han says "making a living with a carrying pole is not good," his elders are indignant. Ma: "He even wants to give up the carrying pole—our precious heirloom [*chuanjiabao*]!" Fang: "This pole was with us in our times of trial, our weapon it was in our hundred years' struggle. Then the Party awakened the toilers' rage, united we broke the shackles on our hands and feet."[21] The need to conserve the bitter memories of erstwhile injury is also expressed in song (an aria by Granny, in *Red Lantern*):

> Remember this debt of blood and tears,
> Be brave and determined to settle accounts with the enemy
>   [*ho diren suan zizhang*],
> A debt of blood must be paid with blood.[22]

Thus Zhao informs collaborator Sun Choucai (*Fighting on the Plain*) prior to killing him that "The time has come to pay your debt of blood. [*xuezhai yuanchou yao ni chang*]."[23]

This hatred is reciprocated by the enemy at whom it is directed; Lao Si, of *Red Detachment,* is depicted as "fuming with rage," for example. Yet the emotional content of enemy hatred is quite different. For one thing, it is more ambivalent, often mixed with grudging respect for the courage and tenacity of the heroic protagonist. Although *Red Lantern's* Hatoyama, the Japanese chief of police, finally succeeds in trapping Li Yuhe, his inability to break Li's spirit leaves him "crestfallen and helpless," for example. "What makes a Communist tougher than steel [*bi gangtie hai yao ying*]?" he marvels. "My persuasion and threats are of no avail."[24] For another, the emotion is based not on the desire to reciprocate sustained or imagined injury, but rather on defiance of a relationship of unconditional subordination. This is because the positive characters in these dramas often play transitional roles: an initial role as *subordinate to* and an ultimate role as *rebel against* the villain; the villain's outrage is precipitated by the switch from the former role to the latter. For his part, the villain (villains in these dramas are for some reason invariably male) seems to fit the classic authoritarian personality syndrome:[25] prone to be ferocious when in a position of dominance and cowardly when vulnerable; his rage when resisted by heroic characters is but a thin veneer concealing panic. Lei Kang of *Azalea Mountain* has but to batter the door of his locked cell with his chain for the Viper to recoil in alarm, for example. Yet even when cringing in submission the defeated enemy is not to be trusted, we discover in *Red Detachment*: "Pretending to be subdued, the kneeling Tyrant begs for his life. Stealthily, he pulls out a dagger .... With two shots she ends the life of the depraved criminal. Red Army soldiers ... pour a volley of bullets into the Tyrant's (dead) body, avenging the laboring people he had oppressed."[26]

THEMES AND PLOTS

The theme that appears with greatest frequency in all of these dramas concerns the inexorability of conflict: its emotional intensity, its moral justifiability, and its inevitably violent resolution. Conflict between the forces of good and evil is utterly ineluctable, and to attempt to reconcile this conflict or to do anything other than pursue it to its violent and cathartic climax is to indulge in corrupt self-deception. Conflict is dramatically realized in the symbolism and imagery of the plays, which identify righteousness with light, purity, publicity, and height; and evil with darkness, filth, concealment, and depth.[27] "The flames of revolution spread far and wide," sings Li Yuhe, martyr/hero of *Red Lantern.* "Once the storm is past flowers will bloom. New China will shine like the morning sun [*xin zhongguo ru chaoyang quangzhao renxiang*], red flags will fly all over the country."[28] Tiemei foresees that "Flames of rage, ten leagues high, will burn away [*shaota*] this reign of the forces of darkness." "The darkest night must end at last in the bright blaze of revolution [*geming ti huoyan yiding yao dafang huang mang*]," affirms Granny Li.[29] The key symbol of this drama is a red lantern, symbolizing steadfast revolutionary ardor and filial continuity in the face of traumatic loss. Height symbolizes not only nobility and lofty aspiration, but confidence in one's ability to surmount formidable obstacles: "As long as we all pull together, there is no mountain top we cannot conquer. [*meiyou kangbupo ti shantou*]," Yang Zerong declaims in *Taking Tiger Mountain*.[30] "The stress is on cleanliness" in depicting heroic and positive characters, a critical discourse on the revolutionary ballet emphasizes—cleanliness of course symbolizing moral purity.

The sharp contrast between the forces of good and evil finds expression not only in the imagery of the libretto, but in the choreography of the dance. In the revolutionary ballet *Red Detachment of Women*, for instance, Wu Qinghua's steps, "filled with cadence, counterpoise, ardent passion, sharp contrast, distinctive nuances and clear-cut vocabulary, deeply reveal the heroine's intrinsic class love and hatred, and sharply set off her flaming enmity for the landlord class and her unyielding rebellious character."[31] The function of all of this symbolism is to exacerbate the polarization of sentiments, and the characters do indeed emote on cue to these symbolic stimuli. Black Shark, the arch villain of *Boulder Bay*, reacts to the sight of a red flag like a bull: "The sight of it burns me up, stabs at my eyes [*wo jiu huoshao xingan li ciyan*]!...Tear it down!" After Granny, nonetheless, manages to fend off the assault of these ruffians with her fisherman's trident, she exults: "Not one of these dogs dares come forward! The red flag is the life of us fisherfolk, the red flag lights up our sky."[32]

The theme—that struggle is zero-sum [*ni huo, wo si*] and inexorable—finds ample underpinning in the more theoretical disquisitions of the major radical thinkers. "Reality means, first of all, the reality of class struggle," declares Yao Wenyuan. "Do you stand on the side of the proletariat or on the side of the bourgeoisie? On the side of imperialism or on the side of the revolutionary people? On the side of Marxism-Leninism, Mao Zedong's Thought, or on the side of revisionism? On the side of the proletarian headquarters headed by Chairman Mao, or on the side of the counterrevolutionary bourgeois headquarters?"[33] "At all times, no matter how fine the situation is, things always have a dark side," points out Lin Biao. "We should (still) be able to see the dark side when the situation is fine."[34] And Zhang Chunqiao writes that "the dictatorship of the proletariat is a persistent struggle—bloody and bloodless, violent and peaceful, military and economic, educational and administrative—against the forces and traditions of the old society."[35]

No fewer than eight (80 percent) of the dramas under consideration here take place in the context of a war, and the remaining two involve violent class struggle. Moreover, the central thrust of the radicals' revisions of the two peacetime dramas was to intensify the starkness of the confrontation. In *Song of the*

Dragon River, for example, the 1963 version concerned a moderate conflict among members of a commune when called upon to build a dam that would destroy their own anticipated harvest so that water could be channeled to higher ground desperately in need of water. Qian Changfu, the middle-peasant nemesis, is not incorrigible, and the Party is ultimately able to redeem him through thought reform. But in the January 1972 Beijing Opera version, the conflict shifts from a struggle against drought to one against a hidden enemy, one Huang Guanzhong, who manifests an insidious ability to infect the minds of good people, even Party members.[36]

A basic plot structure in all the post-Liberation dramas involves the *recrudescence of evil*, thereby illustrating the ineluctability of conflict and the need for eternal vigilance. Thus, in *Raid on White Tiger* Lu avers that the Panmunjon peace talks are "clearly a fraud [*fen ming zhen dajia hotan*]. Since we know that the Yanks are not sincere [*wu chengyi*], why waste our time in talk?" And, sure enough, warfare soon erupts anew.[37] Yet, forgetfulness of the omnipresent reality of struggle seems to be the temptation to which otherwise positive characters are most likely to succumb in post-Liberation China. Several different reasons for such political amnesia are suggested in these dramas. Chief among them, of course, is the self-protective deceptiveness of the enemy; as Fang Haizhen, Party branch secretary in *On the Docks*, explains to young Han:

> We are dockers, we're not the same....We work to support the world revolution and are strict in our demands, vigorous in our work. But he only pretends to work diligently while making trouble behind our backs....Let me remind you, Han, there are enemies with guns who fight openly, but there are also enemies who are well disguised, mouthing sweet words.[38]

Because the enemy is so clever at dissimulation, for a positive character to forget previous misdeeds is pardonable, if not entirely blameless. One reason why otherwise well-intentioned people succumb to these bouts of amnesia is that they become absorbed in productive pursuits. Inasmuch as the enemy is sometimes also able to carve out a useful role in these pursuits, this can give rise to a "liberal" tendency to let bygones be bygones. Thus in *Boulder Bay*, Haiken defends the traitorous Qiu:

> Well, a fellow can change his ways [*kan ren bu neng kan si*], can't he? It isn't right to keep raking up old accounts [*jiuzhang bu neng lao ti*]. The last two years he's turned over a new leaf, he's really keen on his work. Look at the pains he took to get those nets tonight. Without him the business wouldn't have gone through so smoothly.[39]

Qiu then exploits Haiken's zeal for productivity to induce him to abet his escape: "If we miss this chance, the work will suffer. This is the best season for fishing;

what a pity to pass up a really fine catch." In *On the Docks,* too, Zhao defends Qian on the assumption that the latter has reformed through labor:

> We shouldn't look at people with old eyes all the time [*na lao yen guang kan ren*]. The comrades in the dispatcher's office tell me that after the many political movements since Liberation Qian knows better how to behave. He knows his job well and does it pretty well.[40]

As the plot in all of these cases goes on to reveal, however, the enemy remains innately incorrigible over the passage of long periods of time, all appearances or even overt behavior to the contrary notwithstanding.

A second motive for forgetting struggle is the privatization of public spirit. This may take the form of a retreat to home and family, as it does in the case of Lu Zhanghai's wife Jiaolian, who decides to "creep into my shell" after bearing her first child, demanding that her husband likewise abandon his post and return home for the baby's first birthday: "Even a bird has the sense to go back to its nest, but to some people home means nothing." But the militia brigade leader resolutely spurns these blandishments: "A garden of flowers may hide vipers. We must always remember to be vigilant; how can a babe in your arms make you lay down your gun?"[41] A slightly different variant of privatization involves forsaking the public weal in the interest of personal ambition. This type of privatization is precipitated by the fact that memories of evil function not only to stimulate vigilance but to inhibit personal ambition and reinforce the established structure of roles and division of labor: if one's ancestor had such a hard time of it, should one not be reconciled to one's humble station and render eternal thanks to the Party? In *On the Docks* young Han Xiaojiang's dissatisfaction with his "menial" occupation ("My dream was to become a seaman, but now....I'm only a docker.") provides an opening for the villainous Qian to suborn him in his plot to sabotage the wheat shipment. Han is even allowed to make a fairly articulate defense of his ambition in terms of proffering "an even bigger contribution" to the country as a merchant seaman. But to judge from the fervency with which it is repudiated, Han's challenge to the legitimacy of the frozen post-Liberation stratification pyramid must be considered particularly insidious; indeed, old Ma Hongliang, a retired docker, is hard put to refrain from striking the young ingrate with his carrying pole, and even Fang Haizhen, the brigade Party branch secretary, must suppress her anger.[42]

Despite the bitter enmity between the two sides, there are relatively few scenes of direct confrontation in these plays; most of the action involves stealthy and complex maneuvers, climaxing in violence only after a lengthy buildup. Many of the scene titles—"Drawing Up a Plan [*dingji*]," "Sending Out Information [*jisong qingbao*]," in *Taking Tiger Mountain;* "Taking the Blockhouse by Strategy [*zhichu baolou*]," "The Japanese Ruse [*rikou guiji*]," in *Fighting on the Plain*; "Taking the Guard Post by Strategem [*zhiqi shaosuo*]," in *Raid on White Tiger*; "A Battle of Wits [*zhidou*]," "Collaboration [*goujie*]" in *Shajiabang*

—reflect the air of intrigue that pervades these dramas. In fact, the central plot structure that recurs with most striking frequency is the *spy story*. The play typically begins with a situation in which the distinction between good and evil is clearly defined, then develops into a more confused (and more interesting) situation in which the forces of good and evil interpenetrate, and is finally resolved when this interpenetration is publicly exposed and the forces of good triumph over the forces of evil. There are two variants of the spy story: in the pre-Liberation variant, enemy forces are in a position of dominance for much of the play and the spy is a positive character who penetrates the enemy lair. *Shijiabang, Taking Tiger Mountain by Strategy, Red Detachment of Women, Red Lantern, Raid on White Tiger Regiment*, and *Fighting on the Plain* all contain central or peripheral episodes of this form of espionage. In the post-Liberation spy plot, the forces of righteousness command the stage throughout most of the drama but become contaminated by the forces of evil, who penetrate this happy Gemeinschaft in the form of alien (Japanese, KMT, U.S. agents) and invaders. *On the Docks, Song of the Dragon River*, and *Boulder Bay* all dramatize this plot variant.

Each variant of the spy plot exerts its own attractions, but before turning to these I wish to make a few observations about the internal logic and putative appeal of the spy plot in general, which differ from those of the spy story in Western literature.[43] The spy plot represents the assumption that good and evil interpenetrate, even in post-Liberation Chinese society. And there seems to be an ambivalence about this: on the one hand, it is regarded as illegitimate (outrageous, if the spy is an enemy amid the "people"), and the play's resolution invariably involves triumphant exposure of the penetration and a resurrection of clear boundaries between good and evil. On the other hand, there seems to be great fascination with such interpenetration—otherwise, what can account for the persistent recurrence of this theme? Perhaps the reason has to do with the Maoist conception of the "dialectical" interdependence of good and evil. As Lin Biao put it, paraphrasing the Chairman:

> If there is no bad side, it cannot be called good. The good can be good only because there exists a bad side; the bad can be bad only because there exists a good side.[44]

Or perhaps the reason is simply good drama: good and evil should not simply clash on the stage, they should find *personal* embodiment in the form of villains whom the audience can come to know intimately enough to hate. Although there is something to each of these explanations, neither is sufficient, for other plots might also have been utilized—with greater economy—to provide evil with an opportunity for full and intimate dramatic realization. The war story, for example, a genre that *Fighting on the Plain* approximates most closely (the cops-and-robbers story or the American Western would be variants), also permits good and evil characters to dramatize themselves, though they would usually alternate on the stage until appearing in climactic confrontation.

I think that the interest in the spy story, and in the role playing and elaborate deception it involves, may be attributed rather to the conception of authority in Chinese political culture at the time these plays were most popular and to the prevalence of a particular pattern of adaptation to authority. The assumption seems to be that authority is based upon complete consensus and cannot tolerate discrepant or "dystonic" information. For a dissenter to coexist with authority, the former must therefore simulate agreement, or function as a "spy." Any information that does not accord with the maintenance and enhancement needs of authority must be hidden. This accounts for the fascination with passwords, codes, and signals in these plots (e.g., the knife-and-sheath or the lantern in *Boulder Bay*, the "contact map" [*tulong*] in *Tiger Mountain*, the "secret code" [*midianma*] in *Red Lantern*), and for the emphasis on breaking the code or dissembling the password in order to "penetrate" [*charu*] hostile authority. Since authority is based on a monopoly of political communication, to function under any authority involves learning the "language," and the spy plot best illustrates how this is done. The mystery plot might have also been utilized to this end, but because this would keep the identity of the good and bad characters secret from the audience as well as the characters until the denouement of the drama, this would have frustrated the didactic function of the play.

This didactic function contained a somewhat different "moral" for each of the two spy-plot variants. The audience appeal of the pre-Liberation spy plot seems to lie at least partly in identifying with a hero who is allowed to assume— without fear of moral sanction—the role of an archvillain. There must be considerable pleasure in such a fantasy in a society in which wickedness is so rigorously proscribed from "reality." Those who have attended these dramas during tours of the People's Republic have remarked that the audience seemed greatly captivated by the villains, despite the drama reformers' best efforts to minimize their dramatic importance. Villains are, after all, permitted to indulge themselves in many ways not normally permissible to the righteous: they may eat and drink to excess, plunder whatever they desire, gamble, boast, and generally abandon themselves to lustful and sadistic impulses. The enjoyment the audience presumably feels in identifying with a hero who may temporarily participate in such goings-on is however countered by the didactic function of the play, which is to demonstrate how a truly revolutionary character can maintain his (or her) integrity even in the midst of the most vile corruption. One aspect of Jiang Qing's reform involved increasing the ratio of didacticism to fantasy escapism, thus forcing the hero to stay more "in character." But although Yang Zerong's behavior as Luan Ping (in *Taking Tiger Mountain*) therefore remains somewhat more upright in the 1970s version of the play than in the 1963 version (in which he was permitted to "hum obscene ditties," "flirt with Vulture's foster-daughter, Rose," and "tell ribald stories" to ingratiate himself with bandits), he is still allowed to exhibit individual ambition ("I want to join you, Brigadier, and rise in the world [*deng gao*]."), to boast, flatter, steal, and assert his own prowess (by killing a tiger with his pistol, by shooting out two oil lamps with one shot). It is even possible that the off-stage contempt he expresses toward the venal authority to whom he must temporarily submit ("That dumb cluck [*bendan*]," he mutters in an aside. "A fool and a cheat, who plays another trick, it gives me my chance down the mountain.")[45] is a source of humorous catharsis to an audience who must display unremitting allegiance to authority. Sister Ahqing, the doughty and resourceful underground Party worker in *Shajiabang,* makes copious use of flattery to wheedle strategic information from the enemy, while the insensitivity of the enemy commander, Hu Zhuangui, even permits her a mild sally of satire. In all of the spy stories of the pre-Liberation variant, simulating compliance to the enemy while expressing private derision and quietly arranging his undoing implies a none-too-subtle mockery of authority and all its pretensions.

In those dramas (which are in the minority) featuring a post-Liberation spy plot, the didactic tone is dominant. Whereas in the pre-Liberation plot the spy is an Orphean hero, a paean to adaptability, in the post-Liberation variant the audience finds even less reason to identify with the spy than with the villain. A marginal person in a solidary community, the spy shares the worst aspects of both of the "worlds" in which he abides: to the people, he is an isolated, craven figure, inadequately redeemed by the quality of his (apolitical) work; to the enemy, he is a lackey, a "running dog," with no visible opportunity even to enjoy the forbidden fruits for which he has sold his birthright. The didactic function of the spy in these plots is to demonstrate the resilience of evil, even in socialist society. This demonstration serves to vindicate the maintenance of a rigid defensive posture that might otherwise seem unnecessarily harsh, justifying the austere, self-denying aspects of socialist virtue—indeed, Lu Zhanghai would have been hard put to justify yet another abandonment of his neglected family had Black Shark opted *not* to launch his raid over National Day and their baby's first birthday! The presence of a spy also provides a clear and theoretically comprehensible locus for those temptations to which even positive characters, "raised under the Red Flag" of the most impeccably revolutionary forbears, may occasionally fall prey: the desire for a more satisfying career (Han Xiaojiang in *On the Docks*), an exclusive concern with higher productivity (Haiken in *Boulder Bay*), the "liberal" desire to bury the hatchet on ancient enmities (Zhao Zhenshan in *On the Docks*). In the climactic resolution of the plot, the sinister implications of such temptations are publicly exposed along with the spy's true identity ("Look, all of you," warns Zhao upon apprehending Qian Shouwei. "A letter of recommendation from his American boss, an offer of a contract from his Japanese boss and an appointment document issued by the KMT. And here's a lethal weapon!"), and temptation is obliterated along with the spy's sinister career.[46]

DILEMMAS

Having analyzed some of the basic patterns of role relationships, theme, and plot that appear in these revolutionary dramas, we turn now to an examination of areas of tension between different patterns. At least three such internal contradictions seem to be worth closer scrutiny: the problem of moral judgment, ambivalent feelings concerning dependency, and the question of the relationship of heroism to activism and suffering.

Contrary to assertions that China has a "dual" political culture,[47] all of these characters share essentially the same moral world view, greatly simplifying the problem of moral judgment. That villains agree with the general value framework (including their own stigmatization) is amply indicated by the trepidation they show in putting heroes to death, although they hate them. Thus, when Hong Changqing, Party Commissar of the *Red Detachment*, rises to the occasion of his martyrdom, his executioners can only supinely acknowledge his moral superiority:

> The landlord and Lao Se cringe before his piercing gaze and fearless manner....With the utmost contempt and hatred for the class enemy, he grabs the sheet of paper, rips it to shreds, and flings it in the face of the tyrant. What does death matter? The communist creed is the truth! Hong points at the villains in a rage. "Communists are not afraid to die! You'll never escape the people's punishment!" The bandits fall prostrate and trembling in the face of the Communist's splendid courage and heroism.[48]

Because the same view of the moral universe is so widely shared, all characters exhibit far more self-assurance in making moral decisions than has been evident in the more secularized and relativistic West (particularly among elites) for several decades.[49] Whereas Western dramas frequently revolve around a choice between options of apparently equal moral validity, these dramas do not even feature a clash between competing value systems—the choice is between good and evil in a *shared* value system. Based on this tacit concensus, everyone acts from moral intuitionism. The only moral judgment involving cognitive complexity is discovery of the "spy," and this is more a technical exercise in code breaking than in moral reasoning, for the spy's overt behavior is indistinguishable from that of anyone else. The decisions that require greatest ratiocinative acumen are not moral, but instrumental: How can the seemingly impregnable Tiger Mountain be stormed? How can Black Shark and Ding Wenzhai make their escape from the island on which they find themselves stranded? Such decisions involve selection of the most efficient means to an end, not the question of the end itself.

All of which is not to say that these characters all make the same moral decisions, of course, or even that they use similar criteria in making decisions—only that they tend to *evaluate* their judgments in the same light. There are essentially three types of moral decision-makers in these casts, which correspond to three stages of moral maturity: the villain, the non-Communist "apprentice" hero, and the Communist hero.

Villains base their decisions on a hedonic calculus in response to their volatile impulse life, acting in pursuit of short-term gratification. In *Shajiabang*, for example, a KMT soldier no sooner encounters a comely local village girl than he attempts to rob and rape her. Among villain leaders the ability to defer gratification seems to be somewhat better developed than among their underlings, but even here the criteria are relatively short-term and materialistic. In the introductory appearance of bandit chief Vulture of *Tiger Mountain*, both his chief of staff and chief adjutant warn him on the basis of tactical prudence not to plunder the village adjacent to their stronghold: "A rabbit doesn't foul its own nest" [*tuzi bu chi wobian cao*]. But Vulture dismisses such considerations with nonchalance: "Who cares [*hai guan naxie*]? Chief of Staff, go and grab me some of those paupers. We'll put them to work building fortifications. Men and women—take them all."[50] In the scene in which Hu Zhuangui and Dizo Xiaosan agree to collaborate with the Japanese, Hu rationalizes his decision in terms of his troops' need for "money, guns and ammunition," and the prospect of controlling a rich district with "plenty of fish and rice"; his chief of staff explains his choice with delightful candor: "Whoever suckles me is my mother" [*you nai jiu shi niang*].[51] In a conversation with *Red Lantern's* Li, Hatoyama makes his presuppositions equally clear:

> The highest human creed can be condensed into two words.... "For myself" [*wei wo*]....Every man for himself. You know the saying, "Heaven destroys those who don't look out for themselves" [*ren bu wei ji, tian zhu di mie*].[52]

And Vulture crows with egoistic delight upon receiving the prized contacts map. "When the Kuomintang army returns, I'll be a commanding general," he announces proudly, "And I'll make the rest of you brigadiers and division commanders."[53]

Although resentful of the enemy's monopolization and conspicuous consumption of scarce resources, the secondary or apprentice hero is not moved primarily by a desire for material gain (the shortest route to which would have been collaboration), but rather by a desire for reciprocity. Indeed, vengeance, "giving tit for tat" [*zhen feng xiang dui*] has become the overmastering passion in his (or her) life. Two of the most prominent examples of the vengeance seeker are

Lei Kang in *Azalea Mountain* and Wu Qinghua in *Detachment of Women*; Chang Bao in *Tiger Mountain*, Ma Hongliang in *On the Docks*, and the "granny" characters in both *Red Lantern* and *Boulder Bay* (elderly characters frequently dramatize this emotion, for they have lived long enough to have accumulated great suffering) are more peripheral characters moved by similar considerations. As noted above, a desire for vengeance is deemed an ideologically legitimate basis for moral action. Thus, Li Yongqi convinces Shao to allow the precocious Chang Bao to accompany the militia in their assault on the bandits' stronghold simply because "this girl has been through much bitterness and is thirsting for revenge" [*ku da chou shen*].[54] However, the cases of both Lei Kang and Wu Qinghua make clear that for *effective* moral action, vindictiveness is a necessary but insufficient motive. Lei Kang, ignoring Party representative Ko Xiang's advice and driven solely by passion, hastens to the rescue of Granny and thus blunders into an ambush whereby he too is captured. Qinghua breaches discipline to fire on the enemy prematurely ("At the sight of the tyrant, Qinghua's whole being cries out for vengeance. She has only one thought: "Kill the tyrant of the South! Get revenge! Revenge!...Qinghua is in an uncontrollable rage."), with the upshot that although the attack succeeds and the granary is liberated, the tyrant and his bailiff escape. Lei and Wu learn that full moral maturity is possible only by submitting to the moral precepts of the CCP.

The morality of the Communist hero is neither crudely materialistic, like that of the class enemy, nor purely situational and reciprocity based, like that of apprentice heroes, but *principled*. It represents an advance over the morality of the apprentice hero in two respects. First, the pursuit of vengeance is no longer a blind passion, but is tempered by cold prudence. Although Ko Xiang bears a deep personal grievance against the Viper, she "swallows her own grief [*goren chouhen yan zai duli*] and keeps the whole world in view," enabling her to make strategically efficacious decisions.[55] Second, morality is no longer based solely on personal vengeance, but advances claims to universal standards. As Hong admonishes the remorseful Qinghua: "Revolution is not simply a matter of personal vengeance. Its aim is the emancipation of all mankind." This more abstract and universalizable framework for moral judgment explains why the Communist has the most steadfast moral compass and never commits serious errors.

The central contradiction in this moral schema, it seems to me, is between its universalistic pretensions and its situational, reciprocity-based operational code. The universalistic claims are necessary to justify the transcendental status of Communist morality, in terms of which the morality of villains or apprentice heroes may be condemned or subordinated as less "mature" derivatives of a higher law. Yet, these universalistic claims are so vague as to lack operational implications, with the result that the actual decisions of Communist decision makers turn out to be based on reciprocity as well. Lei Kang (an apprentice hero) is initially mistrustful of Ko Xiang's commitment because "My feud with the Viper is a fight to the death; she has no private scores to settle with him" [bing wu jieti zhi hen], whereupon he is informed that Ko Xiang, too, has lost a husband to the Viper.[56]

Resentment of dependency and the endeavor to transcend it is a theme that surfaces quite frequently in these plots. Superficially, there should be no dilemma: dependency is abjured, independence or "self-reliance" (*zili gengsheng*) striven for. Because dependency is based on submission to exigency—needs for food, clothing, shelter, money, praise—these plots feature a concerted attempt by positive characters to renounce their needs. Granny Li thus spurns Hatoyama's blandishments with: "I look upon wealth and fame as dust, we poor people find coarse food very tasty." In a minor incident in *Shajiabang*, young Wang declines to have the dressing on his wound changed. The objection to an excessive emphasis on productivity is also partly based on a desire to mitigate dependence on material commodities.

There is, however, reason to believe that this position of abstemious self-reliance conceals an underlying ambivalence. If the relationships among positive characters are examined, we find that not only is dependency unexceptionable per se, it is pervasive and seems to be heartily appreciated under appropriate conditions. Ardent revolutionaries show every indication that they appreciate being fed when hungry, cared for when sick, hidden or protected from danger, and otherwise placed in a position of dependency on a powerful patron. Auntie Sha and Ahfu of *Shajiabang* make steamed rice cakes for the wounded PLA men and wash their clothes, treating them "like your own sons," while the soldiers in turn help the family with the harvest. In *Red Detachment of Women* (which despite its title and certain superficial trappings does not upset the traditional division of functions between the sexes), a girl soldier mends a tunic for one of the men, and a few female soldiers, "washing vegetables by the river, notice the head cook approaching with a pair of buckets on a shoulder pole. They mischievously block him, snatch the baskets and cheerfully fetch water for him." Then they break into song:

> The river water is clear, oh clear,
> Hats we weave for the Red Army dear,
> Our armymen love the people, we support them delighted,
> And one family we are with them united.[57]

Although dependency is, therefore, not resented in itself, there is clearly a great deal of tension attached to the dependency relationship, probably because it is based upon bonds of affective intimacy (thereby exposing vulnerabilities) and, yet, is subject to abuse. The implicit norms governing the relationship seem to be fairly vague. For example, they demand reciprocity—not necessarily the exchange of equal values, for we have already noted the pervasiveness of hierarchy and the unequal distribution of sacrifice even within the revolutionary "family"—but if *some* degree of reciprocity is not forthcoming then indignation will arise. Any attempt to withhold the food, nurturance, or other needed values upon which the positive characters have become dependent—thereby *imposing* independence—is considered valid grounds for "rebellion." Several plots revolve around elite control of granaries (in one case an ammunition depot) and rebel attempts to capture and redistribute the resources hoarded there. But even if some quid pro quo is offered, the terms of the exchange are subject to dispute. Thus *Red Lantern*'s workmen grouse bitterly about the food:

> It's full of grit (*shazi*)....They just don't treat us like human beings.... How can we eat such swill? We just can't live (*mei fa hua ya*)![58]

In another incident of the same play, Granny Li rejects the terms of an enemy-proferred exchange (viz. her son's life for her secrets) by redefining the transaction as not an exchange at all but as unadulterated victimization:

> What kind of talk is that! You've arrested my son for no reason. Now you want to kill him. You are the criminals, it's you who are cruel. You kill the Chinese, and you want to shift the blame on to the Chinese people, on to me, an old woman?[59]

Ambiguity and friction surround not only the ill-defined terms of the exchange, but its larger purpose: unlike a market exchange, in which the intentions of both parties are a matter of indifference, one of the implicit norms of the dependency relationship seems to be that both sides share the same overarching interests. If this condition does not obtain, the client feels great anxiety about the prospect of being manipulated. In view of the inherent asymmetry of the dependency relationship—tolerated on condition that some higher goal is being attained of interest to the client as well as the patron—such anxiety seems quite rational. Thus, in the following episode we find Li Yuhe accepting a superficially inferior exchange because of his profound mistrust for the patron offering better terms. Hatoyama's emissary, Hou, invites Li to a "feast," in which he will be bribed (or otherwise induced) to give up the code. In parting, Granny offers Li a drink, whereupon Hou assures her there will be plenty for him at the feast. "Bah!...The poor prefer their own wine. Each drop of it warms the heart," she responds. Her son rejoins: "With this wine to put heart into me (*dian di*), mother, I can cope with whatever wine they give me."[60]

The relationship of heroism to activism and suffering is at first glance self-evident: activism is good, suffering is bad—revolution can change everything, the hero should glory in this and seize the initiative to accomplish momentous feats. These traits are so much a part of the revolutionary creed that the hero must seem to retain the initiative even when captured and helpless:

When Yang Zerong makes his entry he enters triumphantly to the accompaniment of militant music and occupies the center of the stage at all times. With the help of singing and dancing, Yang Zerong is shown to hold the initiative with him at every turn and to lead Vulture by the nose round and round the stage.[61]

And whereas in the preradical version of *Red Lantern* Li Yuhe was depicted as a man "who always goes into hiding," in the revised edition he proves to be a most decisive personality: he "pounds the table, jumps to his feet in great anger, and like an erupting volcano spews his hatred at the enemy."[62]

This emphasis on activism, however, leads to the danger of recklessness, unless activism is "tempered" by Party discipline: the organizational implication is that only the primary hero may grasp the initiative without risk of serious error. It also clashes with the older moral belief that it is virtuous to be the passive recipient of affliction—a belief that is still retained in good measure. Indeed, given the above-noted tenuousness of universalistic moral claims, the infliction of pain and death seems to be the major criterion differentiating good and evil in these dramas; good people must suffer in order to justify their assault on the wicked. Yet, they must not suffer so much as to lose hope in an ultimately favorable outcome. A delicate balance must be maintained: positive characters should be weak and passive enough to invite injury, yet not enough to despair or capitulate. Thus, in the revised version of *White-haired Girl*, Yang Bailao, the girl's father, does not commit suicide but, in the spirit of revolt, fights his oppressors until beaten to death; Xi Er herself is cruelly treated but not raped. The ultimate solution to the contradictory needs for both heroic activism and passive suffering is for the condemned hero actively to embrace his destiny in a spirit of Nietszchean *amor fati*. The 1965 version of *Red Lantern* at least permitted Li to approach his death with some sense of foreboding and distaste, but in 1970 he sings "they cannot fetter my spirit that storms the heavens" and moves briskly toward his doom as if in triumph, demonstrating that he is "unyielding and indomitable even though he suffered great torture."[63]

CONCLUSION

From the manifest and latent patterns of meaning detected in these dramas, what inferences may be drawn about Chinese political culture? By monopolizing a highly visible central forum over so long a period and dramatizing a conception of correct relations in public that was, whatever its internal inconsistencies, certainly stark and quite colorful, the revolutionary *yangbanxi* may be assumed to have had a considerable impact on at least the public culture at the time. Whether people were innately convinced by the morals drawn in these morality plays and how long their impact will persist are inherently problematic questions, but if the study of Chinese politics can teach us anything it should teach us not to dismiss a political current or "line" simply because it is no longer in favor. We may assume that those segments of the Chinese public who most intensely identified with the Maoist leadership during the period of radical cultural hegemony, probably comprising a fairly large proportion of activists and younger cadres, internalized the values propagated by the model plays; they might reasonably be expected to retain some loyalty to radical values (even while repudiating the Gang of Four) and to feel disillusioned or cynical should those ideals be abandoned or seriously compromised. In point of fact, the *yangbanxi* have not yet (at time of writing) been repudiated (although they are no longer performed), and although the cultural field is currently dominated by Western-educated "moderates," recent informants report that it is still quite badly split.[64]

If we extrapolate directly from fiction to truth, we arrive at an "ideal typical" characterization of Chinese political culture during the 1966-76 period that may then be corroborated on the basis of journalistic materials, refugee interviews, visitors' impressions, and other available sources. The plays have certain implications concerning the nature of authority in the People's Republic and the types of strain associated with conformity and deviation from authority. Authority seems to be based upon a morally consensual communication system. Solidarity is engendered through mutually reinforcing messages. For a government to be morally legitimate its citizenry must see, hear, and speak only positive things about it. Under these circumstances it is an almost insuperable temptation for the leadership to manipulate the communication system should untoward things occur. (To the extent that this is still true, the prognosis for any permanent liberalization of the cultural or informational media would not seem particularly rosy.) This, however, places the leadership in the quandary of blinding itself to what is actually happening (because people censor their own "bad thoughts"), stifling innovative behavior, and so forth. A split-level pattern of communication arises: one public, one private. The former is useful for purposes of legitimation and the allocation of status, the latter for the transmission of information.

One feasible mode of adapting to such a situation is the "spy" strategy. The government sends spies among the masses to find out what is actually going on ("squat on a point"). Dissidents undergo internal migration, using techniques of espionage to survive in public while pursuing illegitimate private ambitions. While conducting interviews in Hong Kong in 1976-1977, I encountered a sufficient number of respondents who conceded using such techniques to conclude that this was indeed a quite widespread pattern of adaptation. For example, one former sent-down youth of "free professional" (*ceyou shiye*) background, frustrated in his desire to go to Qingua University by the Cultural Revolution and then by his dispatch to a remote Hakka region as a sent-down youth, managed to learn the local dialect and ingratiate himself with the local village community to the extent that he joined the Party and became romantically involved with a local girl, all of which earned him great moral approval. When he finally managed to inveigle an admission to Qinghua, however, he was undone by a frank letter to his old, "real" girl friend (who had been "sent down" to Hainan). His new girl friend, unfortunately, discovered this letter and exposed our young hero, demolishing his reconstructed reputation and eventually inducing him to leave the country. "Is this kind of thought reform ridiculous or pitiful (*bu zhidao xiao hua*)?," he concludes. "I began as a true revolutionary but ended up as a fraud. Such was the transformation of my thought."

Deviation is functionally necessary to this conformity-based system, for it provides an outside reference point for the positive evaluation of the system and a target for the projection of hostile feelings, whose punishment serves further to reinforce internal solidarity. To minimize uncertainty in the search for deviation, it seems to have been "built in" as a permanent category in the stratification system. Munro's observations concerning the "malleability of man" in Maoist thought may have applied to pre-Cultural Revolution China,[65] but the doctrines of the incorrigibility of evil and the inexorability of struggle that acquired currency since that time seem to have had a rigidifying effect upon stratification. At least for the radicals, the prospect of reforming the thoughts of a member of the "black classes" (*hei wulei*) could be totally foreclosed. The moral obligations of members of the good classes toward members of the bad classes are essentially negative: the former should segregate and continuously hold suspect the latter, even when their behavior appears correct; they may also humiliate and physically punish them at the slightest provocation. These circumstances vitiate any possibility of a multiclass united front and necessitate a rigorous dictatorship of the proletariat.

Whereas the deviant role is simple but hard to "play," the conformist role is self-contradictory. Conformity with the Communist moral/political consensus seems to require both rebellion and discipline, obedience and defiance. Support for a revolutionary disposition is evident in the selection of a prerevolutionary setting for most of these dramas, when authority roles were held by the enemy, and by a fairly consistent tendency throughout to attribute assorted misfortunes to the leadership. Yet, revolutionary rhetoric is paradoxically combined with a quite repressive personal regimen. Unless he or she is a hero, the positive character must subordinate self to a hierarchically-structured organization, demonstrating great ability to defer gratification, even to the point of martyrdom, for the ideological objectives of that organization. To villains is attributed an uninhibitedly hedonistic impulse life, and the savage destructiveness that this precipitates stands as a warning to keep one's impulses under control. Even apprentice heroes are allotted a greater range of expression and maneuver than heroes, who may show their imagination only when operating under cover. We have already noted the pervasiveness of hierarchy, the fear of recklessness or error, the dread of ambiguity or lack of structure. Decisions are always clear-cut and made instantaneously, "resolutely."

In its dogmatic severity, its Manichaean moral code, and its emphasis on "worldly asceticism," the radical ethos bears a certain similarity to Puritan Calvinism.[66] Not, however, in its elevation of the martial values and suspicious stance toward productivity, nor in its exclusively collectivist orientation. Nor in its lack of universalism: Puritans also considered themselves members of an "elect" with a morally superior life style, but their creed prescribed the impartial application of ethical rules. The radicals justified discriminatory application of moral precepts on the basis of reciprocity, generalized and given permanence in the context of the class structure. Because the proletariat was in a position of subordination and exploitation in the prerevolutionary class structure, this class is now justified in applying an equally one-sided morality upon the class enemy now that the stratification pyramid has been overturned. Not every member of the proletariat is aware of these structural imperatives, and even after being enlightened they are inclined to forgive and forget. The chief remedy for such amnesia is the commission of some new outrage by the implacable class enemy.

Can the eventual fall of the radicals be explained by the ethos they attempted to promulgate? I would argue that in good part it can. This ethos was based on a desire to perpetuate the morality of revolution in a society in which a revolution could no longer be conducted, resurrecting "revolutionary" issues as a basis for controversy and social cleavage that most people had by now accepted, for better or for worse, as faits accomplis. Such issues did not speak to the problems of national construction to which the nation was increasingly turning its attentions. The radicals inserted into politics a bitter vindictiveness that perpetuated conflicts of all sorts and led to a subterranean politics of plots, spies, codes, and hairsplitting codebreaking. The attempt to perpetuate an ethically superior proletarian life style in a society in which the now subordinate class enemy was, nonetheless, continually indoctrinated to maintain an identical life style (and usually did) led to considerable confusion and a number of shifts on the question of how to define the vanguard class and justify its dominance. In the absence of an exclusive life style, there were tendencies to define the proletariat on the basis of bloodlines, leading to an incipient caste system—or, on the basis of reciprocity, leading to rather indiscriminate anarchistic tendencies against "oppressive" authorities. In sum, radical morality as defined in the revolutionary *yangbanxi* was simply not tenable, and by 1976 this had become clearly apparent.

NOTES

1. Richard Nixon, *RN: The Memoirs of Richard Nixon* (New York: Grosset and Dunlap, 1978), p. 356.

2. E.g., vide Michel Oksenberg, "Sources and Methodological Problems in the Study of Contemporary China," in *Chinese Communist Politics in Action*, ed. A. Doak Barnett (Seattle: University of Washington Press, 1969), pp. 577–607; and Martin K. Whyte, "The Study of Mainland China: Sociological Research and the Minimal Data Problem," *Contemporary China* 1 (March 1977), 1–13.

3. Merle Goldman, *Literary Dissent in Communist China* (Cambridge, Mass.: Harvard University Press, 1967); and, more recently, "The Media Campaign as a Weapon in Political Struggle: The Dictatorship of the Proletariat and Water Margin Campaigns," in *Moving a Mountain: Cultural Change in China*, eds. Godwin Chu and Francis L.K. Hsu (Honolulu: University Press of Hawaii, 1979), pp. 197–207.

4. See Kenneth Jowitt, "Inclusion and Mobilization in European Leninist Regimes," *World Politics*, 28 (October 1975), 69–97; and Lowell Dittmer, "Political Development: Leadership, Politics and Ideology," in *The People's Republic of China after Thirty Years: An Overview*, ed. Joyce Kallgren (Berkeley: Center for Chinese Studies, University of California, Research Monograph No. 15, 1979), pp. 27–49.

5. *Hai Gang* [On the Docks], in *Hongqi* [Red Flag], no. 2, 1972, p. 46.

6. With the sole exception (to my knowledge) of the study by Hua-yuan Li Mowry, *Yang-pan Hsi—New Theater in China* (Berkeley: Center for Chinese Studies, University of California, Studies in Chinese Communist Terminology no. 15, 1973).

7. See John G. Cawelti, *Adventure, Mystery and Romance: Formula Stories in Art and Popular Culture* (Chicago: University of Chicago Press, 1976); and Richard Slotkin, *Regeneration Through Violence: The Mythology of the American Frontier, 1600–1860* (Middletown, Conn.: Wesleyan University Press, 1973).

8. Lois Wheeler Snow, *China On Stage: An American Actress in the People's Republic* (New York: Random House, 1972), p. 122.

9. *Hongse niangzi jun* (Red Detachment of Women) (Beijing: Renmin wenxue chuban she, 1972), p. 55.

10. *Hongdengji* (Red Lantern) (Beijing: Renmin chuban she, 1970), p. 43.

11. *Zhichu weihushan* (Taking the Bandits' Stronghold) (Beijing: Renmin chuban she, 1970), p. 44.

12. *Pingyuan zuo zhan* (Fighting on the Plain) (Beijing: Renmin wenxue chuban she, 1973), p. 22.

13. *Hongdengji*, p. 10.

14. *Hongdengji*, p. 29.

15. Strategy group of the Beijing Opera Troupe of Shanghai, "Strive to Create the Brilliant Images of Proletarian Heroes," *Chinese Literature* no. 1 (1970): 58–72; see also Chu Lan, "A Decade of Revolution in Peking Opera," *Peking Review* 31 (August 2, 1974).

16. "Strive to Create," p. 71.

17. *Zhichu weihushan*, p. 67.

18. *Hongdengji*, p. 49.

19. Ding Xuelei, "Magnificent Ode to People's War: Commentary on 'The Yellow River' Piano Concerto," *Chinese Literature* no. 8 (1970): p. 78.

20. *Hongdengji*, p. 45.

21. *Hai Gang*, p. 43.

22. *Hongdengji*, p. 29.

23. *Pingyuan zuo zhen*, p. 47.

24. *Hongdengji*, p. 33.

25. See T.W. Adorno, et al., *The Authoritarian Personality* (New York: W.W. Norton, 1969 edition).

26. *Hongse Niangze jun*, p. 78.

27. I analyzed this contrasting imagery in a previous article, "Thought Reform and Cultural Revolution: An Analysis of the Symbolism of Chinese Polemics," *American Political Science Review* no. 71 (March 1977): 67–85.

28. *Hongdengji*, p. 43.

29. *Hongdengji*, p. 49.

30. *Zhichu weihushan*, pp. 52, 18.

31. Anon., "A New Road for Chinese Ballet," *Chinese Literature* no. 1 (1971): 93–94, 88.

32. *Panshi wan*, (Boulder Bay) (Beijing: Renmin wenxue chuban she, 1972), p. 35.

33. Yao Wenyuan, *Comments on Tao Chu's Two Books* (Beijing: Foreign Languages Press, 1968), p. 17.

34. Martin Ebon, ed., *Lin Piao* (New York: Stein and Day, 1970), p. 259.

35. Zhang Chunqiao, *On Exercising All-round Dictatorship over the Bourgeoisie* (Beijing: Foreign Languages Press, 1975), p. 5.

36. *Long Jiang Song* (Song of the Dragon River) (Beijing: Renmin wenxue chuban se, 1972).

37. *Qixi baihutuan* (Raid on White Tiger Regiment) (Beijing: Renmin wenxue chuban she, 1972), p. 11.

38. *Hai Gang*, p. 44.

39. *Panxhi wan*, p. 26.

40. *Hai Gang*, p. 32.

41. *Panshi wan*, p. 16.

42. *Hai Gang*, pp. 42–43.

43. Cf. Joan Rockwell, "Normative Attitudes of Spies in Fiction," in *Mass Culture Revisited*, eds. Bernard Rosenberg and David M. White (New York: Van Norstrand Reinhold, 1971).

44. Ebon, ed., p. 259.

45. *Zhichu weihushan*, p. 55.

46. *Hai Gang*, p. 49.

47. Alan P.L. Liu, *Political Culture and Group Conflict in Communist China* (Santa Barbara, Calif.: Clio Press, 1976), pp. 24–41.

48. *Hongse niangzi jun*, p. 70.

49. See Nathan Leites, "Recent Trends in Moral Temper," in *Psychopolitical Analysis*, ed. Elizabeth Marvick (New York: John Wiley, 1977), pp. 59–87.

50. *Zhichu weihushan*, p. 10.

51. *Shajiabang*, p. 19.

52. *Hongdengji*, p. 31.
53. *Zhichu weihushan*, p. 39.
54. *Zhichu weihushan*, p. 58.
55. *Duzhuan shan*, p. 71.
56. *Duzhuan shan*, p. 71.
57. *Hongse niangzi jun*, p. 45.
58. *Hongdengji*, p. 13.
59. *Hongdengji*, p. 43.
60. *Hongdengji*, p. 42.
61. "Strive to Create," p. 68.
62. The Red Lantern group of the China Beijing Opera Troupe, "Struggle for the Creation of Typical Examples of Proletarian Heroes," *Chinese Literature* no. 8 (1970): 53–70.
63. Cf. Hua-yuan Li Mowry, p. 38; also "Struggle for the Creation," passim.
64. See, for example, Jie Zheng, "The 'Gang of Four's' Attack on Progressive Literature and Art," *Chinese Literature* no. 6 (1978): 97–105. The leftist media in Hong Kong have ventured to be somewhat more critical: cf. "Liupai wenti yu 'yangbanxi' di yinxiang," *Dagong Bao* (November 14, 1979): 19.
65. Donald J. Munro, *The Concept of Man in Contemporary China* (Ann Arbor: University of Michigan Press, 1977), pp. 57–84.
66. Max Weber, *The Protestant Ethic and the Spirit of Capitalism*, translated by Talcott Parsons, (New York: Charles Scribner's Sons, 1958).

7 THE MAOIST ETHIC AND THE MORAL BASIS OF POLITICAL ACTIVISM IN RURAL CHINA

Richard P. Madsen

Since the beginnings of the Communist movement in China, the Chinese Communists have propagated an ethos based on the values of hard work, courage, struggle, and self-sacrifice. The essence of this ethos is encapsulated in the Maoist imperative to "serve the people." In this essay, I wish to examine the conduct of some rural political activists who, within a particular social context and under certain historical circumstances, publicly committed themselves to live according to the Maoist ethic. I will try to interpret what those commitments meant to them and to those around them. I will try to explicate the social and cultural contexts that shaped various kinds of commitments, and I will show how different kinds of commitments led to different kinds of social consequences. In doing this I shall have occasion to respond to certain classic issues raised by Max Weber's sociology of ideas, as well as newer issues raised by contemporary theories of moral development.*

---

*The reflections presented in this essay are based on information gathered collectively by Anita Chan, Jonathan Unger, and myself from 24 former residents of Chen Village (a pseudonym), including 14 sent-down youths who came into the village from Guangzhou in 1964 and began leaving in the early 1970s, and ten former peasants who migrated to Hong Kong in the mid 1970s. We have carefully crosschecked the accounts of different interviewees, so as to minimize the effects of bias. A discussion of the methodological issues raised by this research is provided in my doctoral dissertation, *Revolutionary Asceticism in Communist China* (Harvard, 1977), and a more detailed account will appear in a forthcoming book jointly authored with Anita Chan and Jonathan Unger. The ideas on moral behavior presented here, however, are my own and do not necessarily always coincide with the interpretations of my colleagues.

THE MAOIST ETHIC AS A KIND OF INNER-WORLDLY ASCETICISM

"We must all learn the spirit of absolute selflessness.... A man's ability may be great or small, but if he has this spirit, he is already noble-minded and pure, a man of integrity and above vulgar interests."[1] This quote from Mao's homily "In Memory of Norman Bethune"—one of the most important texts articulating Mao's moral message—contains the essentials of that teaching: a commitment to selflessness based upon adherence to certain revolutionary principles rather than "vulgar interests" and proceeding from an individual, personal integrity. The most important characteristic of this ethic, I would argue, is not its injunction to absolute selflessness, to total altruism. Rather, from a sociological and historical point of view, its most important characteristic seems to be its insistence that moral life be based uncompromisingly on principle and be the expression of an individual's personal integrity. It is an ethic that represents what Max Weber would have called a kind of "inner-worldly asceticism."[2]

Traditional Chinese, Confucian ethics always demanded the sacrifice of the individual to social obligations. Our Western-style egocentric individualism, which subordinates in principle the demands of society to the personal integrity of the autonomous self, was always condemned in traditional China and, indeed, seems rarely to have been found there. But the traditional Chinese practiced a type of selflessness that tied him very tightly into the world: the narrow, local world of family and friends, patrons and clients—a world anchored in respect for the past. The life of the traditional Chinese was, as Weber put it in his classic analysis, "determined from without":[3] determined by a person's concrete obligations toward concrete people, whether living or dead—especially members of one's family or extended kinship group. The traditional Chinese lived *in* and very much *of* the world. In contrast to this "ethic of adaptation to the world," Weber opposed the ethic of the devout Puritan, which led the Puritan "to appraise all human relations—including those naturally nearest in life—as mere means and expression of a mentality reaching beyond the organic relations of life."[4] Basing his life on spiritual principles, grasped through solitary personal choice, the Puritan lived in the world but detached from its prevailing institutions, its networks of loyalties, its fabric of "natural" sympathies. He was *in* but not *of* the world and thus committed to changing the world in accordance with what his conscience told him was the will of God.

In contrast to traditional Chinese ethics, the Maoist brand of selflessness enjoins a person to live *in* but not *of* the world. It too is a type of inner-worldly asceticism, and it is this ascetic quality that distinguishes it from traditional Chinese selflessness. The good Communist is supposed to devote his life to "serving the people," and his reward for doing so will be the achievement of ultimate meaning in life, in the Chinese Communist parlance, "revolutionary glory"—a glory that will come from having played a significant part in the progress of history toward its communist goal, a glory that will validate a person's life even in the face of death, will make his death, as Mao put it, "as weighty as Mount Tai."[5] Now the people whom the good communist is supposed to serve are not the concrete individual people who surround a person, but the abstract people-in-general—all of the Chinese people with the exception of class enemies, and, indeed, all of the oppressed people of the world. And to *serve* the people is not to give them what they want or what they think they want at any given time, but rather to lead the people politically to transform their society eventually into a society without classes and without exploitation in conformity with the political and historical theories of Marxism-Leninism and Mao Zedong thought. Thus, the good Maoist is supposed to subordinate all "natural" obligations to family, associates, and friends to the cause of the Chinese revolution—a cause made known to him by his rationally acquired convictions. He is to live in the world in order to create a new world, in a methodical, disciplined way, under the guidance of the Communist Party and the thought of Mao Zedong.

If we grant that the Maoist revolutionary ethos is analogous in some way to Weber's conception of the inner-worldly ascetic Protestant ethos, then by studying certain people and situations in which that ethos came powerfully alive, we might have an interesting opportunity to address ourselves to some unanswered questions coming out of the intellectual tradition launched by Weber's work on the sociology of ideas and the sociology of religion. Weber gave us a brilliant picture of the ways in which the meanings and motivations generated by the Calvinists' solution to the quest for an ultimate meaning in life could have important social and economic consequences. But he did not give us such a clear idea of the social sources of acceptance of Calvinism—the social forces that led certain groups of people under certain circumstances passionately to accept the Calvinist world view and its ascetic ethos, and the exact historical circumstances that enabled the acceptance of that ethos by certain strategic groups of people at a certain time to have a profound influence on the course of history. In the widely reprinted conclusion to his book *The Revolution of the Saints*,[6] Michael Walzer has recently tried to offer suggestions about why Calvinism caught on for certain groups of people during the Reformation, and he has tried to offer suggestions as to why other secular analogues to the Protestant ethic (like Leninism) caught on at other times under similar circumstances. His answer was that an ascetic ethos was born out of an experience of social chaos. It was confused, anxious people who latched on to a rigid ascetic ethos during times of social breakdown—people torn up from traditional roots of family and community, who faced the world as lonely individuals. Such people at such times latched on to a rigid, ascetic ethos because they felt a desperate need for rigid self-discipline and a tightly integrated social order.

But I would like to suggest in this essay that for peasant cadres in rural China during the "high tide" of the propagation of Mao's thought from the mid 1960s to the mid 1970s, a lasting, productive kind of commitment to Mao's austere inner-worldly ascetic ethos came alive not through the destruction of traditional social roots, but through a kind of reaffirmation of them, and not because of the fear of chaos, but because of dissatisfaction with a particular kind of social order. Through a research project carried out in collaboration with two other colleagues into the social history of a particular south China village, I was able to examine the behavior of some local activists whose lives were shaped in significant ways by Mao's ascetic ethos. The most genuinely revolutionary of them drew their commitments not by isolating themselves from their community, but by celebrating their ties with it. And they did not develop their commitment out of fear of chaos, but rather were willing to create chaos in order to realize what they felt to be the truest potential of their community.

Let me now describe those social and cultural characteristics of the village studied by my colleagues and I that are most relevant to an interpretation of the conduct of its political activists. Then let me sketch character portraits of three village activists whose careers point toward major dimensions of the interaction between traditional moral commitments and Maoist ideals.* These three activists are not "typical villagers," in the sense that their behavior represented the average sort of behavior engaged in by a cross section of the village population. The moral life of the average inhabitant of the village, like the moral life of the average inhabitant of the United States, is complex—a tangle of inconsistencies and compromises. But the three persons whose characters I will sketch here were committed in especially vivid ways to particular approaches toward handling the confrontation between Maoist ideals, on the one hand, and traditional forms of Chinese moral behavior, on the other. They, thus, bring into especially sharp focus themes that run in a less clear way through the lives of most ordinary villagers. I will then briefly describe the part these three persons played in the ten years of village history from 1964 to 1974. Finally, I will explain what I think the conduct of these activists suggests about the social basis for commitment to Maoist asceticism in rural China.

---

*Portraits, of course, do not depict reality "just as it is," in all its manifold complexity. The art of portraiture tries only to capture a particular glimpse of a concrete reality. Good portraits manage somehow to capture a glimpse that both suggests the unexplored depth of the image being portrayed and links the image to a broad tradition of asthetic themes. The character portraits presented here are sketches (to be more elaborately detailed in future publications), which cannot convey all of the complexity of their objects. I have chosen these particular "glimpses" because of their relevance to certain theoretical themes I wish to elaborate, and in the limited space of this essay I cannot begin to suggest the subtle nuances of character, the inconsistencies of moral orientation, etc. that the actual persons being portrayed possessed. Thus, these glimpses are more like "ideal types" than good portraits. But I hope, nevertheless, that they capture more of the concreteness of the individuals being portrayed than the "typical" kinds of ideal types employed in sociology.

CHEN VILLAGE AND ITS ACTIVISTS

Chen Village is a small farming village, devoted mainly to rice production, with a population of about 1,200 people, located in Guangdong Province. Like many villages in this part of China, it is a single lineage village: all its members have the same surname—Chen—and all claim to be descended from a single common ancestor. When the boundaries of a single lineage coincide with the boundaries of a village community, the coincidence of lineage ties with community ties has typically given rise to a kind of community organization tightly knit along kinship lines, which could adopt a strong united front against the outside world. In the 1920s and 1930s Chen Village seems to have enjoyed a modest degree of prosperity, but in the turmoil of the late 1930s and 1940s it seems to have lost ground to its neighbors. The women of the village half jokingly say that they must have made some mistake in the process of reincarnation, to be fated to end up in such an unfavorable place. The villagers say that when you go to the commune or county seat you can always easily spot a Chen Villager, because he'll be "thin as a joss stick," ragged, and uncouth. When Chen Villagers go to meetings at the commune or county level, the middle-aged villagers often feel embarrassed because, while their peers from other villages scribble notes with pen and paper, they themselves are unable to read or write. There is a good deal of tension between Chen Village and its better off neighboring communities. When women from neighboring Song Village pass by, the Chen Village men sometimes heckle them with comments like: "Hey, wouldn't you like to get married into our village?" (Since they and their village were so poor, Chen Village men often in the past had trouble getting brides from other villages.) The people of neighboring Song Village, it is said, in turn put broken glass on the path leading from Chen Village to the commune seat, so as to puncture the tires of Chen Village bicycles.

Chen Village constitutes a single production brigade. It is one of nine such production brigades in its people's commune. The political organization (in terms of which the brigade forms a basic unit of the Chinese polity) is, thus, intertwined with the kinship networks (in terms of which the brigade is organized as a traditional lineage) and with the shared memories and sentiments (through which the villagers apprehend each other as occupying a common zone of familiarity and as possessing common interests and hopes).*

Now let me introduce three local leaders who played important parts in the village's history over the ten year period from 1964 to 1974 and who typified

---

*In southeast China it is very common for a single production brigade to be coextensive with the boundaries of a single natural village and very common for a natural village to consist almost exclusively of members of a single lineage. These arrangements do not so commonly exist in other parts of China. In northern China, especially, villages are smaller than in southern China, and several

certain contrasting styles of political conduct to be found in cadres and activists throughout the village.

The first person was nicknamed Old Pockmark, because his face bore the scars of smallpox, which he had had when he was young. In 1964 he was about 32 years old. He was a Communist Party member and was the brigade chief—the head of what used to be called the brigade management committee and is now called the brigade revolutionary committee, the committee in charge of the day to day administration of the brigade. Old Pockmark was a big, strong man. Physically, he was one of the strongest men in the village, and one of its best farm workers. This was an extremely important factor in his ability to gain the respect of the villagers. All of the village's leading cadres were physically strong and first rate farm laborers. The villagers simply would not accept as a leader anyone who was weak and incompetent in manual labor. In addition to his physical strength, Old Pockmark possessed an immensely strong personality. He had a kind of iron willed determination, coupled with a volcanically powerful temper. As one person put it: "his face was always like a cloud," dark and glowering and always ready to break into thunder. In a meeting, if anyone disagreed with him, Old Pockmark would scowl and sometimes yell and pound the table until the dissenter gave in and followed his way. These characteristics made him not much loved, but widely respected in the village. There were a few cadres who were mild-mannered and indecisive—"nice guys" (*shan liang*). But these cadres were never very effective. Villagers would not respect their leadership and would not follow them. They wanted their leaders to be tough, strong, rather authoritarian figures. And among such local leaders, Old Pockmark was pre-eminent.

Old Pockmark lived an austere lifestyle. He lived in what was by village standards a rather small and run down house, and, in the early 1960s at least, ate a rather meager diet of rice and fermented beancurd. This poverty was not simply a show. He was genuinely poor. Even though as a leading cadre he received one of the highest workpoint totals of anyone in the village, he worked so hard at his job that he neglected his family's private plots—private plots that in Chen Village could account for as much as 30 percent of most villagers' incomes.

His leadership style, as we shall see, was characterized by a relentless desire to change and to innovate. It was also marked by an almost rigid fairness. He resolutely refused to accept any kind of gifts from anyone in return for special favors. There was one celebrated incident in which some hapless peasant offered

---

villages usually make up a production brigade. Moreover, the coincidence between a single lineage and a single natural village is not so common in northern China. The patterns of interaction between kinship, community, and political loyalties recounted here should then be seen as fairly typical only of southeastern China.

him a small piece of fish with the apparent hope that Old Pockmark would give him some minor consideration in the future. And Old Pockmark, said an informant, "cursed him out like a beggar." In addition to refusing such gifts himself, Old Pockmark was vehemently opposed to other cadres who did take them.

But when Old Pockmark went outside the village, he often put on a different face. As part of his job, he was responsible for getting scarce items, such as lumber and nails, for the village's collective use. He was very good at making friends with bureaucrats in charge of allocating such supplies, cementing such friendships with meals and warm talk and little favors and in this way putting Chen Village in a favorable position to acquire such scarce resources.

Not many of the villagers felt much liking for Old Pockmark, but most of them respected him, however grudgingly. When asked to enumerate Old Pockmark's good qualities, several persons spontaneously said that one of his greatest virtues was that he "treated the village like his big family." That phrase is not an approved one in contemporary China. People who were sensitive to the official way of talking about correct moral character in China would dutifully say that Old Pockmark was "working selflessly for the collective." But the idea of treating the village like one's big family captures the style of Old Pockmark's dedication better than the officially approved and normally used terminology of working for the good of the collective. The officially approved terminology suggests a group of individuals—a collective—bound together to fulfill the truest common interests of China's laboring classes. In Maoist orthodoxy leadership in the collective should be radically democratic, based on the "mass line": leadership should articulate the truest interests of the "masses." But Old Pockmark acted toward the village like the authoritarian patriarch of a traditional family— not a warm loving father but a stern taskmaster who worked not to fulfill the interests of the individuals in the family but to build up the strength, prosperity, and glory of the family as a whole, as a unit rooted in generations of past ancestors whose well-being transcended and took precedence over the welfare of the individuals within it. Moreover, the orthodox communist idea of the collective suggests a unit nested within a wider society, the welfare of which is fundamentally congruent with the truest interests of the collective. But the patriarch of a traditional family was supposed to behave as if the interests of his family took precedence over all outside interests. In his relations outside of the family, he was supposed to do all that he could to put the good of his own family before all others. Old Pockmark was a harsh husband and a stern father, but he seemed to care little for the immediate well-being of his own small family. He treated the whole village as his big family, even to the point of ignoring the official rules set by outside authorities so as to further the prosperity of the village as a whole. It was this extraordinary "patriarchical" dedication to the village as a whole that made the villagers think of him as a leader worthy to be respected.

In sharp contrast to Old Pockmark was a man nicknamed Old Pepperpot, so nicknamed because, although rather small in stature, he was full of very hot stuff. Old Pepperpot was about the same age as Old Pockmark, but was Old Pockmark's political superior. He was the village's Party branch secretary—the formal head of the whole village. Like Old Pockmark, Old Pepperpot was also a first rate farm laborer and possessed a strong, decisive, hot tempered personality.

But he was not austere like Old Pockmark. He liked to live well and eat well. He had one of the finest houses in the village and his diet was rich in fish, poultry, and meat. Everyone of our informants agreed that he was not as fair in his dealings with villagers as Old Pockmark. He had a large, strategically placed circle of relatives and friends, and he was often seen at the houses of these persons partaking in good meals and friendly talk. In a poor rural community like Chen Village, to kill a chicken or duck or to catch a fish and invite a friend over to share in a good meal is one of the most important favors you have to give. Old Pepperpot very often accepted opportunities to receive such favors, and in exchange for them he was good to his friends, giving them some protection during political campaigns and managing to assure that the areas of the village where they lived would be allocated the best land, irrigation resources, and so forth. To people who were outside this circle of friends, Old Pepperpot acted in the same harsh way as Old Pockmark, badgering them and sometimes even physically pushing them around.

Village reaction to Old Pepperpot was mixed. Some people resented him for his lack of fairness. But many people felt reassured by the fact that, unlike Old Pockmark, he was, as they would put it "full of the taste of human feeling" (*ren qing wei*). For the people of Chen Village, "to have the taste of human feeling" means to respect, cherish, and be faithful to the ties of kinship that bind one to one's contemporaries by virtue of a common ancestry. It means to have sympathy for one's friends (who in a rural context consist mostly of one's relatives), to show kindness and courtesy with them, to exchange favors with them. To have the "taste of human feeling" means to be able to relax and enjoy good food and comfortable lodging if one can, and to share such goods with one's humbler friends and relatives in accordance with their means. It means to respect particularistic relationships, to accept the right of a powerful person to bestow patronage, especially along kinship lines, and to accept the need of the recipients of such patronage to maintain loyalty to him. The "taste of human feeling" remains very important in the consciousness of people throughout the village, and many people feel reassured by the fact that Old Pockmark is sensitive to relationships involving "the taste of human feeling."

Now, both Old Pockmark and Old Pepperpot are members of the Communist Party, and as such they speak in Communist jargon and try to justify what they are doing both to the people of the village and to their higher-level political superiors in terms of the idea that they are serving the people. But neither of them serves the people in the pure sense demanded by Maoist moral ideology. They do not subordinate all "natural" obligations to family and friends to the future good of an abstractly conceived people-in-general. In concrete practice, for Old Pepperpot serving the people means serving the relatively short-term interests of those relatives and friends who have made claims on him by cementing kinship and neighborly ties to him through giving him a steady stream of favors accompanied by appropriate expressions of warm human feeling. Old Pepperpot is not only *in*, but very much *of* a traditional social structure and moral order regulated by traditional moral concerns for the maintenance of "human feeling." For him, his verbal assent to the ascetic communist ideology has been merely a cover for his commitment to a traditional social order and a traditional ethos. For Old Pockmark, on the other hand, the official Maoist ideology has meant something else. It has resonated with a desire to transcend, indeed to struggle against, the ties which have traditionally bound Chinese people to close relatives and friends and to subordinate the interests of those persons to the long range goal of a wider collectivity: Chen Village as a whole. For Old Pockmark, the people he is to serve are the people of the village as a whole, the people who in the recent past were despised and exploited but now under the new communist political system have a chance to gain new wealth, power, and prestige and to look with pride on their neighbors. To serve those people means for him not to cater to their immediate interests but to transform their social relations so that they will be able to take advantage of their new social relations. Old Pockmark has become a revolutionary ascetic, not in the extreme way specified in pure Maoist ideology, but in a relative sense. And as I will show in the next few paragraphs, it is precisely because of those factors that make that asceticism not quite pure that Old Pockmark's brand of asceticism has a chance to endure, in the face of hardships and setbacks.

To help me eventually to make this point, let me describe one other character on the village scene—a young woman named Yang Meihua, who eventually became my research assistant. Yang was born in Hong Kong, but her father was a patriotic physician who returned to China with his family after liberation in 1949, when Yang was one year old. In 1964 Yang had just graduated from lower middle school but had failed to be accepted into senior middle. She was a Young Communist League member with a reputation for being one of the "reddest" students in her class.

This was the time when a vast national movement to send urban youth to the countryside was just gathering momentum. Later in the 1960s great numbers of city youth would be forced to go to the countryside, but for the time being such relocation was still voluntary, although impelled by great propaganda pressure. In response to these propaganda appeals, which said that it was a great and glorious thing for city youth to forgo comfortable careers in an urban environment and to dedicate themselves to serving the poor, lower-middle peasant masses of China, Yang volunteered to go to the Chinese countryside. She came to Chen Village as part of a group of 50 youth from Canton. Like many of the other youths, she initially tried with furious intensity to live a model communist life in Chen Village. She incessantly tried to "serve the people." But for her and many of her urban colleagues, serving the people was interpreted in a narcissistic kind of way. It meant living a personal life style worthy of China's poor, lower-middle peasants, whom the propaganda proclaimed to be the bearers of authentic revolutionary virtue. Thus, Yang and her urban friends tried to identify themselves with the life of poverty and hard work that the official ideology said formed the essence of the poor, lower-middle peasants' revolutionary nature. They went to ridiculous extremes to live poorly and work hard: they ate such meager food that some of them got dangerously thin; they pushed themselves to work so hard that the health of some of them broke down. The peasants whom they were imitating were not the empirically observable peasants who surrounded them, but the idealized peasants of revolutionary propaganda. The actual peasants of Chen Village thought they were crazy to push themselves so hard.

For the urban youth, to serve the people also meant constantly to criticize the people of Chen Village in the light of the lofty ideals of Mao's thought and to participate in political struggles against persons and customs that kept the village from being an ideal socialist village. Because these youth were literate and articulate, some of them—the most fervent and most articulate among them—were given a chance to become important propagandists in the village. They became the leaders of a newly formed organization of Mao Thought Advisers, which had as its purpose the preaching of Maoist virtue and the criticizing of people who did not live up to socialist ideals. Because of her extraordinary fervor and ability, Yang Meihua became a leader of these Mao Thought Advisers and also the person in charge of the local wired broadcasting system in the village. She became one of the most vocal figures in the village propaganda apparatus. More than any native of the village, she adopted an ascetic stance of living *in* but not *of* the village, criticizing all local, particularistic ties for what she perceived to be the revolutionary goals of the Chinese people as a whole. But her righteously "pure" asceticism would burn itself out when she encountered a few setbacks.

THE SOCIAL CONTEXT OF POLITICAL MORALITY IN CHEN VILLAGE

Now that I have introduced these three main characters, let me analyze the social roots of their distinctive styles of political behavior.

To do this, I must first analyze briefly the social structure and political position of Chen Village. The political position of the village can be defined in terms of a dialectic of dependence upon and autonomy from the apparatus of the Chinese state. The Chinese government provides a political/economic framework for assuring public security in the village and its environs; for extracting taxes, for stipulating basic quotas for foodstuffs to be produced by the village and sold at set prices through government channels, for providing limited opportunities for other goods to be sold on a free market, and for providing opportunities for village leaders to receive a limited amount of technical advice on how to improve local agriculture. But the village produces almost everything it needs for its own economic subsistence, with little direct economic aid from the state. Economically, in large degree, the state needs the village more than the village needs the state; and as long as the village hands over its assigned grain quotas, and as long as, from the outside at least, it appears relatively tranquil, the government apparatus often seems reluctant to interfere too greatly in the internal affairs of the village, for fear perhaps that if it did so, it would disrupt the village's economy. Moreover, the villagers are culturally isolated from the rest of China. Most of them are illiterate. Most have never travelled even as far as Canton, and in general they seem to have rather little conception of and interest in the outside world. Since the establishment of the People's Republic of China, the government has on a number of occasions tried to intrude rather actively into the affairs of the village, but these periods of intrusion have usually been followed by a kind of benign neglect, during which the villagers have been left in large degree to their own devices.

Thus, during a large part of the time, the villagers' experience is one of living a relatively self-contained life centered around the hard work of labor-intensive farming. Under such circumstances, their consciousness tends to be structured in terms of the moral idiom, which anthropologists tell us traditionally corresponded to the social relations characteristic of self-sufficient Chinese farming communities. The chief components of the vocabulary of this idiom are symbols expressing the importance of kinship, affirming the importance of the ties that link men together on the basis of descent from a common ancestor and women to their husbands and to the community of their husbands' relatives. This traditional idiom corresponds so closely to the social relations of isolated Chen Village that no villager can completely transcend it, and any villager who aspires to become a local leader must meet local expectations couched in terms of this idiom.

But the village's moral idiom has, as it were, several dialects, related to the fact that the village is not a perfectly integrated social unit, but instead is rent with contradictions. The chief conflicts dividing Chen Village are not simple conflicts between the economically rich and poor, but complex contentions between people rich and poor in terms of various kinds of social relations. The matrix of social life in the village is a complex amalgam of relationships based upon different and sometimes contradictory principles. These different and contradictory principles of social relatedness provide the foci for different and contradictory loyalties. And different loyalties are understood in terms of and justified by different conceptions of the proper moral basis for social commitment in the community.

The first set of principles regulating social relationships in Chen Village is based upon the objective bonds of blood created by possession of a common agnatic ancestor.[7] Thus, as members of a single lineage village, all of the males and the unmarried females in Chen Village are at least distant kin. But some are, of course, closer kin than others. According to classical Chinese moral thinking, under normal circumstances the closer the kinship ties, the closer the amount of mutual loyalty that should obtain. But, although all Chen Village males and unmarried females are distantly related by blood, only a minority belong to relatively extensive networks of close kin—kin related at least on the basis of a common great grandfather.[8] The most extensive such networks tend to be found in the middle part of the village. The eastern and, to an even greater extent, the western sections of the village lack such networks of kin.

The causes of this unequal distribution of extended kinship networks in the village lie in the complex interaction between commitment to cultural ideals, adaptation to economic constraints, and response to political opportunities in the course of the village's history. The Chen lineage had been divided into five "branches"—five lineage segments based upon descent from one of the sons or grandsons of the original founder of the lineage. Some of these branches had prospered more than others. Members of prosperous branches could have more children than members of less prosperous branches. More children eventually meant larger, interlocking networks of related households. Although each household provided the primary focus of loyalty for its members, households related by close ties of kinship were expected to help each other through exchanges of favors made with due respect for "human feeling." Wealthy relatives would provide appropriate material help during times of need, and less wealthy members would reciprocate with commitments of loyal cooperation. More mutual cooperation tended to lead to more general prosperity for members of the lineage branch, more prosperity to more children, more relatives, and more resources to exchange to cement subjectively the objective bonds of kinship. There had been one outstandingly successful branch of the Chen lineage—the Lotus branch—and most of the village's landlords and rich peasants had come from this branch. With the Communist directed land reform in the early 1950s, the landlords and rich peasants were dispossessed and politically neutralized. But the networks of close kin that had often helped people like them to get ahead still existed, and peasants who were officially classified as poor, lower-middle peasants could sometimes use those networks to advance their interests.

Old Pepperpot came from the Lotus branch of the lineage. His father was, in fact, the son of a small landlord and the brother of the village's biggest landlord. But in the early 1940s, Old Pepperpot's father went bankrupt, lost everything he had through opium smoking and gambling, and died an early death. Old Pepperpot was left a destitute orphan, and, when liberation came, he was duly classified as a poor peasant. He, thus, came out of a social milieu in which kinship and exchanges based on the principles of "human feeling" had worked to bring power and relative prosperity. Through his connections with an extended network of kin, he had opportunities to build up a power base by acting as the avuncular head of a traditional kinship network.

In the early 1960s Old Pepperpot had become Party branch secretary and, thus, formal head of the village. In this capacity he presided over the implementation of the 60 Points, the central government document that prescribed the formal economic and political structure that obtains for rural Chinese production brigades to this day. On to the structure of particularistic loyalties supported by the kinship principle, the 60 Points superimposed a set of impersonal relationships that defined the villagers not as kin but as producers and as citizens and regulated their responsibilities as members of collective economic and political organizations. According to the 60 Points, the basic unit of collective production in the countryside was to be the "production team," an organization of approximately 25 neighboring households, which collectively owned the major means of production, managed the labor of its members, and distributed among its members the net profit of its enterprises. A number of these teams—in Chen Village's case, originally ten—made up a production brigade, which was to be the basic unit for political organization in the countryside.[9] Old Pepperpot so arranged matters that most members of the network of kin to which he belonged were made part of the #5 production team, situated in the middle of the village. Then he proceeded to manipulate the assignment of collective lands to the teams in such a way that this team got slightly better land than any other. From the point of view of official communist ethics, of course, this was wrong: Old Pepperpot should have "served the people" by applying the rules for collective organization in a totally impartial way. But for the villagers brought up on the idea that it was somehow "natural" for close kin to be more helpful to each other than to very distant kin, Old Pepperpot's action was not inappropriate. He was acting on the basis of good "human feeling." And he might be expected to extend the scope of his "human feeling" beyond the boundaries of the network of his kin to include "friends" who had helped him with small gifts and favors. Old Pepperpot's conduct toward his kin provided a model for a more generalized kind of particularistic ethic, which could be applied to a patronage politics encompassing most segments of the village.

Although Old Pepperpot's behavior was officially wrong, his political superiors at the commune and county seats tended to overlook it, because it was politically effective. In the early 1960s, in an attempt to heal the chaos created by the Great Leap Forward of the late 1950s, official government policy emphasized the need to build up a stable rural social, economic, and political order. Government officials were more concerned with the effectiveness of grass roots leaders than with their righteousness. And Old Pepperpot was very effective in fulfilling his task of bringing about political stability in the village through his use of patronage politics justified by his respect for good "human feeling."

Old Pockmark, on the other hand, came from the western part of the village. His only close relatives were his mother and a younger brother. He came out of a social milieu in which kinship and exchange based on human feeling had not worked to create lasting loyalties, and he himself had no network of kin upon which to build a power base. To become an effective village leader, he had to appeal to a different set of loyalties focused on a different set of principles than Old Pepperpot. He appealed to the fact that the residents of the village occupy a single zone of familiarity—drawing upon a common heritage of life together, common memories of past glories and of recent bitterness, and common hopes for the future. He appealed to the idea that since this is so, the members of the village must put aside the differentiated loyalties that divide them from one another and work together like a single, closely-united big family in order to glorify their community over the outside world. All the people in the village, perhaps, share this sense of belonging to a single familiar community, just as they all recognize themselves as belonging to specific groupings of close kin and to new kinds of socialist economic and political units. The sense of belonging to a single big family, perhaps, comes most strongly to villagers' minds during times of crisis, when the whole community feels threatened from the outside. But it has a special appeal to people who do not belong to extensive networks of close kin—especially, therefore, to people in the western part of the village.

Now, the idea of making the village one's big family resonates more with the official ideal of serving the people than does Old Pepperpot's moral idiom. Thus, a political cadre like Old Pockmark who puts forth a claim to authority based upon the feeling that he is making the village like a big family can use the idea that he is authentically serving the people to criticize a patronage politician like Old Pepperpot for not being a good Communist. And under certain circumstances, such criticisms may be supported by the power of the Chinese state. Then the resentments and hopes of people like Old Pockmark and his followers can explode with furious power and some important social changes may be produced in the village.

But since the ideology of serving the people—with its implicit command to total commitment to the abstract people-in-general rather than simply to the people of a particular local community—does not fit perfectly with the idea of making the village one's big family, problems can arise from the point of view of central government authorities if people like Old Pockmark are allowed to have their way for too long. We can see this happening if we examine the ways in which Old Pockmark and Old Pepperpot fought with each other in the ten year period from 1964 to 1974.

POWER STRUGGLES, MORAL CONTRADICTIONS, AND ECONOMIC DEVELOPMENT IN CHEN VILLAGE

In 1964 Old Pepperpot was, as I have said, the highest ranking official in Chen Village as well as the most influential person in its informal power structure. He was, as some villagers put it, Chen Village's "local emperor." At this time Old Pockmark was, however, a dangerous rival. In late 1964 the first phase of the "four cleanups campaign"—a movement initiated by Mao to clean up cadre corruption in the Chinese countryside—hit Chen Village. Local Party officials received directives to investigate brigade officials for corrupt economic and political practices and to have the worst offenders "struggled against" in mass political rituals. As Chen Village's highest ranking Party official, Old Pepperpot was in charge of this phase of the campaign. He used the opportunity to get rid of his rival, Old Pockmark. He seized upon a minor indiscretion Old Pockmark had committed a half a decade previously and inflated it into a major transgression. Old Pockmark was then dragged out on a stage before all the peasants of the village, the crowd was whipped up by careful agitation into a frenzy, and the villagers were led to hurl curses and condemnations at Old Pockmark. When the session was over, he was led away in disgrace. It was a devastating experience for Old Pockmark. He went home and tried to commit suicide. Only the strenuous persuasion of his wife kept him from doing so.

But then in early 1965, a new phase of the "four cleanups campaign" began. This time a "workteam," composed of cadres sent into the village from outside, arrived to direct the campaign. After a three month long investigation, the workteam declared Old Pepperpot to be one of the major offenders against proper cadre morality in the village; he had brashly taken bribes, consistently shown favoritism, and so forth. To make a long and complicated story short and simple, Old Pepperpot was "struggled against" and deposed, and Old Pockmark—being in effect vindicated—became for all practical purposes Chen Village's "local emperor."

Old Pockmark then went to work enthusiastically and ruthlessly fighting against all forms of particularism in the village, striving to make people work less on their private plots and more for the collective and to use the extra collective wealth they thus produced not for their own immediate enjoyment but to provide capital improvements such as new roads, irrigation systems, and the beginnings of a local light industry system to benefit the village as a whole. One of his best helpers in this was Yang Meihua, along with some of her zealous young colleagues from Canton. Yang and her colleagues from the city felt no obligations toward and no special sympathies with anyone in the village, and she and her colleagues used this freedom from local ties to badger, criticize, and threaten people who were lazy or concerned more about the good of their families or friends than the good of the village community as a whole. Yang Meihua saw herself as doing glorious deeds for the good of the Chinese revolution as a whole, rather than just for the welfare of the village. But she was really being used by Old Pockmark and people like him to further the interests of the village as a united community.

Old Pockmark was at his fiercest when outside authorities backed him up just enough to assure his domination of the village, but left him relatively free to run the village as he liked. During the Cultural Revolution—from the end of 1966 to the beginning of 1968—the Guangdong provincial government temporarily collapsed, and the disintegration of provincial authority structures left Old Pockmark's grip on the village weakened. Under these circumstances, Old Pepperpot attempted a comeback by organizing the people of his home production team—the team that consisted mostly of his kinsmen and to which he had given special help in the early 1960s—to work against the village order presided over by Old Pockmark. He got the #5 production team to refuse to cooperate with any of the projects of Old Pockmark: so that if, for instance, Old Pockmark wanted the village to work together to build a new irrigation system that would eventually benefit the community as a whole, Old Pepperpot's team would refuse to cooperate as long as the project was not going to be of immediate benefit to it. And when that happened the other production teams would also refuse to cooperate, with the result that no cooperative work could be carried out for the good of the village as a whole.

By early 1968 the most chaotic phases of the Cultural Revolution began to wind down, and a stable structure of state power began to be restored. As this happened, government authorities again intervened in the affairs of the village. They directed that a campaign be carried out to "clean up the class ranks"—the purpose of which was to punish people who had too severely disrupted public order during the Cultural Revolution. County and commune government authorities did not, however, specify clearly who was to be punished during this campaign, and they left the local implementation of the campaign largely unsupervised. It was under these circumstances that Old Pockmark—as the saying went—"jumped the highest." He brutally attacked his old rival Old Pepperpot, along with a large number of alleged troublemakers. Old Pepperpot was locked up in a makeshift jail (the dressing room of the village stage) for almost a year and dragged out every few days for massive struggle sessions. This was a time of emotional frenzy. And the frenzy was not only directed against political offenders; Old Pockmark tried to channel it into efforts to fundamentally change the social and economic order of the village. For a brief time he tried (with the support of policies approved by district officials in his area) to make the villagers give up their private plots and to make production teams turn over their collective land to a single, brigade-wide collective organization. For a brief time, as a local saying went, "the whole village was a single beehive."

But the emotional zeal could not be sustained indefinitely. And when the zeal lagged, villagers' willingness to cooperate in new, radical social experiments lagged. After a few months the villagers were given back their private plots, and the production teams rather than the brigade resumed the main responsibility for the management of agricultural production. Moreover, a more moderate policy line came down from the county and commune levels of government administration; Old Pockmark's political superiors seem to have begun to fear that he was becoming too powerful and too independent and that the village was becoming too impervious to state control. So eventually another outside work-team came into the village to "readjust policy in the light of reality." The work-team criticized Old Pockmark for his "warlord workstyle" and gave Old Pepperpot and other victims of the "clean up class ranks campaign" a chance to rehabilitate themselves. Old Pepperpot turned in a virtuoso confession of repentence: he wept profusely, pummelled an effigy of Liu Shaoqi, and told everyone how he had been swindled by the thought of Liu Shaoqi and had walked down the evil path of capitalism but now was heartfully sorry and would grasp firmly the wise thought of Mao Zedong and was resolved never to walk the capitalist road again. He was so good at this that he was made a model of repentence and paraded around to all other villages in the area as a sterling example of a person who had truly repented.

In the several years that followed Old Pepperpot gradually got back into positions of political trust. He became village militia head and, by 1974, the head of village public security. His rise to official position both reflected and contributed to a change in the village power structure, in which Old Pockmark's influence was balanced out by the influence of people who thought and acted more like Old Pepperpot. By 1974 the intense public fervor that had been generated at times in the latter half of the 1960s had almost disappeared. Villagers tended to be more openly concerned than in those heady days about the welfare of their own household's private plots and less concerned with the collective welfare of their production teams or of the Chen Village brigade as a whole. Particularistic relationships gained more obvious importance.

Old Pepperpot gradually resumed his luxury loving ways. He again began to take advantage of his position to eat well and to avoid hard physical labor. Around 1973 he built himself a new house, a two-story brick structure that was one of the finest houses in the village. Old Pockmark, still maintaining a relatively austere life style (although even Old Pockmark began to slacken his austerity somewhat), was heard to mutter on occasion that someday a new political campaign would come along and then Old Pepperpot would get his just deserts!

The striving of Old Pockmark had left its mark, however. The extra wealth generated in the days when the villagers were working intensely hard for the common good of the whole collective had been invested under the direction of Old Pockmark into a number of new small-scale village industries—for instance a brick kiln, a rice milling factory, a sugar processing factory, a wine making enterprise, and a tool repair shop. These industries were controlled by the brigade as a whole, not by any of the production teams. The industries came to employ about one-sixth of the adult population of the village, committing them to a new village-wide level of economic organization and perhaps preparing the way for the growth someday of new kinds of moral commitment, focused more unambiguously than in the past on the village community as a whole. The profits from the first new village industries were plowed back into more industries. When the limits of small scale industrial expansion were reached, Old Pockmark invested the profits into public works: a new village school and a new village meeting hall. The meeting hall was especially impressive. It was a large two-story brick structure, so big it had to be supported by steel beams. "It was like a theater in Canton," said Yang Meihua. There was nothing like it in the whole commune. Perhaps the meaning of that hall for the villagers can be gathered from a phrase Yang Meihua used to describe it: It was, she said, "our village's glory." Chen Village, once looked down upon by its neighbors, had now put on a modern face, and the villagers could hold up their heads with pride. The hall was Old Pockmark's monument and the whole community's glory.

One casualty of this new state of affairs was the career of Yang Meihua. In the late 1960s Yang had felt that because of the tremendously zealous effort she had poured out in support of the struggle against selfishness and corruption in the village, she would certainly become a cadre in the new brigade administration. In 1968 she was indeed elected to a post on the village revolutionary committee. But her election was nullified by higher level authorities at the county seat. They said that they were concerned because her father had been of middle-class origin—a physician—rather than of proletarian origin. But perhaps they were also concerned about curbing some of Old Pockmark's power and were worried lest someone so effective in his service be put on the brigade revolutionary committee with him. It became clear to Yang that in the future she could play no outstanding political role in the village. Many of her young urban colleagues had already come to this realization, and those who had not yet done so finally came to it now. As this happened, Yang and most of her colleagues became terribly disillusioned. Their fiery zeal vanished and was replaced by a sad kind of cynicism. Like about 15 of her colleagues, Yang went so far as to escape illegally to capitalist Hong Kong, where cut off from family and kin, she began to become a kind of person relatively new to Chinese culture—a Western-style individualist.

Now let me try to use this story of little Chen Village to suggest answers to some of the big questions about commitment to the Maoist ascetic ethos in contemporary China with which I began this essay.

ASCETIC MORAL COMMITMENTS AND COMMUNAL
ATTACHMENTS IN RURAL CHINA

This case study of Chen Village suggests three different ways in which the Maoist ethos might come to have an influence on the tone and tenor of life in Chinese rural communities. The first type of influence is an essentially *external* one, arising from the fact that rural communities like Chen Village, although retaining a partial autonomy, are dominated by a powerful state apparatus which (at least until the recent fall of the Gang of Four) has used the Maoist ethic as its official ideology. Because of the partial autonomy of a community like Chen Village, very traditional particularistic forms of political behavior, as represented by Old Pepperpot, still persist. But because of the domination of a state that uses Maoism as an official ideology, leaders like Old Pepperpot have to pay at least lip service to Maoist ideology, and sometimes at least (especially when the state is making a major effort to penetrate the village) they have to act as if they were really committed to Maoist asceticism. Thus, Old Pepperpot, when he justified his behavior, had to speak in terms of serving the people, and, especially during and immediately after political campaigns, he had to forgo what a Maoist devotee would view as his corrupt behavior. During political campaigns, the contradiction between what he did and what he said sometimes got him into trouble, and to get out of trouble he had to make a convincing show of repentence and conversion to Maoist ideology. Since people like Old Pepperpot have to speak and at times act as if they believed the ideology, social changes take place in the village in accordance with the prescriptions of that ideology. But since the influence of the ideology is in this case mainly external, since the ideology is not fused with the passions of traditionalists like Old Pepperpot, the changes produced by this external influence of the ideology tend to get undone at times when the state is not willing or able to use its coercive power to force an external acceptance of the ideology.

But besides externally influencing the behavior of traditionalists in rural China, the Maoist moral ideology does under certain circumstances become fused with the internal passions and the sense of moral duty of certain groups of people on the rural scene. In places like Chen Village, at least, this internal influence creates two different types of revolutionary ascetics. These two types differ according to the sources of their commitment, the kinds of conduct it produces, the length of time it tends to last, and, accordingly, the kinds of social consequences it is likely to produce.

The first type of person who interiorizes the Maoist ethos is what I call the *individuated ascetic*, represented by Yang Meihua and some of her colleagues from Canton. The individuated ascetic is a rootless person separated from traditional kinds of obligations to family, kin, and friends; separated—typically perhaps by a "modern" formal education stressing abstract concepts—from the concrete, dense, affect-laden symbolic images that communicate the moral ethos of a traditional village community; separated, too, from constant concerns about how he or she is going to earn a living. Such a person's quest for a fundamental meaning and purpose in life can be fulfilled in a commitment to grand, abstractly-conceived visions of the world and history, and the visions might be grasped with special intensity if they are supported by a political system in such a way that the person perceives that commitment to the vision might not only provide an ultimate meaning for life, but might also lead to personal social mobility.

The type of commitment engaged in by individuated ascetics can lead to an extraordinary amount of self-discipline, but a discipline focused by an intense concern for personal purity, personal rectitude. It is a commitment that leads to a kind of ethic of absolute ends, engaged in without primary concern for its effects on society. Because such persons are always concerned with how good they are rather than with the practical business of influencing people who do not share their concerns, they do not directly move people who do not share this type of passion. Their influence on society is indirect. In Chen Village, zealous sent-down youth, like Yang Meihua had an influence in changing the village only insofar as their self-righteous fervor was used by cadres like Old Pockmark to morally terrorize villagers who did not agree with his purposes.

The fervent dedication of the individuated ascetic may be intense for a while, but it is not likely to be long lasting in China. It is, in the first place, vulnerable to shifts in official ideology. Thus, when Lin Biao fell in late 1971, the urban youth in Chen Village were genuinely scandalized and deeply disillusioned, while local village activists—especially the older ones—seemed to take the events in stride. Moreover, the dedication of the individuated ascetic is extremely vulnerable to failure to achieve political success. Finally, the dedication of the typically young individuated ascetic is vulnerable to the need he or she tends to feel with maturity to get married, raise a family, and make a steady living. When the fervor of the individuated ascetic burns out, it quickly devolves into a kind of egocentric individualism—a stance toward life more common to Western than to Chinese morality.*

Any American or European who has ever been in groups like the Peace Corps or perhaps bands of radical political activists in the late 1960s has witnessed a number of examples of this type of individuated asceticism. But because of its familiarity, the individuated ascetic is not, I think, so interesting sociologically as the type represented by the figure of Old Pockmark.

Old Pockmark is what I would call a *communal ascetic*. The communal ascetic is deeply tied to a particular community by bonds that are at once economic, social, and moral. It is through the economic structure of that community that he will have to make his living, so that his material prosperity will clearly depend upon its general prosperity; it is through the respect of that community's members that he will achieve his social status; it is through the common sacred symbols that bind that community together, link it to its past, and generate its hopes that the validity of his moral life will be measured. The commitment of the communal ascetic starts out of frustration; he comes from a sector of his community that has been relatively deprived of access to power, wealth, and prestige. But simple frustration produced by relative deprivation is not sufficient to explain this kind of ascetic commitment. The frustration jells into a fervent ascetic commitment when there is present in the community a set of moral images that can give to such a commitment a name and a goal, and can harness it into a critique of a set of frustrating social structures. These symbols must be consistent with the traditions of the community and correspond to the

---

*The moral stance of the individuated ascetic should not be seen as totally Western, however. According to Professor Thomas Metzger (personal communication), this ethos has analogues with the moral stance traditionally adopted by Chinese intellectuals when they were out of power.

rhythms of its life. But to correspond to the hopes of those marginal to the community, they must be permutations of the community's dominant tradition. Such symbols can provide the moral force for passionate protest.

But the permutations of the symbolic universe of a self-contained rural community cannot by themselves provide an effective program for far reaching, radical social change. The traditional structure of a place like Chen Village can never be overturned unless the structures of similar villages throughout China are also overturned. The resentments and hopes of people like Old Pockmark and his followers focused through a permutation of a traditional community ethos can only be channeled into effective change if they are made part of a national political movement. This is where the over-arching symbols of the Maoist ascetic ethos come in. They resonate with the deep, communally-based hopes of persons like Old Pockmark, and they direct those hopes into involvement with the organizational structure of the new Chinese polity. At various times in the history of the Chinese Communist movement, Chinese Communist propagandists have managed to propagate their ideology in such a way that it does resonate with the tradition-based hopes of persons like Old Pockmark. Resonating in this way, it makes them fervent and faithful workers for the Communist Party. It generates a fervor in them that stands the test of time, perduring in spite of personal setbacks.

And the setbacks are bound to come, because the roots of the commitment of a communal ascetic lie in the soil of his community, and his vision of the world is not perfectly fused with the overarching abstract vision of the official ideology. He is dedicated to the interests of his community, and those interests are not necessarily congruent with the interests of higher–level political organizations. This means that the passions for social change of the communal ascetic will eventually lead him in directions that, from the point of view of government bureaucrats, are harmful to the interests of the state. Old Pockmark gets too intensely involved in concern for the glory of his community. He begins to develop a "warlord work style." So the government clips his wings and lets the revolution move backwards. (The present policy of the Deng Xiaoping controlled government toward the countryside seems to favor the conduct of persons like Old Pepperpot much more than that of Old Pockmark. Within the last few months a friend of mine learned from a letter from someone in Chen Village that Old Pockmark has recently lost his cadre position and is now simply an ordinary citizen; Old Pepperpot, on the other hand, has been promoted to a position of responsibility in the commune seat.)

But political setbacks do not totally destroy the political activism of a communal ascetic like Old Pockmark. He keeps on struggling for social change and economic development in his village even though his power is diminished. What begins to undo him in the end is not political setback, but rather the fruit of his own creativity. One of Old Pockmark's great achievements was the creation of a new kind of small scale industrial enterprise in the village and the consequent development of a more complex village economy, which requires an increasing degree of sophistication to manage. In the early 1970s he began to make some blunders in administrating the small scale industrial expansion of the village. Part of the problem was that he was not good at making the complex calculations required to effectively plan such enterprises. He had, after all, never even learned to read. Now some young peasants who have graduated from rural middle schools are challenging Old Pockmark for leadership and are proving under certain circumstances to be more adapt than he at managing Chen Village's more complex new economic and political order. Old Pockmark helped to make history, but that history he made has tied the village into larger national processes of revolution and modernization. And, therefore, Old Pockmark has as fate the fact that history is coming to pass him by.

MORALITY AS A SOCIAL AND POLITICAL REALITY

The links I have drawn between Maoist inner-worldly asceticism and the actual moral commitments and sociopolitical involvements of Old Pockmark, Old Pepperpot, and Yang Meihua suggest a different way of looking at moral development than that adopted by many contemporary students of moral behavior, especially those influenced by Lawrence Kohlberg.[10] For Western students of morality in the Kohlbergian vein, moral development is a matter of the unfolding of the individual's capacity for reasoning. The highest stages of theoretical reasoning are marked by the ability to subsume particular cases in a systematic way under abstract general principles. Similarly, the highest stages of moral reasoning involve the ability to apply general principles about what is right and wrong to individual cases. The most mature kind of morality is that in which an individual acts according to his personally arrived at appreciation for general moral principles and not according to the sympathies and interests that tie him into a particular social situation. Social involvements, especially involvements that lead a person to desire the approval or fear the disapproval of members of a particular community, tend to create obstacles in the way of the most mature kind of principled moral behavior. Moreover, since the most mature kind of morality is based upon universal principles, fully mature morality is not only individualistic but also universalistic. Its principal cardinal virtue is an impersonal fairness.

The paradigm for "mature morality," then, is the morality springing from "inner-worldly asceticism," with its stress on action according to personally arrived at principles and its rejection of any particularistic loyalties. A Kohlbergian moral theorist would probably say that the ideals expressed in Mao's essays "Serve the People" and "In Memory of Norman Bethune" were the highest ideals of a morally mature person, even though he would say that the practical emphasis of the Communist Party and government apparatuses on automatic conformity to orders would inhibit mature moral development.

But in this essay I have suggested that individuated asceticism—individualized commitment to universalistic ideals—does not provide an adequate foundation for realistic, historically effective action in the world. It is the relatively universalistic asceticism of the person anchored in a particular tradition and committed to the welfare of a particular community that leads to lasting, historically efficacious action. It is certain kinds of community loyalties that nourish a self-transcending project of service for others. I would suggest with Durkheim that character of the self is developed by the character of society, even as the action of the self contributes to the transformation of society.[11]

And I would suggest with Aristotle that to know the content of appropriate moral behavior one cannot simply apply a deductive process to fit universal principles to concrete cases. Moral knowledge is different from theoretical knowledge or technical knowledge. Moral knowledge is tied to intimate involvement with concrete social situations. Moral maturity comes from the acquisition of virtues—habits developed through a lifetime of practical coming to terms with the demands of one's life situation. And the most important of the virtues is prudence—the ability to understand the unique set of responsibilities involved in a particular situation within society. There are no abstract criteria that can be applied to judge moral maturity; such a judgment must be made by considering the commitments and loyalties that make a person a vital member of a particular society.[12]

It was different kinds of social and, in the end, political involvements that shaped the moral conduct of Yang Meihua, Old Pockmark, and Old Pepperpot. To evaluate how "mature" that conduct was one has to understand how vitally it was connected to the cultural traditions and social structures of the concrete social situation into which those people were thrown and how appropriately it intended to transcend that particular situation.

Yet it remains the case that neither Old Pockmark, Old Pepperpot, or Yang Meihua developed a commitment to principles that transcends the community out of a previous involvement in that community for the justice of all communities—a type of moral action that starts in particularistic ties and ends in their rejection in favor of higher principles. Old Pockmark and Old Pepperpot seem forever destined to cyclical struggle. Is this as far as moral action can go? Is the leap to a transcendant moral order a myth?

Is it worth addressing this issue?

NOTES

1.   Mao Zedong, "In Memory of Norman Bethune," *Selected Works* (Beijing: Foreign Languages Press, 1967), vol. 2, pp. 337–338.

2.   Cf. Maurice Meisner, "Utopian Goals and Ascetic Values in Chinese Communist Ideology," *Journal of Asian Studies* 28(November 1968): 101-110.

3.   Max Weber, *The Religion of China*, translated, by Hans Gerth, (New York: Free Press, 1951), p. 247.

4.   Ibid., p. 236.

5.   Mao Zedong, "Serve the People," *Selected Works*, vol 3, pp. 177-178.

6.   Michael Walzer, *The Revolution of the Saints* (New York: Antheum, 1968), pp. 300-320.

7.   Cf. Maurice Freedman's classic work on this subject: *Lineage Organization in Southeastern China* (London: Athlone Press, 1958).

8.   According to the "classical" traditions governing lineage organization (Freedman, op. cit.), a special set of kinship—based loyalties should extend to all the persons related within the "five mourning grades." On the basis of our interviews with former residents of Chen Village, however, it appears that, in fact, Chen Villagers do not attach much importance to any relationships beyond those specified by dependence from a common great grandfather on one's father's side.

9.   For summaries of the formal structure of production teams, production brigades, and people's communes as established in the 60 Points, cf. John Pelzel, "Economic Organization of a Production Brigade in Post-Leap China," in *Economic Organization in Chinese Society*, ed. W.E. Wilmott (Stanford, Calif: Stanford University Press, 1972); and Byung-joon Ahn, "The Political Economy of the People's Commune in China: Changes and Continuities," *Journal of Asian Studies* 34 (May 1975): 631-658.

In 1969, the number of production teams in Chen Village was reduced from ten to five by the consolidation of pairs of teams.

10.   For the line of argument presented here, I am indebted to William M. Sullivan, "Moral Dilemmas and Deductive Ethics: The Limits of Lawrence Kohlberg's Theory of Moral Education," unpublished paper.

11.   Cf. Emile Durkheim, *Elementary Forms of Religious Life* (New York: Free Press, 1965); and Anthony Giddens, *Capitalism and Modern Social Theory* (London: Cambridge University Press, 1971), pp. 95-118.

12.   Aristotle, *Nichomachean Ethics*, Book VI; and Hans-Georg Gadamer, "The Problem of Historical Consciousness," in *Interpretive Social Science: a Reader,* ed. Paul Rabinow and William M. Sullivan (Berkeley: University of California Press, 1979), pp. 135-145.

8 SCARCITY AND MORAL AMBIGUITY IN CONTEMPORARY CHINA

Mitch Meisner

INTRODUCTION

"We are both Poor and Blank"

—Mao Zedong, 1956

Because of the difficult circumstances of its origin, the Chinese revolution, both before and after the seizure of state power in 1949, has had to find virtue in necessity. The flight for the failed working-class revolution from urban bases to underdeveloped but protective rural retreats in south-central China, the tour de force of the Long March—a triumph of necessity—to the even harsher hinterlands of the old northwest, the scene of nearly 25 years of isolated, blockaded struggle against richer Japanese and Guomindang armies, the post-1949 years of economic recovery and construction, first weathering the U.S. embargo and then Soviet divorce, all signified successive moments of severe external limitation within which Chinese revolutionary development was to prosper surprisingly well.

When Mao Zedong not long before the enormous and partially ill-fated take-off into a Great Leap Forward introduced into a complex analysis of China's socioeconomic and political tensions the "poor and blank" metaphor, thus signalling another round of struggle in which ostensible adversity was to be transformed by thought and action into real opportunity, he iterated an ambiguity in interpreting the significance of China's difficult conditions that has figured throughout much of the contemporary revolutionary period. This ambiguity has had a strong moral dimension. As guides for action, prescriptions flowing from behavior that was right and fitting for the heroic overcoming of adverse conditions to bring about radical ends have tended to spill over into calls to exemplify a kind of asceticism of character that finds in hard conditions opportunities to thrive, morally speaking.* It is the contention of this paper that a revolution conditioned by the struggle against and within adversity in an under-developed economic, political, cultural, and military climate of monumental scarcity has led to a major moral ambiguity regarding standards of personal and collective aspirations and behavior in a new stage of development. This ambiguity is most simply expressed as that between "finding" virtue in necessity and seeing necessity as a virtue precisely because it seems to occasion heroic or noble be-havior. If revolutionary virtue grew out of the most rocky and unpromising kind of soil, then success in economic development, especially by modern means, would seem to cut the ground out from under the possibility of further condi-tioning moral action.

Only now, in the post-Mao era, is this ambiguity being clarified by the present government. Dominant portions of the present leadership (and probably masses as well) certainly do recognize the value of the moral gardens cultivated in past historical deserts, but as for now and the future, while continuing to search out virtue in necessity[+] they will outlaw the notion that necessity is to be celebrated as a virtue.

Anyone reading various forms of public commentary issuing from the Peo-ple's Republic of China in the last years of the 1970s or even touring there and engaging in interviews and conversations will now be able to note a positive devotion to the idea that not only is it good to try to work for a "mighty social-ist China" but also to look directly toward your own improvement, your own relative payoff, comfort, and well-being while doing it. It is quite acceptable to expect that socialist development in China will develop a better material and cultural life for yourself, one, moreover, that is not necessarily precisely at the same level as your neighbors' or comrades' or country cousins'. Although there was never a time when Chinese leaders and ideologists, even the most radical, unambiguously articulated moral preachment to the effect that individuals in a period of socialist construction should simply be self-sacrificing and expect no meaningful personal benefit, popular heroic images, propagandized notions of both personal and popular good, certainly leaned in this direction, evincing at times something approaching regret for the absence in post-Liberation China

---

*Nowhere has this been better expressed than in Mao's famous reworking of the tale of Yugong, the foolish old man who set out to move a mountain with pick and shovel plus faith that generations of offspring would remain committed to his heroic but seemingly impossible endeavor.

[+]One extended example of continuing to find virtue in necessity is to be seen in the complex Chinese playing of the "America card" since rapprochement ten years ago.

of the "bad old days." Such attitudes, especially where they figure in economic policy, are straightforward abhorrent to the present leadership.

The significance of glorifying seemingly utopian efforts made necessary by attempts to achieve revolutionary goals within difficult backward conditions and, therefore, increasing the plausibility of success can be understood most dramatically by contrasting the "Sinicized" Marxist morality derived from Chinese historical experience to the original statements of native European Marxism about moral behavior and the objective conditions for its development in history. This comparison will be discussed in the first part of this essay. Then we will take note of present attempts to criticize aspects of past moralism that are aimed at changing the "political culture of economic life" and that speak toward the ambiguity deriving from the Chinese experience. Finally, we will assess possibilities and problems in attempts at establishing a set of values more consistent with present conditions.

THE ORIGINAL MARXIST VIEW OF THE POSSIBILITIES FOR MORAL BEHAVIOR

Marx, like other progeny of the heroic age of European capitalism, admitted that necessity is the mother of invention. But he also recognized that different ages of human history produced different sets of innovating parents. And, on the contrary, inventions (and their human use), following Marx's materialism, tended to sire new types of necessity, the most central of which was, of course, the state of any human society at a given time with its characteristic, reproducible patterns of human interaction and conflict. For Marx the most advanced form of human necessity, and the one to which he paid most attention, was the highly productive and highly oppressive social system of industrial capitalism that matured in the West. Marx's historical critique of capitalism formed the basis for the full explication of his theory of moral behavior and moral development in human society. Some basic aspects of this theory are relevant to our understanding of the Chinese case.

The Marxist view is that the possibility of moral behavior is both created and thwarted by the particular historical forms of existence of human society. Only the development of human society gives people the opportunity to develop their collective powers to the fullest and thus to recognize in their interrelated activities the basis for a truly human existence, one that finds an unforced solidarity between self and the social whole. But human social history to the modern period has been one in which the various societal arrangements, built around changing cores of material necessity, have served to create relationships of unequal wealth and power and to alienate individuals from full unity with their own selves and their fellows. The key to the problem of moral behavior in human development over historical time is the actual material conditions of scarcity. Attempts so far to transcend poverty, only partly successful, have lead to invidious social stratification and lack of full moral sensibility.

Because human interrelationships are seen as moments of historically rooted relations to material life, the possibility for moral behavior among human beings is seen as emerging only in correspondence with the growth of material civilization (and certainly not in fulfillment of divine commandments or other mere statements of ethical ideals). In this process, the appearance of modern capitalism should pave the way for the final realization of those material conditions that for the first time can underpin fully realized, moral human relations. Capitalism makes several advances. First, it provides the economic momentum and technological capability to produce abundance and relieve socially productive labor of the endless backbreaking toil characteristic of scarcity. Thus may be ended the brutal conditions that debase conceptions of human possibility and give rise to religious or spiritual fantasies as sole hopeful responses to bleak and undeveloped life on earth. Second, the expansion of capitalist production and trade tends to universalize existence, brings more people in more places into a relationship through a complex, highly productive division of labor, and reduces scattered, solitary, or provincial ways of life to secondary aspects of integrated and, perhaps, world civilization. Third, and at the core of moral behavior, capitalist production relations are "socialized" to a large extent because of the mass character of work in industry with differentiation and interdependence in the direct production of goods replacing individual, small-scale production as the basis of experience in work. Only ownership and management remain private and separate. When revolution destroys private ownership and control of the means and fruits of production, then the solidarity that has been brewing between workers in one side of an alienated process can lead to complete unification of the individual and the human group—as all work in common, all enjoy the collective fruits of their labor, and the basis is laid for minimizing the competition, to obtain equally hitherto unequal opportunities to survive and prosper. "In the process," the solidarity that grows among members of the working class finally can become rationally connected to the great productivity brought about through capitalist expansion. In capitalist society, the basis for individual antagonism against others—either because of class hatreds or personal jealousies wrought by scarce opportunities or brutal life conditions—are minimized. The capitalist society that lays the basis for abundance but heavily exploits most individuals becomes a socialist society that plans in common, shares wealth, and allows for a mature and nonantagonistic relationship of individual and group or community without demanding submergence of the individual to the group. An important corollary to this analysis, of course, is that, given the lack of fundamental social antagonism, the basis for political domination exercised by a state apparatus is undermined, and governing should become a matter of common economic administration rather than coercive political coordination.*

Therefore, in a socialist system, an historical and material basis for developed moral behavior comes about. Its core is socialized production at a high technological level of productivity and the ending of capitalist class domination over the production system.

In his famous piece on the transition to socialism, "Critique of the Gotha Program," Marx argued that although capitalism in a relatively advanced state will give way via revolutionary socialism, this change would not result immediately in a communist society nor in communist relationships among people or communist self-regulation of behavior. Rather, on the basis of the existing level of economic development, the rational operation of social productive capacity for the first time freed from the irrationality and competitiveness of private capital would be able to bring society to a material condition of full abundance. On that basis, and only on that basis, people would be able to realize fully the kind of mutual relations, moral outlook and behavior that before had only been dreamed about. In writing about the transitional society "which is...in every respect, economically, morally, and intellectually, still stamped with the birth marks of the old society from whose womb it emerges,"[1] Marx makes it quite clear that communist morality will flower only in the complete absence of scarcity—not only in terms of material goods, but also in so far as debilitating structural conditions in the economic division of labor have been eliminated:

> In a higher phase of communist society, after the enslaving subordination of the individual to the division of labour, and therewith also the antithesis between mental and physical labour, has vanished; after labour has become not only a means of life but life's prime want; after the productive forces have also increased with the all-round development of the individual, and all the springs of co-operative wealth flow more abundantly—only then can the narrow horizon of bourgeois right be crossed in its entirety and society inscribe on its banners: from each according to his ability, to each according to his needs![2]

Marx's insistence that the realization of a communist society with equivalent communist values demands full abundance is well known. Somewhat less publicized is another argument, one that looks toward politics, specifically revolutionary action, to complete the remaking of a universal and fully human class and corresponding moral consciousness:

---

*The degree to which this principle, simply put, inheres in Marx's formulation is subject to debate. For a brief survey of opposing points of view concerning politics and freedom in Marx's thought, see Peter Singer's review article, "Dictator Marx?," *New York Review of Books* (September 25, 1980): 62–66.

Both for the production on a mass scale of this communist consciousness, and for the success of the cause itself, the alteration of men on a
mass scale is necessary, an alteration which can only take place in a
practical movement, a revolution; this revolution is necessary, therefore,
not only because the ruling class cannot be overthrown in any other
way, but also because the class overthrowing it can only in a revolution
succeed in ridding itself of all the muck of ages and become fitted to
found society anew....[3]

Conditions of abundance were hardly available to architects of socialism in
China, although economic circumstances have improved measurably since 1949.
But the economic scarcity and other harsh conditions in which the Chinese
Communist movement achieved its initial, perhaps astonishing successes signified by the establishment of state power posed an alternative set of possibilities
for a revolutionary ethic, one that ultimately meant a problem for the Communist moral tradition in the present period: the tendency for political leaders
to continue to advocate the morality appropriate to successful revolutionary
political action within the harsh preconditions of the seizure of state power in
a stage of development in which characteristics more consonant with the approach of abundance should become viable and acceptable. It certainly is true
that the fires of revolution that burned in a protracted struggle of more than 30
years to the time of Liberation provided perceived and actual potential for moral
cleansing and rebuilding of character. And severe economic necessity continued
to impose conditions that *perhaps* called for waging an analogous revolutionary
battle in the material realm from the 1950s to the present. During a significant
part of the latter period, the actual choice was indeed to attempt to sustain the
tradition of communist selflessness and heroic self-sacrifice as the fundamental
image of moral character in Chinese society. And attempts to continue in this
moral pathway despite improvement or potential improvement in productive
forces and material standards of living has been a central dilemma in contemporary Chinese Communist history. The moral legacy of the pre-Liberation period
has been of essentially ambiguous value to the post-Liberation leaders and the
Chinese citizenry. This has been true not only in its reflection on the choice of
personal behavioral models, but also, if we are to believe an avalanche of post-
Mao, post-Gang of Four criticism, the ambiguous moral heritage posed an ideological problem that affected adversely the formation of economic (and political)
policy as well.

THE CHINESE EXPERIENCE: STRUGGLE AGAINST SCARCITY
AND THE LEGACY OF REVOLUTIONARY MORALITY

It may be a commonplace to observe that all communist revolutions to this
day have occurred in societies other than the highly developed capitalist states
of Europe that Marx predicted. From the great Bolshevik revolution of 1917 in

an agrarian bureaucratic empire on the periphery of Europe to the socialist political transformations in former Third World colonies in recent years, all have been characterized by underdeveloped or dependent economies, far from the realm of abundance based on full development of productive forces that Marx emphasized. Today all are doubly burdened by weak positions within the dominant world economy. Additionally, events have shown that the incidence of national rivalries, interstate military competition and fearfulness is far from over, further distorting the conditions of existence in which a transition to communism as Marx envisaged it might be achieved. As Andre Gorz has argued in a path-breaking essay entitled "Arduous Socialism,"

> In no country has socialist revolution taken the form of the collective appropriation of an already developed productive potential, and therefore of the subordination of economic necessities to the demands of collective and individual human liberation, such as the creation of a genuine democracy founded on the power of the producers to regulate production and exchange according to their needs.[4]

Furthermore, following the leading example of the Soviet Union, forced into an agonizingly rapid development mobilization by its isolation in the interwar world, these revolutionary societies have tended to see the primary meaning of socialism as a path to the most intense and rational mobilization of all indigenous resources to achieve economic development, to accumulate the military power to face external enemies and internal counterrevolutionary threats, and so on. Enfranchisement of the former dispossessed classes in the revolutionary process became one and the same with integrating them and their labor power into prodigious economic efforts.

Gorz notes that with strong reason, but problematical results, the association of socialism with developmental mobilization in poor and perhaps beleaguered countries (or liberated portions of countries one might add), required adjustments in the socialist vision about the organization of power and the nature of human relations in the economy and other social spheres, and, by extension, the nature of the dominant morality. Most important, Gorz argued, were outcomes that involved the necessary subordination of democratic bodies of workers or producers to centralized hierarchies that specialize in economic (and political or military) planning and leadership. The nature of the process of socialized accumulation of economic goods for investment and growth (i.e., "socialist construction") within scarcity economies is such that the pressures on the rank and file workers, peasants, and citizens surpass those involving simple or power-neutral economic "coordination" to involve rigorous actions by the state to obtain the surplus products of agriculture or industry in order to boost development. This state-enforced economic behavior becomes the social norm within a context of considerable scarcity in personal income and standard of living (though radical social welfare policies may ease this problem somewhat).

It has therefore been necessary, Gorz argues, for political leaders in such societies to establish collectivist ethics that enforce the need for rapid accumulation within conditions of scarcity, thus, so to speak, "reinventing an *ethic of productivity*" (my emphasis),

> which in certain respects resembled the ethic of the puritan bourgeoisie in the heroic age of capitalism: namely, an ethic of self-denial, frugality, austerity, unremitting labor and self-discipline, and also of moral vigor, prudery, cleanliness, and sexual repression. Man, according to this ethic, was not brought into this world to enjoy himself in his passion for work; he would reap his reward in the future society for the sake of which he was sacrificing in the here and now....[5]

Similarly, Nguyen Khac Vien, a Vietnamese scholar and publicist, describes the virtues of socialism in the Third World with a strong developmentalist thrust. Socialism, he argues, equips Third World populations, in the absence of strong, unified, progressive capitalist classes, with an ethic or ideology of "positive liberty"—the ability and obligation to act energetically and concertedly for development—rather than the "negative liberties"—to be left alone—that are so deeply engrained in developed bourgeois societies.[6] The "ethic of productivity" means the internationalization of a moral standard that will govern everyday economic and other social activity in conditions of "arduous socialism" (Gorz's term).

Gorz's argument on the ethical level, therefore, is an interesting elucidation of the familiar critique of the actual nature of production relations in the experience of the Soviet Union and other would-be socialist societies: the promised socialist liberation of workers and their ensuing "free association" as "masters" of their labor seem engulfed by a powerful political-bureaucratic management apparatus, and the new system fails to overcome the subjugated nature of their former positions under capitalism. But his argument contains an important qualification, and this exception provides a hint to guide us in approaching the complexities of the Chinese situation. Gorz admits that, although the need for an "ethic of productivity" or "socialist Puritan ethic" seems to signify a failure in the realization of nonalienated human relations under socialism, in certain specific phases of revolutionary activity, service based on ethics that call for self-sacrifice and personal abnegation may in fact be quite authentic—not the manipulated product of state bureaucratic leadership. In these conditions, people caught up in common struggle may share genuine, nonmystified, positive commitments that are related to their actual interests.

For example, during periods of active fighting against national enemies (as the Japanese in China) or against clearly identifiable political or class enemies (as the KMT or local and village elites during the civil wars and land reform) by a people enduring common hardships, collective links between heroic endurance and sacrifice and the overcoming of self-interest and individual interest may be forged. In such a period, people on the revolutionary side are not really forced to choose between actions (including cooperative ones) that further their immediate and perceived self-interests and behavior that furthers the greater purposes of the social whole. This special kind of unification of individual and revolutionary movement distinguishes the meaning of the morality or ethical ideal of this period from that of a later one in which an "ethic of productivity," although still based on selfless collectivism, seems to serve primarily the economic imperatives set by leaders of Party and state.

That such conditions were experienced in a protracted way in the Chinese revolution, I will argue, gave a particularly strong practical legacy and popular character to ideologies or personal ethics of collective commitment or selflessness.* And given the special place in practice and theory in China of the post-Lenin Communist Party, a highly conscious "vanguard" of revolutionary leadership and disciplined action, heroic ethics based on the personal conquest of self-interest may become especially strongly embedded in the concept of good Party membership. The Party example, in turn, would provide images for good moral behavior for all individuals committed to the revolutionary society.

In the Chinese case such collectively understood ethics of personal dedication and sacrifice were inculcated into the ideology of the revolutionary military forces. The Red Army, the Eighth Route Army, the PLA, and all other military units of the revolution and national resistance were indoctrinated with a series of ideals calling for personal dedication, overcoming of selfish desires, kindness and rectitude in the treatment of civilians, and, especially, deeply engrained political discipline among those key military personnel for whom being a Communist Party member and a member of the armed forces impose moral responsibilities heightened by the overlapping military and Party identities. (Especially in its later development in the anti-Japanese period, the inculcation in officers and troops of both political and military tasks and identities was much greater in the Chinese army than in the Soviet Red Army, for example.)

To understand the moral vision generated during the protracted revolutionary struggle in China, we may note, for example, the three short pieces by Mao Zedong, significantly revived during the Cultural Revolution as the "Three Constantly Read Articles," (*Lao San Bian*), each of which taught a different lesson about revolutionary heroism. "Serve the People" is the title given to a memorial speech delivered by Mao at a meeting to honor the memory of Zhang Side, a soldier at Central Headquarters and a member of the Communist Party,

---

*The actual relationship between such "revolutionary asceticism" and values flowing from customary peasant village culture in the course of political upheaval is an intensely complicated question and beyond the scope of this essay. See, for example, James Scott's *Moral Economy of the Peasant* (New Haven, Conn.: Yale University Press, 1976) for relevant ideas—also the debate over Chalmers Johnson's concept of "peasant nationalism" in the Chinese revolution.

who had been killed in the collapse of a charcoal kiln. In his address, Mao linked the idea of personal sacrifice to collective service to the Chinese people. Much struggle and personal loss will be necessary to alleviate mass suffering, but it will have great significance because of the reasons for sacrifice. The symbolic significance of the honor done to Zhang involves the fact that he was engaged in a branch of "economic work" and killed in a mundane accident rather than an act of martial glory. Zhang Side, both soldier and Communist Party member, is, structurally, a core exemplar of an ethic of personal sacrifice that finds significance in service to the whole.[7]

In Mao's earlier statement on the death of Norman Bethune, volunteer Canadian battlefield surgeon who died of accidental blood poisoning induced while operating on a wounded soldier, the theme of sacrifice in a large popular cause is also taken up. Bethune's mortal service to the Chinese people is a superb example of the "true communist spirit":

> We must all learn the spirit of absolute selflessness from him. With this spirit everyone can be very useful to the people. A man's ability may be great or small, but if he has this spirit, he is already noble-minded and pure, a man of moral integrity and above vulgar interests, a man who is of value to the people.[8]

Again, a strong egalitarianism, one that defies the logic of economic accounting, is evident here—as in the case of Zhang Side, a case in which Mao advocated that both "cook and soldier" should have a memorial service if killed in the struggle—sacrifice underlaid by a selfless communist spirit defies comparative measurement—all such sacrifice is useful and of value to the people. The emphasis is on sincerity and thoroughness of effort—whether the ability be large or small, recognition will be the same. In contrast, in his "Gotha Program" analysis, Marx specifically argues that in the transitional period before communism workers will receive rewards directly proportional to their (educated) abilities.

The "foolish old man" appears in a fable used by Mao to illustrate the enduring patience and dedication of the Communist Party of China in opposing seemingly insuperable odds to win a victory over domestic and international opposition. Operating in the most primitive of conditions and with the most primitive of tools, backed only by stubborn perseverance and faith, Yugong, the foolish old man, tries to dig away two mountains in front of his house. The job, he knows, can only be completed in succeeding generations—it is obvious that no immediate material reward will be his. However, it is the solidarity of his supporters and followers, inspired by Yugong's moral demonstration, that is gained from such selfless dogged efforts.[9]

The notion that personal sacrifice and a spirit of selflessness, no matter what the degree of ability or centrality of the task, are valued as noble components of a common struggle finds some similarity with the ideas, (also very important to the Chinese Communist victory in a protracted struggle) that poor resources can be utilized for powerful results, that one may view a powerful enemy as strategically weak (the famous "paper tiger" image), that human will and spirit (the essence of human resources) are more powerful than technology and machines or weapons—all of these ideas form the basis of what is sometimes called a *voluntarist* conception of revolution, in which willpower and organization are seen as transcending material inadequacy. One of the most important symbolic statements of this view was made by Mao in his speech on "The Situation and Our Policy After the Victory in the War of Resistance Against Japan," given on August 13, 1945.[10] In this speech, Mao not only raised the slogan of "self-reliance," famous as the Chinese economic development watchword of the 1960s, but also spoke with almost studied self-confidence to potential U.S. supporter of the KMT,

> If you Americans, sated with bread and sleep, want to curse people and back Chiang Kai-shek, that's your business and I won't interfere. What we have now is millet plus rifles, what you have is bread plus cannon.[11]

"Millet plus rifles" against "bread plus cannon" is an enduring image of warfare and revolutionary struggle amidst scarcity and backwardness. There is no implication, of course, that someday the millet and rifles would not be turned into bread and cannon in the event of a successful revolution, but the point is that the great initial act itself can be carried out in the meantime. The secret, or strategic resource, that will be mobilized is the Chinese people:

> To whom does China belong? China definitely does not belong to Chiang Kai-shek, China belongs to the Chinese people. The day will surely come when you will find it impossible to back him any longer.[12]

The moral legacy of the Chinese Communist revolutionary movement is a complex one and easy to characterize in a one-sided way. Despite all emphasis on heroic and selfless virtues, its theorists and propagandists had no intention of arguing that willpower and sacrifice can triumph over absolute impossibilities. Certainly, it is not true that the Chinese revolution was devoid of rational calculation, of genuine regard for the enormous obstacles it faced. Chinese leaders, especially after the 1920s, were quite aware of the distance of the Chinese circumstances from the classic European Marxist vision. But it was also recognized that apparently intractable conditions might hold and reveal hidden resources if bold and decisive actions and patient and persistant organizing were attempted. And these could only find plausibility and impetus if a self-sacrificing collectivist ethic pervaded personal motivations, especially among leaders and core revolutionary activists. So, in many ways, the emphasis of the strengths and hidden potentials within underdeveloped, backward, and beleaguered situations led to incorporation of a revolutionary morality that became very well integrated with a practical possibility it helped create.

The work of the PLA, for example, political and sociological action (transformative of its members) as well as military, became the case in point. In fact, the People's Liberation Army and its earlier forms were as successful as they were and won so much popular adherence and support precisely because their style of work built on a morality attuned to scarcity, to harshness, and to the need for solidarity with the masses in facing these conditions. High morale, politically educated and popularly supported rank and file troops, and an ability to find constant citizen support became strong material conditions backing the military actions taken over the years under the rubric of a people's war. It is extremely revealing, in fact, that the PLA continued to play such a central role, symbolically as well as organizationally, into the time of the Cultural Revolution. The PLA, especially the "reformed" Lin Biao version in the early 1960s, revising the 1950s "military modernization" model, has been a very important vehicle for reproducing the virtues of self-sacrifice, simplicity, hard work, and other aspects of a socialist "Puritan ethic" (as Gorz puts it). The campaigns around young PLA recruits like Lei Feng in the mid 1960s, who made simple, mundane but heroic sacrifices in the name of absolute self-abnegation and collective commitment, carry through this tradition completely. What becomes most striking is the apparent fact that some long-time Party and military leaders preferred the image of a people's army, highly *unmodernized* in technological terms (also cheaper) and depending on the "human factor" first to carry forth the responsibilities of a military force in the contemporary world. This belief, a concerted and dangerous carryover of the past into a different present according to recent critics, is one instance of a more general problem in which solutions quite congenial to the old morality are roundly criticized for being carried over into today's policies. But despite the possible unsuitability of heroic morality, of images drawn from a protracted people's war for contemporary economic development tasks, what other moral images may replace them in order to further the "four modernizations"? And since there is still considerable economic underdevelopment in China, will not some version of the "ethic of productivity" that Gorz pessimistically attributes to a socialist society of scarcity be desirable to leaders, although in a form that is more technocratic and individual-centered and not laden with earlier heroic collectivist trappings? One interesting set of images to consider in this regard, for example, concerns those themes that figured prominently in the so-called "revolutionary dramas" promoted during the Cultural Revolution, linked especially with the name Jiang Qing, and now replaced or repudiated. Many operas, revolutionary ballets, and so on dealt with the heroic days of the periods of revolutionary civil war and anti-Japanese struggle; few effective, acceptable dramas dealing with contemporary struggles for economic development seemed to emerge. More than ever, the military setting was called forth to reaffirm the morality of collective commitment and self-sacrifice; the economic front of post-Liberation China was not replete with such images.

The problem, the ambiguity of the moral legacy of the heroic period of the Chinese revolution in its application to action and policy in the contemporary world, may be stated as follows: Ideals for personal (and group) action that demanded selflessness and personal sacrifice, at the core of the "spirit of communism" as the "Long March generation" conceived it, were rationally conceived and remarkably efficacious in their indigenous setting. They helped inspire action that amazed the world and helped lead to outcomes that reflexively corroborated the seemingly utopian conception of revolution in Chinese circumstances. But, after all, the revolution itself was not simply an act of anger, of class or nationalist passion. It was also carried out in the name of an end to impoverished conditions, of the growth of national prosperity, and of an overall improvement of the Chinese standard of living. In other words, sacrifices of the revolutionary generations should lay the basis for the genuine ending of hardship and sacrifice for succeeding generations.

But, upon revolutionary victory (seizure of state power) and the initiation of a new stage signified by the hard fight to raise an impoverished nation to modernity and well-being, there may be a strong impetus toward central coordination by an expanded state structure pursuing a rapid, arduous movement toward economic accumulation. It is quite likely that progress on the new path will entail the transformation of the earlier authentic revolutionary ethic of the pre-Liberation period, as Gorz argues in general terms, into a social ethic of productivity that may subordinate individual workers to the societal struggle against nature, struggle in the factories and fields, and struggle for national economic development. In its most intensified form, such an ethic could be subverted into a legitimizing ideology for the purposes of managers and bureaucrats in a state-centered economic apparatus, using moral exhortation harking back to the symbolism of the old heroic solidarities to maintain hard work and discipline among a growing industrial work force or a peasantry not yet able to receive much in the way of material layoff from a still underdeveloped economy. And, ironically, because of the great historical appeal of such an ethic due to its earlier rootedness in the real conditions of the liberation movement, the ideologists who now lead the economic struggle may be quite sincere in their approach. Possessing actual beliefs quite consistent with their outward moral preachments, they might advocate wholeheartedly ill-advised strategies of growth in poverty. Gorz does not really seem to deal with this latter possibility, seeing the "ethic of productivity" as primarily a manipulative *ideology* of socialist management, albeit a necessary evil in a scarcity economy.

It is, in fact, even possible that leaders of the modernizing Chinese state and economy would go so far as to look with some suspicions or doubts at the appearance of "shoots" of prosperity and modern ways and look with favor, perhaps nostalgia, at the old, more simple days when a genuine solidarity and revolutionary fervor was underlined by everyday experience and gave an elevated ethical flavor of mass commitment to the practical work of society (and strengthened their own legitimacy). For it was clear that seeking a successful outcome to post-Liberation work of building a modern, prosperous, powerful socialist China called precisely for eliminating the old conditions, plowing under the soil in which so many of the revolutionary ideals had flourished, so many socialist relations had flowered, and so many sacrifices had been made. Thus, through the kind of development that must surely be the ultimate end of revolutionary aspirations, the moral basis of historical revolutionary successes might be undermined. What might then appear but a new era of selfishness, narrow materialist thinking, lack of regard for the hardships *and* the solidarities of revolutionary ancestors in the past—a vulgar turning to material payoffs to encourage effort, invidious and hierarchical distinctions made between different levels of skill and output where once a spirit of sacrifice had been a great leveler of the value of different personal efforts. In other words, there would be a risk, in the very success of the economic development sought, of bourgeoisification, of capitalist attitudes growing in socialist ground. Thus, why rush away from the heroic past to a modernized but morally compromised future? Hence, the once extraordinary ability to perceive at work in primitive circumstances dialectical forces that could allow for so much genuine revolutionary power to be generated might now under new conditions become a flawed perception that was at best romanticized and at worst opportunistically used to gain privilege, and that ignored the imperatives of change and growth and the satisfaction of new wants.

For many years, attempts at maintaining a revolutionary ethic, or developing "new socialist persons," enlightening mass consciousness, and insuring mass input in the development process were regarded by sympathetic observers as special qualities of the Chinese revolutionary experience. The antibureaucratic intentions of the Cultural Revolution, the attempts to continue revolutionary education, the links between the realms of modern, urban government, culture, and high technology and manual, especially rural, productive labor, attacks on stratification in the production system according to pursuit of egoistic payoffs and routinization of command structures all seemed admirable—the "serve the people" orientation of the PLA was to be widely emulated. The determined pursuit of self-reliance, the economic autarky in the work system, and the emphasis on continuing political mobilization was admired and celebrated by many, this author included.* But in attempting to understand the dramatic reversal of slogans, of political platforms, of economic and social policy in the years since Mao's death and the demise of the Gang of Four, attention to some of the ambiguities in the post-Liberation use of the moral legacy of the pre-Liberation period and some issues affecting the possibility of its continuance into the present (especially that of the so-called Yanan Spirit) may help us understand some of the rationale and perhaps the popular support for the reversals. We will discuss briefly a number of examples below.

---

*Hence the interest in Marx's political *praxis* condition for transforming through revolutionary struggle in the direction of communism—Mao's political concerns seemed in line with this issue. See p. 181.

SACRIFICE AND EGOISM IN THE POST-MAO ERA:
DOES CHINA SEEK A "MORAL MODERNIZATION"?

Considerable criticism has been vested in the past several years on policies or political attitudes extant since the Cultural Revolution began, if not before. Many of these involve issues we have raised above. For example, Cultural Revolution criticism of what was called the erroneous "theory of productive forces" has in turn been subjected to scathing counter criticism. The "theory of productive forces," ascribed to Liu Shaoqi, Deng Xiaoping, and many others was, in a sense, a restatement of the original Marxist proposition: that many basic aspects of the human relations of socialism could only appear on the basis of sufficient development of the productive capacities of society—that socialist or communist politics, morality, and human relations could not be forced into existence. Critics stated that this "theory" contained a refutation of politics as the leading element in the revolution, denied the significance of the human factor, denied Mao's theoretical leadership, and in general repudiated the lessons of the Chinese revolution in favor of a doctrine reminiscent of the Soviet experience—one that would emphasize bureaucratic leadership and the power of specialists built around the perceived need to develop the production apparatus at the expense of fostering revolutionary political attitudes and ideals as the key to rapid progress utilizing resources already at hand. The present day has seen the critics criticized, much renewed emphasis given to the limits that economic and technological underdevelopment places on human relations and on the nation, and much abuse heaped upon most of the 20 years' record of economic policies from the Great Leap Forward on.[13]

One of the most vivid early attacks made on Jiang Qing was that she would prefer a "socialist train that runs late to a capitalist train that runs on time"—in other words, she believed that the characteristics of poverty or scarcity or backwardness, on the one hand, and socialism, on the other, might well exist harmoniously—a view far removed from Marx's notion that socialism and the transition to communism would have to rest on a highly developed economy. Such criticism now pervades attention to many areas of past policy, notably that pertaining to the countryside. Frequent charges are made today against policies alleged to have linked rural development cum socialist institutionalization in a "radical forward 'transit regardless of poverty'."[14] Related to the now excoriated goal of hastening the amalgamation of richer and poorer production teams to bring more egalitarian accounting at the brigade level, or other forms of rural institutional experiments, such policies are now caricatured by critics as endorsing continued poverty to bring about a distorted version of socialism.[15] Similarly, many characteristic statements single out for attack apparent attempts to stifle personal or group enrichment on the grounds that "when there is plenty of money, there is capitalism."[16] The Gang of Four did not like individually-owned business and small-scale private trade, but, given the relatively small scope that exists for its expansion into large endeavors even today with the new economic policies, it will seem that their main complaint may have involved the symbolic, *moral* defectiveness of so-called "Capitalist tails."

The Dazhai work-point system has been criticized, with production units returning to an earlier system of fixed norms and quotas that allow for a much wider spread of remuneration depending on the amount and type of work done in the collective rural economy. The Dazhai system had allowed for payment of work points according to political attitude and contribution as well as production achievement alone. In general, it had led to a narrowing of the gap in work-points received for work rendered by different commune members and tended toward egalitarian distribution of the collectively-distributed product. In many ways, the Dazhai system, with its emphasis on attitude and zeal as well as actual measurable physical accomplishment and its innovation of different modes for being distinguished as a valuable worker, resembles the egalitarian revolutionary moral ideal that whatever the ability, it is the spirit of dedication and personal sacrifice that is important. Current criticisms argue that all this became window-dressing for a guaranteed income for slackers and militated against actual consci-entious effort—a symptom of scarcity-centered attitudes not tempered, appar-ently, by political inspiration. Notably, much of the Dazhai model and the actual political position of its defenders are now under severe attack.

A more general reinstitution of so-called material incentives has also occurred. Wages and bonuses, especially in industry, are linked to performance by individ-uals (sometimes small work groups). Such reemphasis is held to be an implemen-tation of Marx's notion of pay in the socialist period "according to work" (related to "removing the iron rice bowl") and a criticism of egalitarian systems that stifled just desires for reward based on effort (although the close link be-tween individual effort and material reward may be considered as an instrument for aiding the process of inculcating an "ethic of productivity"). In relation to this, attempts have been made to raise wages for much of the work force and to recognize the problems of underpayment and low standards of living (instead of arguing that working for low pay is an incorporation of revolutionary morality). Also, emphasis today is placed, in policy terms at least, on upgrading housing and other necessities of life. Quite clearly, present leaders believe that long-term revolutionary aspirations must fairly include demands by the Chinese masses for higher material standards, for perceptible improvements in life style within tangible, visible lifetimes. They must have ascribed much of the unrest and in-tense political factionalism and violence of the Cultural Revolution to a basic disquiet arising from low material payoffs and lack of economic and career mobility, rather than to revolutionary political motives.

Of enormous significance is the appearance in recent major economic state-ments of arguments blaming much past economic policy for focusing on produc-tion rather than consumption and on accumulation over distribution. Even though the Cultural Revolution critique of the "theory of productive forces" is repudiated, "production for production's sake" is also attacked—not in the name of renewing socialist-minded revolutionary asceticism, but in the cause of more consumption and of a higher personal standard of living, in other words, satisfaction of popular material longings. Statements today attack the pace of accumulation as historically too rapid (at least since the end of the first five-year plan). The noteworthy element in these very far-reaching criticisms is that they bring under a critical light both possible moral spinoffs of a socialism originating from scarce and difficult conditions: the first and more familiar is the "ethic of productivity," designed to foster accumulation and submerge workers' autonomy in the name of centralized societal coordination of scarce resources. The second is a backward-looking heroic image of the moral legacy of scarcity and hardship that views harsh conditions as a continuing basis for revolutionary achievements (and human socialization). The goal, it is argued instead, is that people should receive more now.

The last significant criticism of the present period to be mentioned concerns the nature of political leadership. In a September 1979 major address in honor of the thirtieth anniversary of the People's Republic, Party elder, Ye Jian-ying argued for a new type of cadre recruitment policy—one that specifically recognized the need for the recruitment of leaders who were experts and specialists. He argued that:

> The development of a modern economy, modern culture, and modern politics demands a gradual change in the composition of our cadre contingent with a reduction in the general run of administrative cadres and an increase in the number of specialist cadres in all trades and professions....Those who rest content with being laymen and indulge in political claptrap certainly can't run the country but can only ruin it.[17]

Given the terms of Ye's criticism, it is hard to dispute his judgment leveled at the apparently empty claims of ill-trained windbags. But, we will take the liberty of broadening the sense of his conclusion to relate to our earlier discussion. The criticism against relying on generalist cadres resonates with wider suspicion of the hortatory slogans of the past, those emphasizing zeal as such, sacrifice as such, hard work as such, or discipline as such—things that gave a particular stamp to a heroic revolutionary period but can be a hollow basis for unproductive privilege and officeholding in the present, not to mention a platform, apparently, for attacking much needed specialists for being "expert" rather than "red."*

---

*The basic argument here is reasonable on the face of it. I have argued elsewhere that long ago Mao sought a slogan to harmonize the needs for political integration of socialist construction with well-considered appreciation of the premises of scientific and technological development [see Mitch Meisner, "From

CONCLUSION: NEUTERED EGOISM?

In an early essay, Karl Marx implied that the moral concerns of a revolution-ized world need not be understood as entangled in a choice between personal abnegation or selfishness:

> ...communists do not put egoism against self-sacrifice or self-sacrifice against egoism, nor do they express this contradiction theoretically either in its sentimental or high-flown ideological form; on the contrary, they demonstrate the material basis engendering it, with which it dis-appears of itself...they are very well aware that egoism, just as much as self-sacrifice, is in definite circumstances a necessary form of the self-assertion of individuals. Hence, the communists by no means want...to do away with the 'private individual' for the sake of the "general", self-sacrificing man...[18]

In many ways, the moral dilemma that Marx rejected for communists has, in fact, come to life as a troubling ambiguity in China because of the remarkable successes of the Chinese revolution in its heroic period of struggle amidst scarcity. The attitude of self-sacrifice and commitment beyond self was brought forward as an official, i.e., state-sponsored morality, well into the period of post-Libera-tion economic development or "socialist construction." If the plethora of contemporary criticisms are to be believed, such attitudes, including a genuine sentimentalization of poverty or hard times as the basis for desirable behavior, has had a serious and debilitating influence on economic and social policy making and perhaps slowed down the pace of development. An heroic, romantic scarcity-based morality, or alternatively, an organization-serving ethic of pro-ductivity have both persisted. At times they have been tied strongly together, especially in the boosting of values of collective manual labor as a means toward accumulation, at times separated as varying preferences between conflicting political factions. The latter is reminiscent of the Soviet hierarchical, worker-subordinate morality of "primitive socialist accumulation." The former infuses romantic claims for "human-factor"-centered development at the expense of modern technology. It involves suspicion of efforts toward achieving tangible

---

Theory to Practice, Science, and Revolution: The Three Great Revolutionary Movements in China, 1963–1966," in *Selected Seminar Papers on Contempo-rary China I,* eds. Chin and King (Hong Kong: University of Hong Kong, 1971), pp. 44–90.] The emphasis in Ye's speech is so extreme, however, that it comes close to arguing against any special political realm of expertise for the CCP as such. In a different approach, Fox Butterfield argues (June 1, 1980, *New York Times*) that actions taken by middle government bureaucrats to thwart technical modernization policies may reflect their antiintellectual attributes derived from peasant backgrounds.

living standard benefits for the post-Liberation generations. Such undertakings are seen as dangerously reminiscent of a "revisionist" "goulash communism."

The above characterizations certainly must be examined with circumspection. The original vision and much of the strategy of the Chinese revolution was a dialectical one. When Mao found strengths in poverty and ignorance, he also found weakness and urged China to learn from all courses, including the full range of foreign ones. Also, the gains to be achieved in the short run by Chinese patriots as a whole in rebelling against the occupying Japanese and the corrupt, ineffectual KMT were considerable, as were the immediate goals of poorer peasant strata in Chinese rural society against landlords and other elements of the old power structure—all of this led to a very visible solidarity that gave heroic assertions of the revolutionary struggle's strong underpinnings of individual and communal interest. But after the establishment of the People's Republic and during the building of an enlarged revolutionary state apparatus amidst complicated debate over how to stage a Chinese war on poverty, the ambiguities of a morality of scarcity heading (hopefully) toward prosperity were considerable. Would efforts toward success in the new period of socialist construction, or the very success itself, induce a falling away from the much valued communist spirit of sacrifice to a morality founded in "egoism"? (or, to "new bourgeois ideas"). The following example from an interview carried out by the author in 1972 illustrates part of the dilemma:

> A factory manager was criticized by workers for eating separately from them during a period at a special worksite. It turned out that there was not enough food brought for the whole body of workers, so the manager had opted to sacrifice himself along with other high-ranking colleagues by eating inadequate lunches to make up for the shortfall. They ate in private to avoid any controversy. However, when this situation finally surfaced, the manager still was criticized. The point for leading cadres was not, as one might have thought, to sacrifice themselves for the good of the masses. Rather, he should have managed the food supply better![19]

Perhaps neither sacrifice *nor* egoism but an apparently neutral efficiency is the ethic to be preferred in China today. True, the general pronouncements of the present leadership (not assuming total unanimity) tend to allow some leeway, even attribute positive value to motives of self-satisfaction of basic desires. At least in the area of perceived benefit in personal income and standard of living these desires have been pent up for a long time. But the leadership would very much like to tie motives of individual satisfaction to standards of efficient or effective task performance. With the repeated mention of "economic laws," scientific methods, and management "systems," they would seem to externalize the moral dilemma by placing the direction or control of behavior in a neutral realm beyond choice or social antagonism. In a sense, by reviving emphasis on modernization and productivity, the present period in Chinese revolutionary history has restated in policy terms the original Marxist premises that developed human morality appears only on the basis of the full unfolding of productive forces and the availability of abundance.

There is great concern, in fact, that continuing lack of progress in economic development, including meeting people's real desires for full desirable employment and improved material standards of living, as well as a recent legacy of political strife and chaos in public life, has led to a real moral crisis in Chinese society. Much of these themes can be found in a wealth of current discussions about the problem of juvenile delinquency. Certainly, disturbing evidence of social and moral pathologies, the appearance of a kind of socialist anomie, as well as economic slowdown, is at the heart of present criticisms of the now-repudiated "ultra left" and "egalitarian" policies and attitudes. But it is not at all clear that such criticism, including a rearguing of a socialist rationale for egoistic motives or claims (as realistic and understandable as they may be) or invoking the gods of science, system, and efficiency—sidestepping the moral questions, in a sense, if not reworking the "ethic of productivity" in a new form—will provide the basis of an ethical behavioral framework that can transcend the once-integrated moral universe of an earlier heroic period.

NOTES

1. Karl Marx, "Critique of the Gotha Program," in *Karl Marx: Selected Writings*, ed. David McLellan (Oxford: Oxford University Press, 1977), p. 568.

2. Ibid., p. 569.

3. Karl Marx, "The German Ideology," in McLellan, ed., p. 179.

4. Andre Gorz, *Socialism and Revolution* (New York: Anchor, 1973), p. 184.

5. Ibid., p. 188.

6. Nguyen Khac Vien, *Tradition and Revolution in Vietnam* (Berkeley: Indochina Resource Center, 1974), p. 132.

7. Mao Zedong, *Selected Readings from the Works of Mao Tsetung* (Beijing: Foreign Languages Press, 1967), pp. 310–312.

8. Ibid., pp. 180–181.

9. Ibid., pp. 320–323. It is reported that the Yugong tale itslef is now criticized in some Chinese circles as silly.

10. Ibid., pp. 324–342.

11. Ibid., p. 336.

12. Ibid., p. 336. It is interesting to read back over these words delivered over 35 years ago now that the day Mao mentioned *has* come!

13. See, for example, Deng Xiaoping's statement about post-1957 economic policy in his interview with Oriana Fallaci, *Washington Post*, August 31, 1980, 01.

14.   Xu Zhigang and Zhou Jinghua, "Economic Policies in Rural Areas," *Beijing Review* (April 20, 1979): 15–26, furnishes extremely rich documentation of such criticism pertaining to rural policies.

15.   Ibid., p. 22.

16.   Ibid.

17.   Ye Jianying, "Comrade Ye Jianying's Speech," *Beijing Review* (October 5, 1979): 28.

18.   Karl Marx, "The German Ideology," in McLellan, ed., p. 183.

19.   The example is taken from an interview described in Mitch Meisner, "The Shenyang Transformer Factory: A Profile," *China Quarterly* (October–December 1972): 724–725.

INDEX

ABOUT THE EDITORS AND CONTRIBUTORS

RICHARD W. WILSON is professor of political science and director of international programs at Rutgers University. He has published widely in the area of political socialization. In addition to writing numerous articles, Professor Wilson is author of *Learning to be Chinese* (1970) and *The Moral State* (1974) and is co-editor of *Deviance and Social Control in Chinese Society* (1977), *Value Change in Chinese Society* (1979), *Moral Development and Politics* (1980), and *Organizational Behavior in Chinese Society* (1980).

SIDNEY L. GREENBLATT, associate professor of the Department of Sociology at Drew University, Madison, New Jersey, is editor of *Chinese Sociology and Anthropology*, a quarterly journal of translation published by International Arts and Sciences Press, White Plains, New York. He is also editor of *The People of Taihang: An Anthology of Family Histories* (1976) and co-editor of *Deviance and Social Control in Chinese Society* (1977), *Value Change in Chinese Society* (1979), and *Organizational Behavior in Chinese Society* (1980), as well as *Social Interaction: An Introductory Reader in Sociology* (1979). He is currently working on a book on claims to human rights. He has delivered papers to various conferences in the social sciences and the China field. Professor Greenblatt holds a B.A. from Harper College of the State University of New York and an M.A. and East Asian Institute Certificate from Columbia University.

AMY AUERBACHER WILSON is a professional associate with the Committee on Scholarly Communication with the People's Republic of China, National Academy of Sciences, Washington, D.C. She is co-editor of and contributor to *Deviance and Social Control in Chinese Society*, *Value Change in Chinese Society* and *Organizational Behavior in Chinese Society*. Dr. Wilson received her B.A. from Douglass College, Rutgers University, and her M.A. and Ph.D.

in sociology from Princeton University. She has taught sociology at both Princeton University and Rutgers University.

ALFRED H. BLOOM is associate professor of psychology and linguistics, director of the linguistics program, and coordinator of Asian studies at Swarthmore College, Swarthmore, Pennsylvania. He received his Ph.D. in social psychology from Harvard University in 1974. His research interests focus on the impact of language and culture on cognition and cognitive development. He has written articles for, among others, the *Journal of Social Psychology, The Handbook of Political Psychology*, the *Journal of Peace Science*, and *Current Anthropology* and has just completed a book entitled *The Linguistic Shaping of Thought: A Study in the Impact of Language on Thinking in China and the West* (Hillsdale, N.J.: Lawrence Erlbaum Associates, in press).

LOWELL DITTMER is chairman of the Center for Chinese Studies and a member of the Political Science Department at the University of California at Berkeley. He has taught previously at the University of Michigan (Ann Arbor) and the State University of New York at Buffalo.

Professor Dittmer received his M.A. and Ph.D. degrees from the University of Chicago. He is the author of *Liu Shao-ch'i and the Chinese Cultural Revolution* (University of California Press, 1974) and has published articles in *World Politics, China Quarterly*, the *American Political Science Review*, and other scholarly journals.

PETER LI was born in China and educated in the United States. He received his B.A. from the University of Washington and Ph.D. in Chinese literature from the University of Chicago. At present associate professor of Chinese and comparative literature at Rutgers University, he is a contributor to *Chinese Narrative* (Princeton University Press, 1977), *Traditional Chinese Stories* (Columbia University Press, 1978), *The Chinese Novel at the Turn of the Century* (University of Toronto Press, 1980), co-author of *Classical Chinese Fiction* (G.K. Hall, 1978), and author of *Tseng P'u* (Twayne, 1980). His interests also lie in the area of intercultural literature and the relationship between literature and society.

RICHARD P. MADSEN is assistant professor of sociology at the University of California, San Diego. He is completing a social history of Chen Village, together with Anita Chan and Jonathan Unger. He is also completing a book length monograph on "The Moral Basis of Political Commitment in China."

MITCH MEISNER is assistant professor of political science and international relations at James Madison College, Michigan State University, East Lansing, Michigan. Until 1978, he was lecturer in politics at the University of California at Santa Cruz.

Dr. Meisner has published widely in the area of contemporary Chinese politics with an emphasis on local politics and rural development. His articles have appeared in *China Quarterly, Modern China,* and *Politics and Society.* He is presently involved in collaborative research on development administration in China at the county level based on fieldwork conducted in 1979.

Dr. Meisner holds a B.A. from Amherst College and an M.A. and Ph.D. from the University of Chicago.

THOMAS A. METZGER is professor of Chinese history at the University of California, San Diego. He received his Ph.D. from Harvard University in 1967. He is the author of *The Internal Organization of Ch'ing Bureaucracy* (Harvard University Press, 1973) and *Escape from Predicament—Neo-Confucianism and China's Evolving Political Culture* (Columbia University Press, 1977). Among his articles is "The Organizational Capabilities of the Ch'ing State in the Field of Commerce: The Liang-huai Salt Monopoly, 1740-1840," in *Economic Organization in Chinese Society*, ed. W.E. Willmott (Stanford University Press, 1972).

JAMES REEVE PUSEY is associate professor of Chinese history at Bucknell University. He has also taught Chinese for ten summers at the Middlebury Chinese School. His research has mainly been in modern Chinese intellectual history. He is author of *Wu Han: Attacking the Present through the Past* and a long thesis, "China and Charles Darwin," now being readied for publication at the Harvard East Asian Research Center. Mr. Pusey received his A.B., M.A., and Ph.D. from Harvard.

STEPHEN B. YOUNG is a research associate at the Harvard Law School. He was educated at Harvard College (A.B. 1967) and Harvard Law School (J.D. 1971). He has undertaken ethnographic field work in Chiapas Mexico and northeast Thailand. For three years (1968-1971) he served in the Republic of Vietnam with the Agency for International Development, specializing on political development and village government. He has written on the political cultures of the Zinacantecan Maya, the Thai, and the Vietnamese. He has also written on the legal history of Vietnam and on Vietnamese nationalism. He has recently completed at the Harvard Law School under a grant from the Rockefeller Brothers Fund a study of the basis for human rights in the jurisprudence of traditional China and Vietnam.